MANAGING
THE
TELECOMMUTING
EMPLOYEE

MANAGING
THE
TELECOMMUTING
EMPLOYEE

**Set Goals, Monitor Progress, and
Maximize Profit and Productivity**

Michael Amigoni and Sandra Gurvis

BUSINESS

Avon, Massachusetts

Published by Adams Business, an imprint of
Adams Media, a division of F+W Media, Inc.
57 Littlefield Street, Avon, MA 02322. U.S.A.
www.adamsmedia.com

ISBN 10: 1-59869-887-7
ISBN 13: 978-1-59869-887-9

Printed in the United States of America.

J I H G F E D C B A

Library of Congress Cataloging-in-Publication Data
is available from the publisher.

This publication is designed to provide accurate and authoritative
information with regard to the subject matter covered. It is sold with
the understanding that the publisher is not engaged in rendering legal,
accounting, or other professional advice. If legal advice or other expert
assistance is required, the services of a competent professional person
should be sought.
—From a *Declaration of Principles* jointly adopted
by a Committee of the American Bar Association
and a Committee of Publishers and Associations

Many of the designations used by manufacturers and sellers to distinguish their product are claimed as trademarks. Where those designations
appear in this book and Adams Media was aware of a trademark claim,
the designations have been printed with initial capital letters.

This book is available at quantity discounts for bulk purchases.
For information, please call 1-800-289-0963.

*To our respective families and pets, who provide
diversion, comfort, and support, and keep us
grounded in the realities of working at home.*

Contents

PART ONE

Acknowledgments

Any book is a team effort, and we'd like to thank the following people for their help:

Chuck Wilsker of the Telework Coalition, who made this collaboration possible.

Susan Harrington of Harrington Software Associations for her excellent information and generous sharing of same.

Mark Goldstein, whose excellent glossary adds a dimension of understanding to those both new and familiar with telecommuting.

All the dedicated entrepreneurs at ARO—Lester Ham, Joye Moore, RJ Johnson, Brad Frederick, and David Devoy.

For Michael: Professor Darrel Sutter whose insistence on pursuing your goals has remained for a lifetime.

For Sandra: Nancy Harding, who despite many obstacles, showed that no matter who you are, you can succeed with determination and a clear vision.

How to Use This Guide

This book is designed for anyone concerned with managing tele-commuting employees. More and more managers are supervising employees who are physically distant from them, and these employees may work in a variety of settings—in an office, at home, or on the road. So, ready or not, managers are confronted with new ways of thinking and doing things.

However, such changes don't have to be painful; they can be enjoyable, interesting, and downright productive. If you are managing workers properly, they're motivated, doing their job well, and making money for the company. Why not train employees to work from the comfort of their homes, saving money and the environment?

Hence, this book, intended to be a manager's comprehensive guide to the brave new world of telecommuting. Part One covers the basics—what telecommuting is and what it means to you and your employees. Along with defining the different kinds of tele-work, and delineating the advantages and disadvantages of them, the chapters explain the various types of nontraditional work arrangements and virtual teams. We also define the all-important "Telecommuting Personality," characteristics of which are essential to any successful off-site effort. This section also includes the challenges of dealing with diversity, as well as employee's rights, in addition to methods of designing and implementing virtual teams.

Then it's on to Part Two, the nuts and bolts of managing tele-workers: how to set up a team through cost analysis, defining goals and types of jobs, and other implementation issues. Ways of over-coming managers' resistance are also included, for without their cooperation and support, any workforce effort is doomed. We cover hiring, training, and equipping teleworkers; in many ways, they are different from office-based employees, requiring a much more results-oriented approach, as opposed to merely focusing on processes. Not only do you need to make sure their home office is in a safe, secure, and work-conducive environment, but they must be educated as to the importance of ergonomics, proper equip-ment, and ways to avoid computer viruses and data theft.

Other complexities facing managers of telecommuters include insurance, benefits, and tax issues, the fine points of which are still being debated in courts and among legislators.

Once you've got workers in place, how do you actually manage them? We offer insight on how to set clear boundaries, goals, and methods of communication; provide feedback; keep track and in touch; and perhaps most important, establish trust between and among employees and managers.

Telecommuting employees, especially those just beginning, face a number of challenges. Other chapters provide suggestions for dealing with distraction, procrastination, and lack of self-discipline. We discuss how to overcome isolation and help ease the transition into home officing. Still other chapters will help manag-ers distinguish between normal adjustment problems and red flags indicating that the telecommuting program might not be working.

Telecommuters are often concerned with becoming "invis-ible" and left out of the loop, so as a manager you'll need to help them feel like a cohesive and vital part of the organization. Part of this is finding inventive ways to reward and communicate with employees "from a distance"; being direct and clear regarding per-formance standards, expectations, and goals; and promptly deal-ing with problems. Such things may initially require extra effort and imagination on your part, but it could pay off big time with *all* employees, boosting productivity and leading to more effective and creative ways of working. Such procedures also make employee discipline and termination more clear-cut and easier to deal with.

Part Three of this book discusses guiding and managing your telecommuting team, now and in the future. As with the brick-and-mortar office, different telecommuting jobs require diverse skill sets. For example, a graphic designer who works alone does not necessarily have to be a "people person" or even very social, as long as she produces timely work that satisfies clients. Understanding these differences is especially important with telecommuters as they will be pretty much on their own and you will not be physically supervising them.

Meetings are another aspect of work life that are different for telecommuters; they are more frequently held virtually or through teleconferencing. We'll talk about ways to handle different kinds of meetings and the best circumstances for each.

Finally, how (and when) do you determine whether your telecommuting program is a success? We'll suggest some methods of measuring this.

Although no one knows everything the future holds, it's a good bet that telecommuting is here to stay. Technology is burgeoning and morphing in such a way that many obstacles confronting worldwide virtual teams such as incompatible programs or communications issues are being overcome even as of this writing.

So why not explore the possibility of telecommuting for yourself and your employees? The only things you have to lose are four walls and a desk . . . And there's a world to gain!

Michael Amigoni
Sandra Gurvis

Foreword

Telework and telecommuting have been covered in every major newspaper, on television, and in magazines. It's a hot topic in the federal government and among the states. Also known as virtual work, mobile work, and distributed work, telework and telecommuting are still the most commonly used descriptive terms. They suggest work@home, mobility, and flexibility. I find I use "telework" more than any other word to describe the concept that "work is something you do, not a place you go." Telework can thrive in both the public and private sectors. In most cases if a job is done by talking on a phone and/or working on a computer, it can be done from almost anywhere.

Although over 99 percent of people I speak to at different events and conferences admit to working, at least some of the time, from locations other than their primary place of employment, only about 10 percent ever admit to "teleworking." In a telework benchmarking study done by the Telework Coalition (TelCoa) in 2006, we asked the leaders of telework programs for several major private corporations and government agencies what they called their programs. Most said they didn't call them telework any more; the most frequent response was "it's just work" to us.

THE PAST

The term "telework" has been with us for many years—since the 1970s when it was coined by Jack Nilles, the "father of telecommuting." Since the early-to-mid 1990s it's been what I call "technology enabled telework," accomplished with the prolif-eration of more affordable computers, greatly augmented by the Internet and broadband connectivity. As we transitioned into the twenty-first century, broadband Internet access became more ubiq-uitous, and computer prices dropped even more. These changes have driven the tremendous growth in telework as much as the many other benefits.

Because of their desire to be compliant with the Clean Air Act, AT&T was an early adopter of telework. This act addressed the elimination of air pollution and burning of fossil fuels, specifically gasoline. One of the recommended ways to lower gas use was to leave your car parked for as many days as possible—hence, by working at home.

With the positive conclusions published in their annual employee telework survey, even more organizations followed in their footsteps and let employees work from home. Companies realized that while doing something favorable for the environ-ment, their employees also experienced a new degree of work/life balance, enjoyed wasting less time sitting in traffic, and realized other savings related to commuting costs. The Telework Coalition presented AT&T with an award for their research in 2003.

As companies measured these benefits, it became obvious that since employees no longer needed their offices, the compa-nies could get by with less office space and fewer parking places, therefore saving significantly on real estate costs. Teleworking employee productivity increased due to fewer distractions, less travel/commuting fatigue and frustration, and their ability to focus on accountable tasks. Retention increased because most employees were very pleased with their new working arrangements. Added benefits for the employer that the TelCoa's benchmarking study acknowledged included the ability to recruit and hire from a wider geographically dispersed pool of candidates with better educa-tion and qualifications; higher morale; and reduced costs related to absenteeism.

THE PRESENT

The number of telecommuters grew slowly but steadily in both the public and private sectors over the next several years for all of the aforementioned reasons. Then came September 11, 2001.

An interesting paradox about telework is that "bad things" often happen that encourage people and organizations to discover its benefits. September 11 was one such instance in which the value of a distributed workforce really struck home. After the attacks, many organizations with telework programs found they had a significant part of a business continuity plan already in place. Several firms whose primary offices were destroyed during the terrorist attacks were back in business within forty-eight hours thanks to their work-at-home employees as well as those working from satellite offices, hotels, client offices, and so forth.

Other situations positively affected by telework include the aftermath of hurricanes, floods, transit strikes, bridge collapses, earthquakes, blizzards, ice storms, disease epidemics (such as SARS and the possibility of a pandemic), or severe traffic congestion.

But more than calamities are shifting management's thinking in favor of telework. Employment opportunities for the disabled, including war veterans; older workers who either want or need to remain in or reenter the workforce; and rural workers unable to commute to distant places to find employment are playing roles in this. And we can't forget, no matter how hard we try, about rising gas prices. For each day that one's vehicle remains parked at home, 20 percent of that week's commuter gas consumption and cost are eliminated. Throw in reduced wear and tear on the car, "low mileage vehicle" reduced insurance rates, parking expenses, lower food bills by eating at home rather than in a restaurant, lower dry cleaning expenses, and fewer expensive work clothes, and employees save many after-tax dollars.

TelCoa estimates that a full-time teleworker receives an $8,000 indirect pay raise, regardless of his or her salary rate. This alone makes teleworking extremely attractive in the call center and other service industry functions not requiring a physical presence in a defined location.

However, it's interesting to note that although long the poster child of how to have a successful telework program and run it properly, at&t—the new, lowercase at&t, formed when SBC bought the original AT&T, Bell South, and Cingular—recently started to notify its full-time teleworkers that they will be required to return to the office while and until new policies on telework are determined. The reason behind the change was never made clear. Although this cutback has not yet become a trend, in February 2008, Governor Ted Strickland of Ohio called for a severe limitation of teleworking policies for state employees. This affected not just those who worked from home or alternative locations but also those who took advantage of flex-time and compressed work weeks. This reversed the telework initiatives advocated by former Governor Taft.

A change to new management can occasionally have a negative effect on telework, requiring that the new boss become educated as to its many benefits and overcome erroneous perceptions concerning exactly what it involves. However, organizations, whether public or private, that reduce or eliminate telework are taking a giant step backward.

THE FUTURE

The baby boomer section of the workforce is getting grayer. Gas prices will continue to rise, and we must reduce our need for imported oil and dependence on foreign suppliers. Reducing global warming and air pollution should be handled sooner, not later.

All these things are reasons telecommuting is the future.

Comprehensive telework programs can be initiated relatively quickly at a low cost. There are proven return on investment (ROI) models that CEOs, CFOs, and investors are now demanding. There is no reason to wait.

If you find even only *one* of these reasons beneficial, that's all you should need to consider telework attractive. But you'll get the rest of the benefits, too!

DOWNSIDES

You'd think that with the advantages to employers, employees, and society in general that everyone would be lining up to get their telework programs started. That's not the case. Resistance comes from the very top of an organization, mid-level managers, and from some employees themselves.

Employers want to know how they can be assured that their employees are actually working. Managers like the power they think they have by being able to physically view those they supervise. Some feel this power will be minimized if staff isn't there all of the time. Perhaps more important, the vast majority of supervisors need to learn how to manage remotely. This is something that must be addressed in the evolving global and mobile economy.

I have sensed reluctance to telecommute by many employees themselves for more than one reason. As a friend and associate, Dr. Jay Hellman, who calls telework "virtual adjacency," says, "Work is where you go to socialize; home is where you go to work." I have spoken with many workers who cringe at the idea of not going to work each day and seeing their friends and coworkers. For some, the idea of staying at home one day a week is objectionable let alone full-time. The success of the work-at-home agents in call centers is due partly to the fact the majority of the workers are older, more settled in their ways, and prefer to socialize away from work.

Other workers are bothered by what they see as the more intense monitoring of their productivity. Instead of being measured on the time spent at work, measurement of telework is based on work output and productivity. Too many people in an office environment "get by" by doing as little as possible, and they know it. They are frightened by the prospect of having to produce more than the minimum.

Full-time teleworkers sometimes feel isolated. However, web-based video collaboration can greatly reduce, if not eliminate this.

IN CONCLUSION

In many of my talks on the topic of telework I and my friend Dr. Hellman shy away from the words "telework" and "telecommuting." With some audiences, these terms have a negative connotation. So I often use the term "The 'T' word."

Whatever you want to call it, the time to telework is *now*. It has evolved from "we want to do it" to "we *need* to do it." The environment and global warming? Traffic congestion, the expense to replace/repair our dilapidated transportation infrastructure? Our dependence on imported oil? Work/life balance? Improved rural economic development? Pick one and you—and we—are affected by them all. Teleworking addresses each of these problems.

Chuck Wilsker
President and CEO
The Telework Coalition
Washington, D.C.

PART ONE

TELECOMMUTING

What It Is and What It Means

CHAPTER 1

What Is Telecommuting?

INTRODUCTION

You'd have to be Rip Van Winkle not to have heard of telecommuting, but as a manager who has probably dealt primarily with full-time, on-site office staff, you may be unsure as to exactly what the term encompasses. Currently 21 million Americans telecommute in one way or another.

Suddenly you're faced with the daunting and, at the very least, unfamiliar task of managing one or more telecommuters. Possibly you may even have to manage *virtual teams*, a group of people who rely on electronic forms of communication to communicate in order to achieve goals, some (or all) of whom may work off-site, often in geographically dispersed areas. The first step in your education then, is understanding what telecommuting is, how it came about, and the various advantages and disadvantages as well as the kinds of jobs it most frequently encompasses.

DEFINITION

Telecommuting is the practice of working outside the traditional office or workplace, usually at a small office or home office environment. This workspace is sometimes called a virtual office. Communication with a main office is handled through a computer and/or other technology. More recently, telecommuters also worked through voice and picture communication like voice over Internet protocol (VOIP) via broadband or high-speed Internet, and through groupware/Internet conferencing tools such as Live-Meeting or Windows Meeting Space.

Some people use other terms for telecommuting: e-commuting, e-work, and working at and/or from home. *Telework*, also frequently used interchangeably with *telecommuting*, and in this book as well, is in fact a much broader term. Jack M. Nilles, often called the "father of telecommuting," says telework involves *any* form of substitution of information technologies for work-related travel; that is anything that moves the work to the workers instead of vice versa. So although all telecommuters are teleworkers, the reverse is not always true.

HISTORY

Modern telecommuting was spurred by the development of (no surprise here) the personal computer. In the early 1970s, when programmers were at a premium, companies such as Control Data Corporation (CDC) began offering the option of working at home, an attractive incentive to independent-minded programmers who really hated driving the clogged freeways of Silicon Valley.

Almost at the same time, Jack Nilles was working with the federal government to study how telecommuting might prevent massive traffic jams and ongoing pollution. States, particularly California, continued the studies in the eighties and began adopting telecommuting plans. Private companies, intrigued by the concept, jumped into the act. However, it wasn't until the 1990s, helped by the passage of the Federal Clean Air Act and the Americans with Disabilities Act that telecommuting came into its own. The Clean Air Act helped raise awareness regarding elimination of pollution and the conservation of fuel and other natural resources; and the Americans with Disabilities Act encouraged equal opportunity for and hiring of physically or otherwise disabled workers. Since 1990, states one study, it has been growing at a rate of 15 percent a year. Other sources claim that 80 percent of Fortune 1000 companies will likely introduce telecommuting by 2010.

Michael Amigoni
The Good Old (?) Days of Telecommuting

Based in Kansas City, Missouri, my company ARO, Inc. provides various industries with leading-edge business process outsourcing (BPO). Over the past several years, our business model drastically changed to employees who worked at home or were otherwise geographically distributed. This means we can save a lot of costs by using at-home workers. Since then, we have deployed this distributed workforce for an array of industries such as insurance, healthcare, pharmaceutical, energy, and seminar/training. ARO's business model centers on using our remote workforce for the majority of these processes.

In 1997, when we first implemented our first call center for work-at-home reps, they had to use dial-up to reach a modem bank of phones so they could connect to our computer system. Whether they had a 24kbs or 56kbs modem made all the difference in the world; between say, the speed of molasses and the speed of Heinz ketchup. Both were sluggish—it was just a matter of degree.

Regardless of what they used, if the speed connection was low they would have to sit and wait patiently for the screen to refresh—however long that took. The screen was monochromatic with either green or orange cursors, so that was hard on their eyes. No one had even thought of an ergonomic keyboard or wrist rest to avoid carpal tunnel or other repetitive motion injuries.

Then, as now, the most challenging times occurred during inclement weather. The connection would have to be reset multiple times since the modem was so unstable, and calls often got dropped. When that happened the worker would have to start all over again and wait for the model to slowly reconnect. And does anyone remember DOS?

Sandra Gurvis
The Good Old (?) Days of Telecommuting

I've been working from home since Generation X was in diapers, including my own daughter Amy, who is now almost thirty. Back in 1979, it wasn't known as "telecommuting" but rather a "hobby to prevent Mom from losing her mind." The only people who were in business for themselves were professionals (such as doctors or lawyers), entrepreneurs, or franchisers. Except for the occasional consultant (then, as now, sometimes a buzzword for the terminally underemployed) most the rest of the jobs were in offices, factories, or other on-site locations. As a female professional, it was hard to be taken seriously; women either stayed at home full-time or worked in offices. In an era when we were supposed to have it all, I was somewhere in between.

Early on, however, I decided to separate my work from my home life and established my own space, usually in the spare bedroom or basement. I spent several hundred dollars on expensive stationery and business cards. In 1984, several months after my son Alex was born, I took out my first bank loan to pay for an Atari computer so I could do word processing. I bought a then-extremely expensive thermal paper fax so I could send and receive articles and information from sources. It raised a few eyebrows. Why go into debt to put such items in your home?

Today, of course, all that has changed. In my condo complex alone (and in the neighborhood where I lived in the late 1990s) about 20 percent of the residents work from their home offices. Who would have thought back in 1979 that I would have as much—if not possibly more—job security than some of my peers whose positions have been downsized or abolished by mergers and acquisitions?

ADVANTAGES/DISADVANTAGES TO THE WORKER

Telecommuting has many advantages for employees. Not only do they have control of their time, but they no longer have to deal with dress codes, office politics, and stressful and sometimes dangerous rush hour traffic. No one's breathing down their neck to make sure they get their work done. Telecommuting also allows groups that might otherwise be considered marginal to compete in the employment pool: families with young children or ill parents whom the worker must care for; those living in rural or other remote areas; and people with disabilities. As long as you get the job done—and as long as it doesn't have to be performed within specific hours—you can take the kid to the doctor, wait for the furnace repair person, and even sneak off to a movie during the day. An added advantage is being able to work to the ticking of your own personal clock, when you are most creative and alert.

According to studies, telecommuting reduces stress for over half of the workers who opt for this form of employment. Another factor that contributes to this is that the telecommuter can choose his or her own environment—a telecommuter can work in a yurt as long as it has electricity and Internet access. They are freed from office interruptions. In this sense, the telecommuter's life is his or her own.

As with everything, there are challenges. The biggest problem facing telecommuters, especially for those new to this type of work, is motivation. The telecommuting employee needs to be a self-starter and disciplined enough to get the job done. For some people this is difficult if not impossible; they need the presence of others—and a "business" atmosphere where work is accomplished—to get them going. Telecommuters—again, often those who are starting out—can feel lonely and isolated, which can have a negative impact on both their work and personal lives.

Many of the issues that make telecommuting so attractive can also contribute to its downfall. Sure, you can work in your pajamas, but do you really want to? Every day of her telecommuting life, Sandra has gotten up, put on makeup and "real" clothes, eaten breakfast, and gone into her office. The ability to spend time with her family (and now, her two cats) could result in procrastination and detract from productivity unless she remains organized and focused. Telecommuters can also have difficulty separating their work life from their home and may become overburdened, putting in all kinds of hours on evenings and weekends, becoming stressed-out and exhausted.

Although telecommuting is growing, there is still a dearth of employers willing to consider how work can be accomplished through telecommuting. They may be intimidated by the technology required or have security concerns. However, there are signs that this is changing. Someday soon every manager may well have to deal with at least some remote workers.

ADVANTAGES/DISADVANTAGES TO THE MANAGER

Because they are happier with their work environments, telecommuters are generally more productive. As any manager knows, employee satisfaction equals increased productivity. Along with a reduction in absenteeism, there's a decrease in staff turnover. Employees who are effective telecommuters rarely leave their jobs.

Another boon to managers is a reduction in time spent commuting to and from work. Employees who only have to go as far as the next room to get to their desks save hundreds of hours that can be used in actually getting the job done. Not to mention the money they save on gas and the cut in pollution! Telecommuting also reduces the number of unnecessary meetings. Yet, almost paradoxically, telecommuters who work in well-organized programs state that they communicate more effectively with supervisory and other company personnel than when they were in the office every day.

If you're having difficulty recruiting and retaining skilled employees, telecommuters can fill the gap, possibly saving you six months (or more) in searching for, training, and replacing the lost worker. As the world shrinks, it's also easier and more convenient to "expand" your team nationally and even globally by having tele-workers located in target areas. They can act as eyes and ears, spotting trends and providing information about the region that you might not otherwise be able to obtain.

However, although telecommuting can decrease overhead, the technology involved can be expensive and problematical. Many times telecommuters will need both a PC (for the office) and a lap-top (for on-site meetings and business trips), as well as a company BlackBerry, cell phone, or other PDA. There may also be issues with program incompatibility and platforms—if, for example, the team member owns an Apple, but the company requires Windows. Someone will need to pony up funds for a software patch, replace equipment, and/or train the individual. Often that responsibility falls on the manager.

There's also the question of whether the telecommuters are actually doing their jobs, a major concern especially among more traditional managers. If the kind of management you do is by observation—for example, if the employee has face-to-face con-tact with the public and needs to be courteous at all times—tele-commuting may not be practical.

However, if your management evaluation of an employee is by objective, measurable results, telecommuting may be effec-tive because you're looking at the end product (e.g., goals met or number of widgets made or sold) and not the process itself. The challenge then lies in hiring someone you trust and who will do the work.

Telecommuting also forces the elimination of guesswork. In the past, you might occasionally be a bit vague in assigning the project. After all, you could make sure it was on track and define specifics as you went, since you were in close proximity to the worker. All you had to do was walk over to her cube. Business writer and analyst Constantine von Hoffman cites the need to make previously informal systems explicit, a challenge for many managers. Not only must they be better able to communicate, they must provide "a higher level of mindfulness, planning, and attention to detail."

If equipment breaks down or there is a crisis, the telecommuter may be unable to respond or get in touch as quickly as if he were in an office. There may be a gap or lag time in resolving the situation that might not otherwise occur.

Finally, you may have to deal with employees still working in the office who resent telecommuters. If you're a telecommuting manager yourself, it's possible you may be passed over for promotion. Out of "site," out of mind—not being in the office every day reduces visibility and a chance for decision-makers to shine, get your team members noticed, or give out plum assignments. Many of these and other issues can be resolved with effective planning and implementation and will be addressed in upcoming chapters.

Some Pros and Cons of Telecommuting

Pros:

- Save space and money by eliminating or reducing a brick-and-mortar office
- Benefit the environment by limiting or doing away with the commute to work
- Increase employee morale and loyalty by offering them work in an environment of their choice
- Choose from a wider geographic pool of workers and those who may otherwise be considered unemployable due to physical limitations or family commitments
- Motivate workers more effectively, thus making them more productive
- Provide a better work/life balance for all parties involved

Cons:

- Lose day-to-day physical contact with employees. How do you know that they're really working?
- Face additional challenge of possibly selecting the wrong employees for telework—and you may not know that right away
- Leave employees feeling "invisible" and out of the loop, believing that teleworking reduces their chances for promotion
- Reduce productivity if the job does not lend itself to telework
- Give rise to miscommunications and misunderstandings due to limited face-to-face contact

ADVANTAGES/DISADVANTAGES TO THE COMPANY

Primarily, companies use telecommuters for one reason: cost reduction. It could be real estate—they don't need to set up an office or can open up something smaller—or they could avoid incurring additional expenses in moving or transferring skilled and/or experienced employees.

Telecommuting also makes sense for companies located in high-income areas. Your main office may be located in New York, San Francisco, or even London, but—depending upon the type of work needed and how it's transmitted—you can use people who live in Oshkosh or Bombay, reducing the need for premium salaries or relocation expenses. Companies that need to be open around-the-clock, such as service or retail organizations, can find workers in different time zones, or even internationally, providing 24/7 global availability. Because of this and because of increased productivity, telecommuting also reduces the need for overtime.

Another benefit to the company is the ability to recruit workers with specific skills, regardless of where they're located. A company located in St. Louis that uses teleworkers can draw from the entire country, rather than just their metro area. Telecommuting provides such companies with a larger pool of applicants with experience in similar jobs.

Legally, companies are at an advantage as well. They're complying with the Federal Clean Air Act by reducing the number of commuters and taking automobiles and pollution off the streets; and they're in compliance with the Americans with Disabilities Act by making it easier for them to hire qualified employees who are unable to leave home due to physical or other ailments.

The chief downside of telecommuting from companies' standpoint—it is a huge one and an increasing risk—is the potential loss and compromised security of important data. The geographical diversity of the network and the reduction of direct corporate control over the physical work environment greatly adds to the vulnerability of confidential information. For instance, in 2006, an employee of the United States Department of Veterans Affairs who worked at home part of the time took home a laptop with the Social Security numbers of as many as 26.5 million veterans and their families; it was taken when his residence was burglarized.

Companies considering telecommuting may find also themselves entangled in a complicated mire of local legal regulations, union issues, and zoning laws. Such issues must be investigated carefully before establishing a telecommuting presence and hiring employees.

COMMON TELECOMMUTING JOBS

Most telecommuting jobs are fairly specialized. Author and World Privacy Forum founder Pam Dixon lists computer programming, customer service (especially online support), and graphic design (particularly on the web), as well as translating, data entry, and writing and editing as being fields that lend themselves to telecommuting.

The legal, medical, and publishing professions use telecommuters. For example, training programs for home workers are available in litigation coding, medical and legal transcription, and medical coding. Even those in the front lines of the medical profession—RNs, PhDs, PharmDs, and even MDs—can earn six-figure incomes from their homes by doing drug studies, medical writing, and other types of research for hospitals and pharmaceutical and related firms.

Following is a brief list of jobs that may help managers define the kind of work that lends itself to telecommuting:

- *Computers:* Software designer, systems troubleshooter, computer scientist, hardware product developer, industrial engineer, information systems manager, manual tester/writer, security specialist, systems analyst
- *Hospitality and Service:* Food consultant, relocation consultant, virtual assistant
- *Medical and Insurance:* Billing, claims, actuary, adjuster, cost containment specialist, underwriter
- *Legal:* Deposition taker, collections, accident reconstructor, investigator, transcriptionist
- *Writing/Research:* Journalist, copywriter, marketing specialist, researcher, abstractor, technical writer/editor
- *Video:* Electronic media designer, video animation specialist, computer graphics specialist, photographer/videographer, photo researcher

A large and rapidly expanding area consists of *call center representatives,* who comprise the bulk of the employees in Michael's company, ARO. Positions can range from customer service to order taking to providing medical and other specialized information. These are not telemarketers in the traditional sense—the National Do Not Call Registry pretty much put the kibosh on many of those jobs. Rather these workers acquire information about specific products and services, as well as answer consumers' questions and inquiries. In short, they're the folks you want to talk to, once you get past the voice-bot. (By the time you get to them you may be frustrated and irritable yourself.)

Yet another well-established area for telecommuting is *sales*, including pharmaceutical, educational (textbooks/training materials), business to business, manufacturing, inside sales, and more. While requiring different skill sets than many other telecommuting jobs, often sales forces are partially or wholly home or satellite office based. This is becoming the norm as companies downsize or try to save on overhead.

Finding—and Retaining—the Right Person(s) for the Job(s)

Freelance writer Sherry Beck Paprocki has worked in many positions within the publishing and education industry, from being an editor at newspapers and magazines to overseeing summer camps that encourage scientific inquiry. In her years of managing and dealing with long-distance employees, she's learned to discern qualities and character traits that help define effective telecommuters.

With interns, or those just starting out, managers "need to establish benchmarks regarding expectations," she advises. "Have them report to you, say, on Wednesday and Friday of every week." More inexperienced employees (e.g., those just out of high school or college) "tend to postpone things and only work on deadline. Let them know what you expect and when you expect it, even if you don't need it so much by that particular date." This "deadline training" will go a long way towards helping them develop good habits as an independent worker.

Given that the team member is diligent, experienced, and a self-starter, Paprocki believes that the responsibility for the success of a telecommuting program lies with the manager. "The most important thing is to maintain good verbal and written communication via telephone or e-mail." You should disseminate information in short, easily managed chunks so the employee can process and integrate it into his workload. To this end, Paprocki has developed weekly newsletters that are e-mailed to all regional coordinators and camp leaders, "with a calendar section at the top, so they know what to do and when."

As with any office employee, "you need to let them know they're being monitored and their work evaluated." Her team members understand, for example that she regularly checks whether fliers promoting the camps have been distributed to the proper outlets. She offers rewards for positive behavior as well. "They receive financial incentives if they recruit X number of campers."

In the final analysis, she says, the relationship between team member and manager should be tempered with flexibility and mutual respect. "While you need to be understanding of their schedule and other responsibilities, make sure that a regular reporting system is implemented and that they can come to you with any problems and concerns. Nothing takes the place of one-to-one contact."

SUMMARY

Thanks to the influx of technology and desire for companies to be "lean and green," telecommuting is here to stay. Although, like everything else, it has both advantages and pitfalls, telecommuting can be beneficial for all concerned. Along with flexibility and convenience, it allows for employment of previously marginal groups like those who are housebound due to family ties or disabilities and others living in remote areas. Managers of telecommuters find their employees to be more productive, motivated, and stable in terms of job tenure and satisfaction. This is due in part to the reduction in stress by eliminating the commute and dealing with office-related issues. Companies also opt for telecommuting because of its adaptability—they can recruit and retain workers from anywhere in the world and be open around the clock. Telecommuting also (most importantly) saves money in reduced overhead and retraining.

Of course, there are problems in telecommuting: loneliness, isolation, and possible overwork for the employee; apprehension for the manager about whether the team member is really doing the job; and security issues and potential legal complications for companies. But an intelligently designed and well-organized and executed telecommuting system can alleviate many of these issues.

Finally, managers need to make sure the jobs lend themselves to telecommuting. Many of these positions fall into certain categories: computers, customer service, graphics and video, legal, medical, writing/editing, and sales, among others. Although it's important that the teleworker carry out his or her responsibilities, the burden of success falls on the manager to make sure that the job is being done.

CHAPTER 2

Types of Nontraditional Work Arrangements

INTRODUCTION

This chapter will discuss the many flavors of telecommuting, from "chocolate"—the most popular and traditional home office—to the more exotic "lime cardamom frozen yogurt with lingonberries," using Skype in the virtual office and hot desking (when employees share a communal desk as needed).

We'll cover some other aspects of telecommuting, such as determining the difference between independent contractors (IC) versus regular (W-2) employees. Classification of these different types is monitored by several government agencies (most notably the IRS) and in some cases involves complicated criteria. Finally, this chapter will address the question of whether employees should be paid by the hour, by the piece/project, or by commission.

INDEPENDENT CONTRACTORS (IC) AND REGULAR (W-2) EMPLOYEES

Due to the very nature of the work arrangement the distinction between independent contractors (IC) or regular (W-2) employees more easily becomes blurred than for traditional office workers. However, it's extremely important you be aware of the difference, because you must pay taxes for employees; for independent contractors, you don't have to pay taxes.

The price for misclassification can be steep. If you incorrectly categorize an employee as an independent contractor, the government can hold you liable for benefits as well as employment taxes for that worker. In addition, it can impose a penalty. Rules change and new interpretations are common—as are misinterpretations, especially if you are unfamiliar with the nuances of the various regulations. So it's best to consult an accountant or a labor relations expert (or lawyer specializing in same) when making this determination.

Along with other state and federal agencies, the Internal Revenue Service (IRS) serves as a watchdog on this matter and has set forth guidelines about who controls what. According to the IRS, you must withhold income taxes, withhold and pay Social Security and Medicare taxes, and pay unemployment tax on wages paid to an employee (Form W-2 worker). You do not generally have to withhold or pay any taxes on payments to independent contractors (Form 1099 worker).

Types of Classifications

According to the IRS, when dealing with an independent contractor "you, the payer, have the right to control or direct only the *result* of the work done . . . and not the *means and methods* of accomplishing the result." Examples of independent contractors include an electrician, a transcriptionist, or anyone who works independently for several different companies or clients from a separate site (such as a home office) and who supplies their own equipment.

In contrast, an employee is anyone who performs services for you in which *you control how and when* it will be done. These can be people who work at a call center (whether based in their homes or at a separate site) or do the majority of their work for one company, even if they are based at home. Many of these telecommuting workers have full corporate jobs with benefits and are on a schedule dictated by the employer. Such employees have jobs as underwriters, software engineers, financial analysts, marketing managers, or many others. The point here, though, is that you, the employer, tell them how to do the job and when to do it.

Then there are *statutory employees*, who, under the law, while they may be based at home or are otherwise away from the office are to be treated as employees.. For example:

- A full-time life insurance sales agent whose principal business activity is selling life insurance or annuity contracts, or both, primarily for one life insurance company.
- An individual who works at home on materials or goods that you supply and that must be returned to you or to a person you name, if you also furnish specifications for the work to be done. This can include someone who produces items by the piece or does other light manufacturing, similar to a factory worker whose assembly line is at home.
- A full-time traveling or city salesperson who works on your behalf and turns in orders to you from wholesalers, retailers, contractors, or operators of hotels, restaurants, or other similar establishments. The goods sold must be merchandise for resale or supplies for use in the buyer's business operation. The work performed for you must be the salesperson's principal business activity.

Categories of Control

In deciding on the tax status of the people who work for you, the IRS looks at questions of control and independence. Conveniently, they've broken this down into three categories.

1. *Behavioral control.* This deals with the kind of instructions given to the worker as well as when and where they work and train. "The key consideration," the IRS guidelines state, "is whether the business has retained the right to control the details of a worker's performance or instead has given up that right." If you've given up this kind of control, then the employee is an independent contractor.

2. *Financial control.* This includes such issues as unre-
   imbursed business expenses (usually the case with
   independent contractors, although there are exceptions);
   the extent of the worker's investment (independent
   contractors often invest in their own equipment and
   facilities); and whether or not the worker makes his
   services available to the marketplace in general (as
   independent contractors often do). The IRS guidelines
   say, "An employee is generally guaranteed a regular
   wage amount for an hourly, weekly, or other period of
   time . . . even when the wage or salary is supplemented
   by a commission." On the other hand, "An independent
   contractor is usually paid . . . a flat fee for the job"
   although there are exceptions (see "Hourly vs. 'By the
   Piece' work" on page 27).
3. *Type of relationship.* The nature of the work arrangement may be defined by such things as a written contract
   which describes the relationship between you and the
   worker; whether the business will provide employee
   benefits such as a pension plan, vacation, or health insurance; and the permanency of the relationship. Employees
   are generally hired indefinitely while independent contractors are engaged for specific projects or time periods.

Finally, the IRS looks at the extent to which the services are a
key aspect of the company's regular business. If the worker's duties
are so integral to your business that you must direct and control
his activities, you're probably in an employee-employer relationship—and you'll be responsible for taxes for the employee.

The IRS lists some twenty factors that provide even more detail
and clarification as to whether the employer has enough control to
establish an employer-employee relationship. Known as Revenue
Ruling 87-41, the list can be found on page 139 and will be discussed further in Chapter 11.

HOME OFFICE

Now that you know the kind of employees or contractors you'll need, the next logical question is where to put them. Many companies take the environmentally friendly path of least resistance—the home office. This is the most commonly known form of telecommuting. For most people it's what comes to mind when they think of this type of work. It's also where the vast majority of telecommuting jobs are located. According to the US Census, nearly 4.2 million people worked from home in 2000, up from 3.4 million in 1990, and it's a good guess that these figures are probably very low. This 23 percent increase doesn't even include those who worked at home during part of the week (but elsewhere more days than at home), so the numbers of home-based telecommuters are probably higher.

The concept is simple: Your employee sets up a workspace in a well-defined area, such as a spare bedroom or basement. If no other space is available and there are no kids, pets, or other potentially destructive entities, she can use the dining room table or other central location. But this is a short-term fix, because eventually workers will need a room of their own where they can store their stuff and close the door, if only for psychological distance.

Telecommuting workers purchase equipment and furniture with the sole purpose of using it for their jobs. If they are independent contractors, they also pay quarterly taxes to the IRS, city, and state and are allowed deductibles for having a business in their home.

Workers classified as company employees receive regular paychecks with deductions for taxes, Social Security, and benefits (health insurance, 401(k), etc.).

Depending upon what kind of equipment they buy and whether or not they are reimbursed, employees may also qualify for deductibles. However if they use the office for other purposes such as personal computing or answering ads on Match.com, then only a percentage may be allowed for the equipment and space. Given the fluid nature of tax laws, that may change, so always check with an accountant or other expert.

THE HOME OFFICE DREAM

Although the home office may seem like a dream come true for a cubicle-farm refugee, it can present many challenges. Those with small children will need to figure out a way to keep them away from the space. Pets, too can cause problems, with hair that can clog equipment, and "accidents" and chewing incidents wreaking havoc on furniture, computer cords, and important pieces of paper.

Barking, meowing, and chirping can also present problems when considering background noise, as Michael can attest. One of his former call center employees used her home office to breed birds. Customers soon grew curious about all the non-human twittering that was going on in the background. Needless to say, she was soon asked to hang up her headset. So it's best to work behind a closed door, especially if there is a bathroom nearby.

As a manager, you should consider what your employee will need in terms of equipment, workspace, storage, and inventory. Generally a home office is impractical if a large amount of equipment and/or space is required, as is the case with retail or manufacturing. Service businesses, such as editing, medical transcription, and call center/customer service can lend themselves very well to this type of environment. However, if the job requires that a client visit the site or the work requires highly specialized and expensive equipment, then a home office may not be the solution.

REMOTE WORK CENTER

While not as convenient for the teleworker as the home office— having your desk and computer a few feet away from the rest of the house is the ultimate dream commute—remote work centers (also known as satellite telework centers) are mini-facilities owned by the company. As with a traditional office, employees report for work during regular hours, and the center has the usual desks, chairs, and office equipment, although on a smaller and sometimes more casual scale than a traditional office setting. A company can own or lease several remote work centers in different areas, increasing its national or global presence at less than it would cost to open full-scale operations in these areas.

The main difference between satellite and regular offices is proximity—employees live closer to the remote facility than the main office. The employees are still telecommuters in the broad sense of the term. This type of arrangement works with a variety of jobs because of the advantages of operating from an office setting. For example, telecommuters working from a remote work center may have meetings with clients at the center, something that would be more difficult if they were working from their homes. If you choose to set up such a center, you may wish to arrange for employees to work part-time from their homes and the rest of the week from the remote work center.

SHARED SPACE

Job sharing was a big deal in the 1980s and early 1990s. Job sharing involves two (occasionally more) employees who divide the duties of a forty-hours-a-week job and split the pay between them. It is more common these days in government positions and overseas. However, the twenty-first century has given rise to a different but a similar-sounding concept: shared office space (or serviced office space). This phenomenon seems to be on the rise, as evidenced by the proliferation of real estate ads for this type of arrangement on the Internet and elsewhere.

Shared space is the use of a fully equipped and furnished office by more than one employee, usually at different times. (Think of it as an office time share.) Setting up shared space allows you to quickly establish a branch office and may be ideal for the independent contractor who would rather not work from home and wants to present an office setting to suppliers and clients. Like remote work centers, shared spaces can be a solution to the sense of loneliness and isolation common to home offices. In a shared space there are other workers present, often in the same occupation (for instance, in a shared sales office).

Also known as business centers and executive suites, these facilities provide mail, telephone, and Internet services. Shared office space also offers professional facilities at a lower cost than traditional office rents, since the cost is split between several different companies. They work well for telecommuters who report to the office in staggered shifts or who are in the same or similar professions and need the same kinds of equipment and facilities.

Shared space can even improve your business opportunities. Your employees, sharing their workspace with other professionals, can use the opportunity to establish beneficial relationships (such as finding a lawyer or accountant) as well as generating referrals for new clients.

Use of this type of space is generally short-term and flexible; leases can run six to twelve months (or longer, for greater discounts); some even have three-month options. *Subleasing* is similarly open-ended; a larger company will rent out desk space or a group of offices. Renters share kitchens, conference rooms, and other facilities with the leasing company.

Shared space can present scheduling problems (if an employee needs to work at the same time another worker is scheduled). As well the desk, phone, computer, and other equipment are yours only for the time that your employee is on duty. This can present a problem if information is sensitive. If your employee has sloppy work habits such as keeping a messy desk, this can create difficulties with the other professionals who share the space.

Still the arrangement can be ideal for small business owners, start-up companies, or those looking to establish a branch for telecommuters. As always with any leasing arrangement, you should consider such factors as the location, the other tenants—ideally, they do the same or similar kinds of work and use the same equipment—and of course the terms of the contract.

VIRTUAL OFFICE

Described as "the business with no office to telecommute from," a virtual office has no actual physical location but enables workers to run a business by using online communication technologies. The employee's car, back porch, or the neighborhood coffee shop can be her or his virtual office.

In many ways a virtual office is ideal for telecommuters. Not only does it require little if any money, but even though the employee's coworkers may be hundreds or possibly thousands of miles away, she is in constant communication through the Internet and other technologies. Virtual offices are very similar to home telecommuting arrangements.

Members of Generations X and Y are familiar and comfortable with the concept of the virtual office. It allows for inexpensive (if not free) communication by instant messaging, blogging, and Skype, as well as more established forms like web conferencing, e-mail, fax, and for transportation of physical items (such as order fulfillment) good old-fashioned snail-mail, FedEx, and UPS. (A software program created by entrepreneurs Niklas Zennström and Janus Friis, Skype allows computer users to make free telephone calls to other Skype users anywhere in the world, along with enabling computer calls to land lines and cell phones for a small fee. Additional features include instant messaging, file transfer, short message service, video conferencing and the ability to circumvent firewalls.)

This arrangement can be especially comfortable for people who have limited living space and don't have room to set up a home office. As well, it works for people who enjoy getting out and working away from home in a different environment or for a change of pace.

As with home-based offices, time management can be a problem—where does the employee's personal life begin and business day end? But the instant-gratification factor is high, always a big selling point with Generations X and Y.

The "Dirt" on a Virtual Office

Dennis Yang works at Techdirt, a virtual company that provides daily news and analysis to corporate clients. While Yang does not sit with coworkers, he is never lonely. He typically has about seven conversations going on at any one time on his computer screen, and he can work anywhere he wants—for example, his grandmother's living room.

A typical day involves constant instant messaging, occasional e-mails with clients, and Skype for Internet-based phone calls, which are free—though Yang adds, "We don't like to have phone conversations because it's difficult to have more than one at a time."

Techdirt's fourteen employees hang out in a virtual conference room, which is really a chat room, and when the once-a-week phone call happens, someone types in the chat room that it's time to move to the conference call.

OFFICE HOTELING

Yet another type of telecommuting arrangement is known as office hoteling (or simply hoteling). Rather than having their own offices, cubicles, or even desks, workers or their managers reserve whatever space or resources they think they will need ahead of time. This can be in an office or other building or even in a hotel itself and unlike shared space, can be more of a temporary or as-needed arrangement.

Some companies even provide areas especially designed for hoteling. Introduced in 1994 by the advertising agency Chiat/Day, businesses ranging from real estate agencies to consulting and law firms to sales reps have "checked in" to the concept.

According to *techtarget.com*, hoteling "reduces the amount of physical space that an enterprise needs, lowering overhead cost while (ideally) ensuring that every worker can access office resources when necessary." Because of its flexible nature, hoteling is especially conducive to telecommuting, particularly when large numbers of workers are constantly on the road.

Hoteling is also advantageous to employees who work independently, such as consultants, salespeople, and others based out of their cars or home offices. "In this scenario, employees can call ahead and reserve an office space for the day or for a few hours," observe authors Kimball and Mareen Duncan Fisher. "This allows at least occasional office interaction."

However, hoteling may fail if you neglect to communicate the reasons for implementing it. Workers may resent losing their desks and offices, even if they are only part-time or already sharing. And if a hoteling policy is inconsistent—if you apply it to some workers and not others for seemingly arbitrary reasons—it can cause even more dissatisfaction and misunderstandings. When setting up a hoteling arrangement, clearly explain the reasons for it and the benefits it provides to all workers. Pay close attention to details, such as making sure that desks, software, and office supplies are replenished, reliable, and up-to-date.

HOURLY VERSUS "BY THE PIECE" WORK

In setting up a telecommuting program, the next question you as a manager will face is how will the telecommuting workers be paid? Some telecommuting jobs—for instance, administrative or virtual assistants or call center workers—are usually paid by the hour. Generally speaking, jobs that involve easily measurable results (typist, phone sales or solicitation) receive an hourly wage. They include but are not limited to billing, claims, actuary, adjuster, underwriter, deposition taker, collections, and transcriptionist.

However, consultant or creative positions may not be as clear-cut. You will have to decide if these are paid hourly or by the project. Such jobs may include software designer, systems trouble-shooter, computer scientist, hardware product developer, industrial engineering, information systems manager, manual tester/writer, security specialist, systems analyst, food consultant, relocation consultant, journalist, copywriter, marketing specialist, researcher, abstractor, technical writer/editor, electronic media designer, video animation specialist, computer graphics specialist, photographer/videographer, photo researcher, and others. With these types of jobs, results are often less readily measurable; whether or not a design or software program effectively meets your company's needs can be open to interpretation.

Several factors need to be considered regarding the hourly versus project pay structure.

How much time will the project take? Because hourly workers keep time sheets and are paid for the exact amount of time spent, costs could add up quickly if extra work is involved. And as a manager you must also consider what constitutes a work hour—does it include coffee breaks, socializing with members of the team, and other nonessentials? And it needs to be the same for everyone: ARO call center workers are allowed one fifteen-minute break for each four hours that they work. An eight-hour worker gets two paid fifteen-minute breaks and an unpaid half-hour for lunch.

What is the project worth? With piece/project work, you and the contractor will usually agree on the price at the beginning of the project, based on a quote from the contractor. But this can create problems as well. What if the project is considerably less involved than either of you thought? Spending twice as much money on something that requires half the anticipated time and effort is hardly cost-effective. Nor is it fair to the worker if the opposite is true, and the contractor ends up having to do much more work for the same wage.

How long is it going to take? In the planning stages, you or the telecommuting contractor should provide a basic timeline and estimate of how long the project will take. You can do this by developing benchmarks—milestones defined by certain features. For example, in writing this book, the authors agreed to a schedule based on a certain number of chapters to be written per month, with a turnaround time of about one week to incorporate all final revisions and changes. Although your initial planning may involve extra work, you will catch schedule slips or delays early, keeping everyone in the loop and preventing overruns of time, cost, and effort.

To ensure the success of a task, make a list of what needs to be done. Once tasks are written down, you will get a clearer idea of what the task involves. It's important to agree on details about exactly what must be accomplished. This applies particularly to longer-term projects, although these tactics are useful in estimating shorter projects as well. You can even do this for call centers, which can measure the progress of some projects by the number of calls processed per hour.

Still other telecommuting jobs, such as sales (and also some telephone work) may be paid on commission: a base hourly salary, plus extra compensation for however many measurable phone calls/referrals/sales the employee makes or receives over a certain limit or quota. This type of arrangement can motivate people to work harder and rewards achievement. However, if the sale or referral falls through, the employee is not paid commensurate with the time and effort he has spent, even if he's given it his best attempt.

SUMMARY
Welcome to the brave new world of telecommuting with its many sizes and shapes, and even more cutting-edge ideas and arrangements developing as of this writing. So how do you figure out what's the best for your workers?

The first question to address is whether they are hourly wage workers (W-2s) or independent contractors. The IRS guidelines can help you figure this out by referring to the three kinds of control as well as twenty additional criteria.

The main difference is that with independent contractors you only direct the result. With W-2 employees, you are overseeing the means and methods by which they accomplish that result. It's an important concept, as failure to correctly classify employees could cost you and your company big bucks in taxes and other penalties.

Then it's on to *where* they should accomplish the work—in a home office, remote center, shared space, virtual office, or via a "hoteling" arrangement. Each type has advantages and disadvantages, and often distinctions between the different kinds of setups can be blurred. Concentrate on your desired results or goals and figure out which arrangement best and most cost-effectively suits the needs of both your business and its telecommuters.

Finally, you must address *how* you should pay your workers—by the hour or by the piece/project. Although some categories such as administrative assistant and customer service have traditionally received an hourly wage, many others can go either (or both) ways. Again, it's up to you to determine how the work is best compensated to benefit both the company and its employees. Key to this is figuring out what needs to be done, when it needs to be done, and how long it will take. You can also consider whether or not employees should receive a commission.

No matter what you decide, the determination needs to be within the parameters of the law and requirements of the job. The IRS and labor relations experts can provide you with additional criteria and guidance.

CHAPTER 3

The Telecommuting "Personality"

INTRODUCTION

Is there a "telecommuter personality"? Yes, but . . .

In truth, many of the characteristics of effective telecommuters are desirable in office workers as well. However, there are also important distinctions. As a manager you probably *don't* want to hire someone with an unrealistic concept of telework. ("Oh, I can take care of my kids and the neighbors' kids and clean the house *and* watch *Oprah*!") Nor do you want someone who is psychologically incapable of handling the unique challenges of a non-office environment. This chapter will help you determine the characteristics of someone best suited for telecommuting, be it a bookkeeper, technical writer, or traveling salesperson.

POOR CANDIDATES

In general, poor telecommuting candidates include those who:

- Need to meet face-to-face with people in the workplace every day
- Must operate complicated, expensive, and large machinery, such as in manufacturing operations
- Require extensive training or supervision
- Need a large amount of reassurance and positive reinforcement

In his book *Managing Telework*, Jack Nilles points out that, along with bureaucrats and other individuals who have inflexible work habits, socializers who need face-to-face interaction should stick to the office.

When interviewing for telecommuting positions, human resources people should not only modify what they're looking for but also whom. Joye Moore, the general manager of Michael's company, ARO, had to make major adjustments when they began selecting customer services reps who worked at home. "When hiring an individual for the office, I focused on three things: image, attitude, and skills," she recalls. Physical appearance—in the sense that the person is neat and presentable in their dress and manners—is vital, if only to present the impression of professionalism to coworkers and clients.

Habits and mannerisms are also important when considering office work. Does the person talk loudly on the phone and with coworkers or chew with his mouth open, leaving crumbs all over the desk? Does she over-share the personal details of her life or, at the opposite end, appear unsociable? Although such things may seem petty and irrelevant to the tasks at hand, when you're working with a team forty hours a week in what is usually an open environment, even the smallest quirks can grate on others' nerves and eventually interfere with productivity.

Face-to-face contact is important but may not be as much when hiring telecommuters. If you're conducting a job interview over the phone, "you miss out on body language, which can speak volumes," continues Moore. "If the person has his arms folded or avoids your gaze, it's a good bet they're lying, and there's no way to tell that over the phone." On the other hand, however, "we've hired some really good people that we might not have otherwise considered, based on their phone skills. And for this job that's exactly what we're looking for—someone who is well spoken, articulate, and focused." In the case of the telecommuter who works entirely from home and has no contact with customers other than by phone or e-mail, personal appearance and grooming become immaterial. Whether the individual fails to brush his hair, prefers the window open in the dead of winter, or even works in the nude is irrelevant, as long as he gets the work done. (Although if the latter, he should definitely keep it to himself.)

QUALITIES TO LOOK FOR

Although experts may not exactly agree on what constitutes an ideal "telecommuting personality"—much depends on the characteristics of the job itself and what it requires—they do find common traits among successful telecommuters. Number one is self-discipline, with a willingness to work independently and ability to manage time running a close second and third. Communications skills are also vital, as is conscientiousness. As someone who has juggled various clients for years, Sandra knows the importance of constant contact with them, whether by phone, fax, or e-mail.

What Makes A Good Telecommuter?

Skill Set
- Results-oriented
- Excellent communications skills
- Doesn't require a lot of supervision
- Adaptable
- Very organized
- Solid job knowledge
- Thorough understanding of organization's objectives
- Strong focus on job goals and objectives
- Can establish priorities and manage time well

Other considerations
- Candidate has been successful in current and prior positions
- Candidate's home environment is favorable to telework
- Job has tasks suited for telework
- Job has clearly defined work objectives

Telecommuters also need to be more concerned than their office counterparts with deadlines, work products, and results. For one thing, they're not around to observe nuances from managers and coworkers that can provide tip-offs to real feelings, like off-the-cuff comments or body language hints such as eye-rolling. You, as a manager, need to make sure that telecommuters know exactly where they stand.

Sylvie Charrier, author of "You Can Work in Your PJs," believes that successful telecommuters have four personality traits.

1. *Self-Motivated.* Telecommuters "are completely reliant on [their] own steam to get things done . . . and don't need anyone to remind [them] about deadlines," she writes. Rather than looking for constant guidance from others, they tend to find their own answers (although they should never hesitate in asking questions if they need clarification).

2. *Obsessive-Compulsive.* Adrian Monk from the hit detective TV show of the same name has obsessive-compulsive disorder. But his attention to detail and ability to follow through is validated when he solves every case! Telecommuters "have the type of personality that feels compelled to finish what [they] start," no matter what the inconvenience, continues Charrier. They "simply refuse to fail."

3. *Perfectionist.* Another Adrian Monk trait, "this refers to individuals who are never quite satisfied with the work that they do," she adds. Because they look for logic and patterns in everything, perfectionists are quick to spot mistakes in themselves or others. They're often so diligent that they'll point out their errors to you, rather than have you find it and catch it at a later time. It goes without saying that this trait would benefit almost any workplace, telecommuting or otherwise.

4. *Cheerful and Optimistic.* These traits are essential in telecommuters, because they'll need an inner resilience to be able to continue to focus on their work despite the many interruptions and distractions that life can present. They also need to be comfortable being alone.

Unlike an office, which provides a cushion against the worries of home and temptations of procrastination ("What if the boss walks in?"), the teleworker is often in the home environment all day long. They must be able to compartmentalize and say, "I know the bills need to be paid and Johnny's grades have fallen, but I have to get this job done and will deal with that later."

Some of the above traits seem contradictory: An optimistic perfectionist? Someone who's willing to compartmentalize but is obsessive-compulsive? But when in the right proportion and combination they can add up, because the "ideal" telecommuter maintains a *sense of balance* in her work and personal life.

According to the Telecommuter Work Life Balance Survey, "telecommuters who reported greater work/life balance had a personality profile that included being less neurotic (i.e., less anxious, angry, nervous), more conscientious (i.e., organized, self-disciplined, goal-oriented), more extroverted, and indicated their central life interest to be work-related." Besides having the support of their managers and families, and an environment conducive to their work, they were able to balance work, life, family and other outside interests, even when these demands clashed or competed against each other.

Personal Traits Checklist for Employer

A telecommuter:
- Is good at organization
- Can set goals and meet them
- Can develop schedules and stick to them

- Can deal with the isolation of telecommuting
- Can deal well with distractions
- Can work well with a minimum of supervision
- Can communicate well using technologies such as phones, fax, and e-mail
- Is self-motivated and mostly avoids procrastination
- Is flexible
- Is able to balance work and life: not a workaholic yet able to set limits with personal issues
- Is good at meeting deadlines
- Is a competent time manager
- Can deal autonomously with roadblocks and setbacks
- Can make decisions independently
- Can manage stress

LIFE STAGES AND THE TELECOMMUTER

Some of the advantages of telecommuting discussed in Chapter 1 included its convenience for those who care for elderly parents and/or young children. However that only works if the employee has encouragement from all family members. "If the family environment is supportive, productivity and morale can soar," observes Nilles. But family members can also be intrusive and drain attention away from work. Family care works best when those individuals needing care receive it separately so the telecommuter can work uninterrupted. If a telecommuter has a child at home, encourage her to hire a babysitter at least part-time or to drop the child at a care center a few days a week. Such arrangements should be in place before you hire the telecommuter.

"Many successful home teleworkers are at stages in their lives when working at home has positive tradeoffs," continues Nilles. "As a counter example, young singles, who often depend on peer contact to meet and form social relationships, may want to be on site . . . with access to a pool of potential leisure, as well as work friends."

Michael has found this to be true at ARO as well, where most of the workers are in their late forties and older, often within the Baby Boomer age range. He attributes this to the fact that they've "been there, done that" in the office and simply don't want to be bothered with the day-to-day annoyances and politics that can sometimes crop up when you're penned in with the same people 9 to 5, week after week. Teleworkers, he finds, simply want to get the job done, do it well, get paid, and get on with their lives.

There is some indication, however, that this may be changing. Jade Harris, a frequent contributor to *www.telecooler.com*, a website and blog geared toward younger professionals, recently took Nilles's observation to task. "It should be clear that [the positive tradeoffs] are not desired solely by middle-age and senior employees," she writes. "Many 'young singles' would strive to work from home in order to reap the same rewards. . . . And while it is true that the office can be an excellent place to meet people and make friends, the growing trend toward making connections over the Internet drives holes into the theory that if not for workplace socialization, casual interaction would cease to exist."

A recent study at North Carolina A & T University bears out the fact that telecommuting is an option the emerging generation is widely considering. In addition to finding that successful telecommuters needed to possess many of the traits discussed in this chapter, the study added that a desirable quality in telecommuters was flexibility—"being able to move from one [problem-solving] approach to another"—and "technological inclination . . . skill in harnessing the power of information technology for problem solving." The latter is especially true of Generations X and Y.

The graduate students in the 2001 study were "keenly aware . . . of the unique demands of the telecommuting work environment." While it was understood that telecommuting was not for everyone, the study "suggests the importance of fostering and reinforcing [traits] in both the academic setting and the workplace." So it may not be your grandmother's telecommuting for much longer.

SUMMARY

Although there is no "perfect" telecommuter, certain characteristics are required to succeed in this type of work. You, as a manager, should know in advance what to expect from your teleworker. If she or he seems unable to work independently or has difficulty making decisions or meeting deadlines, then the situation will likely be problematic. Let's face it, some people are born to work in an office, while others are born—or are driven—to work away from it!

Successful telecommuters possess four important but seemingly contradictory traits—self-motivated, obsessive-compulsive, perfectionist, and cheerful/optimistic. The first three appear consistent with one another, while the fourth seems completely at odds with the others. However, when you consider another important characteristic—the ability to balance and coordinate competing demands—the need for the fourth quality becomes more understandable. If the worker has a supportive family and conducive work environment, his situation is as close as possible to the ideal.

Conventional thinking has been that telecommuting is best for older workers or those with families or eldercare needs. However, with the prevalence of technology and the fact that telecommuting has become more accepted and widely used, it's no surprise that the younger generation is getting in on the act. With that in mind, academic institutions are becoming aware of the need to train workers in developing the traits necessary to succeed as a telecommuter in addition to those needed in the office environment.

Regardless, you need to be cognizant of the "telecommuting personality" in order to make at least some basic decisions about whom you hire to work at home or otherwise independently.

CHAPTER 4

Types of Virtual Teams

INTRODUCTION

Virtual teams have become a part of the everyday workscape, both for telecommuters and office workers. This chapter defines virtual teams and their functions as well as the different types of teams.

"Real-time" communication, that is, "live" interaction either face-to-face or in a virtual environment (as opposed to "offline" done at varying times in an electronic bulletin board or e-mail type environment, with no direct interaction), is vital to the success of your virtual teams. So you need to find and select the best software and applications that will facilitate operations. Some suggestions as to how to do this are included as well.

WHAT ARE VIRTUAL TEAMS?

Sometimes known as Geographically Dispersed Teams (GDT), virtual teams allow organizations to hire and retain the most qualified people regardless of where they are located.

Virtual teams can consist of employees who work either at home and/or at one or more offices in different areas.

Why Virtual Teams?

Today's global environment, with its continued shift from production to service/knowledge increasingly places less emphasis on physical location. While there will always be a use for office workers and manufacturing facilities, many companies outsource work to individuals or groups. Tasks assigned to virtual teams range from the more routine, such as customer care, to highly specialized design or computer programming. The bottom line for creating a virtual team is that in order for the job to get done you don't need everybody physically there to do it.

Even as recently as the 1980s, office workers had a modicum of job security. However, in the current corporate climate, with its cost-cutting measures and mergers and acquisitions, no position is safe. Yet it is this very atmosphere that has fostered the proliferation of virtual teams. In creating these teams, management looks at such factors as organization-wide projects or initiatives; alliances with different organizations, some of which may be in other countries; and emerging markets in different geographic locations.

Companies focused on the bottom line know it is cheaper to have someone on board who can do the job and who has the proper equipment and skills, no matter where they are based. Hiring a telecommuter can be cheaper than relocating a worker or paying for training or travel. The following section discusses different types of virtual teams.

NETWORKED TEAMS

According to authors Deborah Duarte and Nancy Tennant Snyder, networked teams typically cross time, distance, and organizational boundaries and lack a clear definition between the team and the organization. "Membership is frequently diffuse and fluid, with team members rotating on and off . . . as their expertise is needed." In fact, the structure of this type of team is so loosely based that its members may not even be aware of everyone who is in the network. Team members may be drawn, on a permanent or part-time basis, from universities, think tanks, corporations, or even different countries.

Networked teams can be found in consulting firms and high-tech organizations such as research and development companies that need specialized expertise or problem-solving that break out of traditional boundaries. For example, if a healthcare certification firm was assigned to define best practices for its member hospitals, and the company did not have the information on hand, it could use its various partners and databases as a resource to obtain the information.

Such teams often draw in telecommuting workers, depending on their needs of the moment.

PARALLEL TEAMS

Like the Special Forces or Navy Seals, parallel teams implement unusual or specialized assignments, tasks, or functions. Often these projects are ones that the organization has neither the time, equipment, or interest in performing. These types of teams are used when the skill required cannot be found in the organization or at a particular location. As with networked teams, they cross time, distance, and organizational boundaries, but unlike networked teams, parallel teams have a distinct membership. Everyone knows who is on the team, and team members work closely to achieve a goal. These teams are often found in multinational and global organizations when there is a need to define and provide a broad overview of worldwide processes and systems.

Once the project is completed and the goal achieved, the team is disbanded.

PROJECT/PRODUCT TEAMS

Like the first two types of teams, project or product development teams cross time, distance, and organizational boundaries. And like parallel teams they are assigned with the task of conducting or developing a specific project. Similar to networked teams, people move off and on the team as their expertise is required. Yet these teams are unique in several important ways:

1. The focus is on a new product, information system, or organizational process
2. The teams usually exist for a longer period of time and have the authority to make decisions, not just recommendations

Members of such teams are clearly delineated, and the goals of the teams are explicitly stated.

Project/product teams are likely to be found in companies developing a specific product or technology or engaging in scientific research. Along with having a great deal of influence and potential impact, this type of team uses a variety of resources to create new offerings or projects that can provide a competitive edge.

PRODUCTION TEAMS

Also known as work or functional teams, production teams perform more routine or ongoing types of tasks. In the past, members of such teams were office workers, but today they can also be telecommuters, operating virtually and crossing boundaries of time and distance because they can work in any time zone or live in any place. These types of teams are often located, whether virtually or face-to-face, in global call or business centers and operate around-the-clock so they can provide service to customers 24/7.

As telecommuters, they have access to the company's intranet, so they can log on any time and document their activities/goals. They may meet face-to-face during training or for conferences, but even this they may do virtually.

SERVICE TEAMS

This type of team provides support or technical assistance. They may work around-the-clock dealing with problems and providing help, passing along any unresolved workload and issues to the next shift. Located anywhere and available whenever needed, they are distributed across distance and time. Many times finding individuals with specialized technical expertise from a single geographical area is nearly impossible. If you're putting together this kind of team, you'll need to be able to recruit from all over the U.S. and possibly other countries.

MANAGEMENT TEAMS

Like service teams, management teams too can be dispersed across distance and time. They work together, often on a daily basis, to achieve corporate objectives and goals via audio and video conferences as well as through e-mail and other forms of electronic messaging.

ACTION TEAMS

These teams offer immediate responses, many times to an emergency. Crossing distance and organizational boundaries, their membership may be fluid. A national or international news organization is a good example of an action team (in fact, that's what they often call themselves). They have regular reporters or anchors and also use area correspondents or "stringers" for specific locations. Along with the camera crew or photographers who send images and film, they provide information that is transmitted to the editor and disseminated to the public via print or broadcast.

HOW VIRTUAL TEAMS WORK TOGETHER

Because they are disbursed across time, space, and organization, virtual teams are faced with many more communications challenges than traditional office-based teams. However, the obstacles caused by physical separation—lack of communication, misunderstandings resulting from discrepancies in language and culture, and time zone differences—can often be resolved by collaborative technologies, including software specifically designed to help virtual teams accomplish their goals.

Duarte and Snyder list software as among the seven primary factors in virtual teams' success. They cite the importance of consistent standards for and management support of electronic communication and collaboration tools; the need for resources to purchase the best and most effective software; and the importance of making sure that all team members have access to and training in technology.

Software must also provide ease of communication and include such features as presence awareness, instant messaging, and web conferencing. You and your team need constant access that transcends time differences even for members located across the globe. By participating in "real-time" virtual conversations, you can deal with the situation directly and immediately and eliminate confusion.

Software must also enable organization of team tasks and documents via a central program that is accessible to all members. Team members should be able to locate key information, track progress, assign and organize tasks, and maintain calendars with important dates, schedules, and specific goals so everyone is on the same virtual page.

For example, ARO uses an easy-to-use, collaborative program similar to Google Docs (*docs.google.com*), which allows a project to be defined as a spreadsheet of action items. Each member of the team can update the same project outline, and everyone is kept in the loop in "real-time" with a clear idea of which tasks have been completed. Perhaps best of all, the Google Docs shareware is free.

Not surprisingly, the proliferation of virtual teams has resulted in a figurative explosion of software. Programs include Microsoft Office Groove, a peer-to-peer platform used for collaboration; TeamDirection intended for communications and information sharing; and SharePoint, which allows for project collaboration, document sharing, meeting management, discussion boards, and mobile access. These programs may be used together, separately, or in conjunction with other applications. Other systems used by virtual teams are IBM's Lotus, Facilitate.com, and Thinktank.

The software is ever evolving, so when choosing a system look closely at the functionality of applications as it relates to your workload. Another option is selecting a la carte applications that can be chosen individually based on the company's requirements—some of which are mentioned in the sidebar below.

Regardless of whether it's a package deal or one of your own making, the goal of the system is to keep team members engaged in "real-time" rather than "offline," which can result in misunderstandings, problems, and inadequate results.

A Virtual Team "Toolbox"

In the kaleidoscopic world of virtual team technology, finding the right tools can be a challenge. The following is a list of some of the more commonly used applications—at least, as of this writing.

Communication Tools (replaces face-to-face communication)
- Skype
- Gizmo
- Jajah
- Google Talk
- Google Docs

Presentation (the best offer real-time screens, which help with brainstorming and design)
- GoToMeeting
- webEx
- BudgetConferencing
- LiveMeeting

Project Management (helps with planning, scheduling, division of tasks, and tracking)
- Basecamp
- CentralDesktop
- ActiveCollab
- TeamWork Live
- QuickBase

Calendar (so everybody knows who is doing what and when they need to get it done)
- Google Calendar
- Yahoo! Calendar
- 30 Boxes

Code Repository (for software developers, provides source code version control)
- CVSDude
- SourceHosting
- Versionhost

Backup
- ElephantDrive
- JungleDisk
- Mozy

Accounting/Payroll (in lieu of or to supplement a bookkeeper)
- QuickBooks
- Intacct
- KeepMore

SUMMARY

This chapter provided an introduction to virtual teams and described their importance as well as the different types of teams. When setting up a team, think about the kind of team you're looking for and how it will accomplish the specific task at hand. Incorrectly matching a team and task could greatly reduce efficiency and possibly even result in disaster. For example, using an "action team" to create a new product or provide a service would not only tap into the wrong resources but would greatly limit the outcome.

Another aspect to consider when setting up your virtual team is facilitation of communication. Thus you (and your designated computer wiz) should examine the various software packages available in the current marketplace, possibly even looking at older, cheaper, or even free versions such as Google Docs, as long as the software presents the most efficient way of working. Ask yourself if your team will need all the bells and whistles that come with many software packages.

You can also set up team communications a la carte. This way, you can pick and choose relevant features as well as investigating those that are most cost-effective. Many of these software programs have a free or reduced-fee trial period, which can be immensely helpful, especially in the beginning of the process when you are defining parameters.

This chapter provided the nuts-and-bolts of working in a virtual team environment. The next chapter will describe some of the complexities, challenges, and nuances involved in setting up and implementing a successful team.

CHAPTER 5

The Challenges of Virtual Teams

INTRODUCTION

Virtual teams are complex entities that are becoming even more interdependent as the global economy grows smaller and communications continue to evolve. This chapter will discuss the challenges faced by virtual teams and how to overcome them. It will also provide information on factors to consider when setting up and assessing virtual teams, as well as the dynamics that contribute to their success.

Differences in culture are among the biggest obstacles facing virtual teams, so we'll look at ways of overcoming disparities within and outside of the company as well as among the different nationalities and orientations of team members. We also have some suggestions about how to get team members on the same virtual page.

CULTURE AND THE VIRTUAL TEAM

Understanding the variables of time, space, and organization are vital in choosing and setting up virtual teams as well as designing strategies to improve them. Kimball and Mareen Duncan Fisher point out, and rightly so, that the biggest challenges facing managers of virtual teams can be those dealing with culture. Team members may have different goals and conflicting frames of reference—union versus nonunion and manufacturing versus customer service, for instance. Some team members—especially those who telecommute—may feel that the day shift gets preferential treatment, because most meetings and decisions occur from 9 to 5 while others may resent having to participate in teleconferences on evenings and weekends to accommodate team members who are working from home and are located in different tune zones. Other conflicts may occur due to a worker's orientation—a marketing member of the team may feel differently about a project than, say, someone who is in research.

Cultural clashes can be common occurrences in global teams. "South Americans . . . may see timelines as approximate, while Germans may view them as precise, even though both sit through the same discussion in the same language at the same time," state Fisher and Fisher. "Asians may smile and nod their heads when asked if they agree to something that they know they cannot later support because the rudeness of overt disagreement is culturally intolerable. North Americans may run roughshod over respected but time-consuming practices of other cultures." And so on.

SETTING UP AND ASSESSING VIRTUAL TEAMS

Yet cultural and other obstacles can be overcome—or at least anticipated—when you set up and organize the team. One factor to consider are the kinds of interactions members will have. Generally, they fall into four categories.

1. *Same time, same place* (like traditional teams, telecommuters can come into the office on certain times and days so they can meet face-to-face)
2. *Same time, different place* (using audio/videoconferencing)
3. *Different time, same place* (using a chat room, shared file, or even something as low tech as a bulletin board that everyone has access to)
4. *Different time, different place* (e-mail, voice mail, or even Podcasting)

Obviously the more different kinds of communication used by the team, the more complicated the exchange of information becomes. Understanding the who, what, when, and where of communication will also help you assess software and technology needs.

Another aspect is to evaluate the complexity of your team. For example:

- How many organizations do team members represent?
- How many functions do they have?
- Will members be transitioning off and on the team, and when?
- How geographically disbursed is the team?
- How many different countries do they represent?
- Do some team members speak different languages?
- Do they all have access to e-mail and other software that allows for collaboration?
- Are there members who are not formally assigned to the team?

The more items you add to the list, the more complex team interaction will get.

Recognizing the dynamics of the team beforehand can help head off potential problems. For instance, if a team member in Africa lacks appropriate Internet access, you can arrange for equipment to be sent to him or set up a time where he can be online at an Internet café or shared office and get the information in conjunction with the rest of the team.

SUCCESS FACTORS FOR VIRTUAL TEAMS

Including technology, which was discussed in Chapter 4, several factors contribute to the success of virtual teams. They include:

Human resource policies. If your company makes extensive use of virtual teams, it must have in place career development systems that address the needs of team members; rewards that recognize working across boundaries or virtually; systems to ensure results and goals are properly acknowledged; and support of non-traditional work arrangements, such as telecommuting.

Training, education, and development. These include ensuring that team members have good access to technical training; that they are trained in working across relevant cultures; that continual and immediate learning processes are available, such as web training; and that lessons-learned databases are available for sharing by everyone.

Standard organizational and team processes. There must be standard, consistent, and mutually agreed-upon team processes that apply throughout the organization, both technical and "soft." The latter include team rules and modes of operation, both formal and informal; conflict resolution procedures; and methods of communication. Additionally processes need to be flexible so they can be adapted to situations as they arise. The team should also be designed so it supports shared ways of doing business across teams/partners.

Organizational culture. The organization must foster trust within and outside itself and show that all team members and cultures are equally valued. The organization's leadership must place an emphasis on collaboration and teamwork.

Leadership. Leaders should set high expectations for performance, gain the support of customers and other stakeholders, allocate resources for training and technology, and provide models for working across boundaries and effective use of technology.

Competencies of team leaders and members. Both team members and leaders need experience working virtually as well as across organizational and cultural boundaries.

While it may be unrealistic—and probably too time-consuming—to have all of these in place at the beginning of the project, they should at least initially be addressed, and you should attempt to take care of as many as possible in advance. Some aspects may already be in place, such as having an experienced and trained team on hand or enabling the support of management regarding technology, telecommuters, and rewards systems.

GETTING ON THE SAME VIRTUAL PAGE

Cultural differences between team members may seem inevitable, especially in the beginning. When and if they do occur ask yourself whether the problem stems from differences in organizations, technology, or the country itself. Whatever the case, you'll have to establish procedures to deal with and overcome these problems. Fashion such procedures in such a way that all team members are comfortable with them. The same is true of country-of-origin and technical disparities. Teams can work together in creating guidelines for those as well as taking language and technical courses and cross-cultural sensitivity training to gain a greater understanding of each other.

Other important strategies for overcoming cultural differences include:

- Hold an initial face-to-face start-up meeting
- Have periodic face-to-face meetings, especially to resolve conflict and maintain team cohesiveness
- Establish a clear code of conduct or set of norms and protocols for behavior; this will help avoid delays and allow for timely processing of requests
- Do not allow team members to "fall off the radar." Have a calendar for each team member so that everyone's schedule is available to view
- Recognize and reward performance
- Use visuals in communications
- Recognize that many communications will be nonverbal—use caution in tone and language

"Face time" is especially important, particularly in early days when the team is just getting off the ground and members are becoming acquainted with processes, projects, and each other. Along with regularly holding meetings via webcams and video conferencing (or other "live" Internet conferencing tools or conference calls if video is unavailable), you can also create an online Facebook, which includes information about each member's background, skills, and interests. (The members of course would provide the information.)

During the ARO virtual training sessions, time is allowed so people can introduce themselves and talk about their hobbies, interests, likes, and dislikes. Not only is this a team-building activity but it allows insight into employee behavior. The instructor takes notes, so as training progresses, she can ask specific questions related to their interests to get to know them better.

No matter what the medium, activities that involve team members getting to know each other encourage camaraderie and relationship building. It will also help provide guideposts as to where the project is going and how it is progressing, who is responsible for what, and how the team member fits into the overall picture.

SUMMARY

Virtual teams have hit the big time in recent years. This is due in part to the explosion of telecommuting and the use of a global economy for outsourcing and knowledge building. So while virtual teams are here to stay, they are still being developed under a steep learning curve, which may result in trial-and-error implementation as well as a confusing and sometimes costly smorgasbord of technology and software that may or may not fit the needs of your particular program.

However, many pitfalls can be avoided by using the guidelines and checklists discussed in this chapter and making sure that various policies, procedures and norms are consistent and considered fair and equitable by all parties (or cultures) involved. This is best accomplished through direct communication, whether in realtime, webcam, or conference calls. If you are working globally, it's important to understand each culture's nuances in getting things done, even if it's contrary to your preferred or usual way.

As a manager, you'll need to keep track of each team member's progress and responsibility as well as make sure they are kept in the loop. Even if they are thousands of miles away or work part-time from home, team members should feel as if they are an important part of the process and vital to the project's success. Managing virtual teams can be far more challenging than traditional ones; however, they also allow for unprecedented growth and expansion, not only on a personal level but a professional one as well.

CHAPTER 6

Dealing with Diversity

INTRODUCTION

Telecommuters are coming into their own, so much so that a law is being considered by Congress that will give provide them (and your company) tax breaks. Conversely, they may also be found in remote areas with limited communication access and other obstacles that you'll need to overcome to get the job done.

TELECOMMUTERS AND THEIR LEGAL RIGHTS

Diversity in the workplace is here to stay. Not only within the types of telecommuting jobs—from a full-time home office to switching between home and office days to "on the road" workers—but within the kinds of people who fill the various positions. In addition to eliminating cultural and physical barriers (such as those caused by disabilities), telecommuting opens up possibilities for dual-income families, singles, and one-parent families, not to mention older workers and those with specialized skills who live thousands of miles away from the home office.

Yet it is this very flexibility that on one hand can be good for business, yet on the other makes managing even more complicated. You'll need to be more aware of the various laws affecting workers (see page 58) than managers of "regular" workers. Telecommuters are more likely to be older, disabled, or have issues dealing with elders or children, among other things.

The Occupational Safety and Health Administration (OSHA) and worker's compensation organizations have also gotten involved, with mixed results. These and other safety and liability considerations will be covered in Chapter 11.

Labor Laws for Regular (W-2) Workers

Although many of the laws have been around for decades, some are more recent, with implications still being felt today. These laws affect all regular workers, regardless of whether they are full-time telecommuters or office personnel. (The key words here are "full-time.")

The federal laws prohibiting job discrimination are:

- Title VII of the Civil Rights Act of 1964, which prohibits employment discrimination based on race, color, religion, sex, or national origin
- The Equal Pay Act of 1963 (EPA), which protects men and women who perform substantially equal work in the same establishment from sex-based wage discrimination
- The Age Discrimination in Employment Act of 1967 (ADEA), which protects individuals who are forty years of age or older
- Title I and Title V of the Americans with Disabilities Act of 1990 (ADA), which prohibit employment discrimination against qualified individuals with disabilities in the private sector, and in state and local governments
- Sections 501 and 505 of the Rehabilitation Act of 1973, which prohibit discrimination against qualified individuals with disabilities who work in the federal government
- The Civil Rights Act of 1991, which, among other things, provides monetary damages in cases of intentional employment discrimination

The U.S. Equal Employment Opportunity Commission (EEOC) enforces all of these laws. The EEOC also provides oversight and coordination of all federal equal employment opportunity regulations, practices, and policies.

Another federal law, the Family and Medical Leave Act of 1993 (FMLA) allows for up to twelve work weeks of unpaid leave during any twelve-month period for eligible employees to care for a newborn child, seriously ill family member, or if they themselves develop a serious health condition, among other contingencies.

Each state has its own laws against discrimination in addition to enforcement agencies. Although there are few laws preventing discrimination regarding sexual orientation (homosexual, transgender), managers should be sensitive to this area as well. Given the recent controversy about same-sex marriage, it only follows that the rights of homosexuals will eventually be addressed in the workplace. The cold reality is that many of these issues—particularly relating to age and sex—come into play in decisions regarding hiring and promotion more often than they should.

To protect themselves legally, managers should avoid knowing an employee's age, sexual orientation, or family situation. Although this may seem somewhat stringent, consider the fact that upon legal review, you as a manager may be perceived as having used this information to make decisions regarding which employee to promote, terminate, and so forth. Information about equal labor laws can be found at *www.eeoc.gov*; most states also have a specific website for workplace regulations.

The Fair Labor Standards Act (FLSA) establishes minimum wage, overtime pay, recordkeeping, and child labor standards affecting full-time and part-time workers in the private sector and in federal, state, and local governments. There may soon be a law geared specifically for telecommuters. The recent introduction in Congress of the Parents' Tax Relief Act of 2007 by Senator Sam Brownback (R-Kan.) and Representative Lee Terry (R-Neb.), promises tax incentives for employers who support remote workers, such as a vastly simplified home office deduction ($2,500 or the profit from the home-based business, whichever is less) and a telecommuting tax credit for employers of up to $2,400 per telecommuter. In addition, employers who provide telecommuters with computers and broadband access equipment can write off the expense. Passage of this bill may make telecommuting more attractive to managers and employees.

UNDERSTANDING DIFFERENT FRAMES OF REFERENCES

Chapter 5 discussed the challenges of working with a diverse virtual team in terms of company culture, job orientation, and nationality. Many of the same principles apply in dealing with telecommuters. Author and business consultant Paul Tulenko suggests the following steps in managing a workforce that operates from many different frames of reference.

1. **Identify the diversity.** Find out about the various cultures represented by your workforce. Each has a different way of processing information and dealing with situations.
2. **Discover the norms.** Find out everything you can about their culture—from books, from others who have lived and worked in the culture, and perhaps most important from the employees themselves.
3. **Discern the differences.** As mentioned earlier, each culture does things its own way. What may be acceptable in one is completely offensive in another (consider the disparities between American English and that of the UK!). If you get an inkling that you might have done something wrong or offensive in your dealings with a worker from another culture, find a trusted expert and discuss the situation (in some cultures, direct questions in themselves are considered offensive).
4. **Recognize the necessity.** There is no "textbook" way of dealing with different cultures. The most effective way to understand a culture is to spend time in the country yourself. If that's physically impossible, hire or consult with those who have expertise in multicultural relationships.

Religiously diverse work forces also present challenges. Observance of holidays and the Sabbath can have an impact on work hours and overtime. Managers must also be sensitive to implications regarding customs of dress if employees are dealing directly with customers.

It's vitally important to understand multicultural implications and nuances both within your team and as it relates to your business. Culture change agents and even courses in multiculturalism can help bridge the gap.

Telecommuters vs. "Regular" Employees

Telecommuters may experience resistance and resentment from office coworkers and in some cases even clients who know about their work-from-home status. Sandra Gurvis has encountered everything from clients who call after hours to discuss matters that can be handled during office hours—one memorable incident involved an out-of-control author screaming over the cell phone while Sandra was out to dinner with several friends—to downright envy from peers who feel trapped in office jobs. However, managers can take steps to avoid "tele-resentment."

Make sure that work is properly and evenly distributed and that office employees are aware of exactly what the teleworker is doing, and when. Communication is key; otherwise the teleworker becomes invisible and cut out of the loop. Managers should constantly emphasize and reinforce the fact that everyone is a member of the team, despite the diversity in the working conditions and physical locations.

Sometimes office workers do have legitimate complaints. "In my workshops for soon-to-be teleworkers, I urge them to be sensitive to what could result in their colleagues having to put out all the fires in the office," states David Fleming, organizer for the California Task Force on Interactive Telecommunications in Government. To help forestall resentment, managers can assign teleworkers their fair share of routine duties.

Another way of boosting team morale and facilitating communications is through a forum or blog where everyone can discuss telecommuting, office scheduling, and workload problems. As mentioned in Chapter 4, have software for all members of the team to access. Arranging for a specific day or time period for "virtual brainstorming" by all team members helps identify any ongoing issues before they become a full-blown crisis.

Set specific boundaries.

Along with clearly identifying the workload and setting goals, make sure that teleworkers know what hours they are to be available and that they are responsible for being reachable during this time. Coworkers and clients should also be aware of when the teleworkers are "off duty." As Sandra can attest, the advent of the cell phone has eliminated many of these boundaries, so it's good to set them in the initial work plan.

Arrange face-to-face meetings, especially at the beginning.

Most teleworkers are glad for an occasional excuse to get out of their home office, especially if it provides a chance to socialize and become acquainted with the other employees and visit the organization. Putting a "face" on things not only increases comfort levels (in most cases, anyway) but provides all parties with a sense of being vested in the project or organization.

DOING BUSINESS OVERSEAS—SPECIAL CONSIDERATIONS

As communications increase and the virtual world shrinks, the argument for doing business overseas becomes stronger, even for smaller companies. But as anyone who has tried to work with or in a foreign culture knows, such dealings can be fraught with complications.

In addition to the differences in language, ways of doing business, customs, and time zones, variances in *infrastructure* can present challenges. These can range from wide disparities in telecommunications systems that fail to support technology (for example, hampering interactive software) to inconsistencies in availability and dependability of mobile or land lines. Another issue is the quality of support and services—import restrictions can slow down the repair of vital equipment, as can inadequately trained or a scarcity of technicians. The cost of importing replacement parts might be exorbitant as well.

Also consider how the population is distributed. Are teleworkers concentrated in small apartments with limited or no space for home offices or villages where cable and Internet access are much less common than in bigger cities? If so, then you may be faced with the cost and requirements of establishing a telework center.

In addition to time zones, what are the discrepancies in work customs? For example, countries in Mediterranean Europe tend to take two-hour lunch breaks, while Germans rarely if ever work on the weekends. It's well-known that most of the rest of the world takes much longer in getting projects done and making decisions than the U.S.

You'll also need to address issues relating to taxes and statutory compliance. For example: Who pays taxes on the salaries of overseas workers, and to which country? What about currency? If workers are located in India, will they be paid in rupees or U.S. dollars? Another sticking point is whether or not workers are to be considered regular employees or independent contractors. Each country has different laws and requirements, raising even more questions regarding healthcare and other benefits.

However, gaps between countries are narrowing, especially regarding technology. Asia and Europe are ahead of North America in terms of sophistication and speed of Internet access, according to the website internetworldstats.com, while Sweden and Finland lead the world in cellular services. So-called Third World countries in Africa and the Middle East have increasingly widespread mobile phone technology (although land lines might not be as readily available); in recent years, both show several hundred percent's worth of growth in the use of Internet technology. Trade agreements have also helped lower prices for some equipment.

None of these obstacles is insurmountable, especially if you are flexible and willing to use your imagination. For example, one independent contractor, while in remote areas of Scotland, took along his laptop, cell phone, and trusty international calling card. When attempts to connect with clients via the first two failed, he was able to locate a phone booth, and do business from there.

Case Study: Making Diversity Work

Since 1994, IBM in Phoenix, Arizona, has used a telecommuting program involving approximately one-fourth of its full-time employees. Jobs ranged from sales to marketing to technicians and systems consultants to customer service. Along with developing hardware and software specifically for telecommuters, they allowed for flexible work settings—desks at customer sites, off-site telework centers, and work from home options—and created handbooks/policies geared for telecommuters. They also provided some equipment for employees.

According to manager Skip Richards, "Our telework program allows IBM to be at the forefront of the technology industry. It has enabled us to have a regional, instead of a geographic, organizational structure. Now, people are managed in different cities across geographic boundaries."

Additionally, "our telecommuters are more culturally diverse. There are fewer cliques. It has created much wider diversity in IBM's company culture." Telecommuting is also no longer considered an oddity: "Since there are so many teleworkers at IBM, it doesn't affect them too much. If employees want to telework, the resources are available."

SUMMARY

You, as a manager, are only limited by your imagination and flexibility in working with a variety of telecommuters. However, the best way to deal with any telecommuting arrangement is, if possible, to plan ahead. This can be done by asking questions.

Does a specific telecommuting arrangement make good business sense? Although overseas outsourcing may seem to save money, the costs of doing business—and the complications and delays that may ensue—may more than make up for the difference.

Which telecommuting arrangement works for which kind of job? Consider how productive employees might be in a given telework/traditional office environment. If a team works most effectively in a "cubicle farm" arrangement, that may be a better choice. Depending upon what duties the job entails, you may use one or more combinations.

What guidelines should be used? These should be developed in advance and not only measure the employee productivity and goals but also how, where, and when the team will communicate. When dealing with a diverse work group, it is essential that all members feel equal and part of the team.

PART TWO

LAWS OF THE JUNGLE

Nuts and Bolts of Managing Telecommuting Employees

CHAPTER 7

Setting Up a Telecommuting Team

INTRODUCTION

As idyllic as telecommuting might sound in theory—not to mention the many obvious reasons for it discussed in earlier chapters—managers and companies need to ask themselves some hard questions before establishing a telecommuting program. For example: Who will organize and support the team and how much will it cost? What does the company hope to gain, in terms of its goals, mission, and end results? Which employees should comprise the team and how will they contribute? Finally, how can you, as a manager, learn how to deal with the changes inherent in leading the new team? This chapter addresses these and other questions.

WHO WILL SUPPORT THE TEAM?

The first step in implementing a telecommuting program is evaluation. This is best accomplished through forming an interdisciplinary group that acts as a telecommuting committee. Members can come from many areas: human resources, information systems (IS), facilities, public relations, upper-level management, and if possible, customers or end users. Consultants should include anyone whose job might be affected by the telecommuter.

The committee's job is to evaluate such areas as:

- Is this organization a good candidate for telecommuting?
- Does the company have the right jobs and people for this type of arrangement?

- Who will support the program and how will supervisors and workers react?
- Does it suit the company's bottom line to institute telecommuting?

The committee should solicit the opinions of employees and managers who will be affected by the program. "Identify what's negotiable—what can and can't be changed—ahead of time," advises Diana Francis, senior consultant for Steelcase, Inc. in Grand Rapids, Michigan. "Solicit feedback and make changes as a result of the feedback."

Everyone should also be kept in the loop regarding the committee's progress via a bulletin board, newsletter, e-mail, web-based interactive sites, or casual events such as departmental coffees and "lunch and learn." Francis also suggests workshops and training sessions for both employees and supervisors to introduce the telecommuting program as well as any resultant changes and new work methods. "It's important for managers and peers to clearly understand what to expect from [telecommuters]."

Sponsors, Stakeholders, and Champions

In finding support for the telecommuting effort, Duarte and Snyder recommend identifying sponsors, stakeholders, and champions.

Sponsors work closely with the team leader and act "on the team's behalf to cross organizational barriers, resolve conflicts of interest, obtain resources, and provide a link with upper management." The sponsor should be in an influential position that transcends organizational boundaries.

Stakeholders have the greatest impact on the team's success and . . . will be most affected by the team's result. They may be from vastly different functional and geographical areas, levels of management, or partner organizations. It is vital that stakeholders be kept in the loop regarding the committee's (and later the team's) progress. Duarte and Snyder recommend focusing on what they call Type 1 stakeholders: "Two to four people whose opinions and sponsorship are critical to your team's success."

Champions, while a bit further removed from day-to-day processes, "may be able to find resources, promote the team's activities, remove barriers and provide advice." Often members of upper management, champions may be found in any area of the company or partner organizations.

Defined at the beginning of the evaluation process, these individuals should be involved from Day One, if possible. The more time and effort they invest in the program, the more likely they are to support it throughout.

COST ANALYSIS

Although at first glance telecommuting might appear to save money, further examination might reveal little or no savings, or even added expense. The issue of cost should be faced early in the evaluation process. When considering costs, look at three major areas:

1. *Technology.* This includes the price of setting up the system: computer hardware and software, networks, and any other necessary equipment, such as wireless modems or phone headsets. At this point, you might want to decide who will pay for the home worker's office setup—the company, the employee, or a combination of the two.

2. *Training.* Here, costs can mount up quickly. Not only do they encompass loss of actual work time by the employee when training but also the expense of developing a training program. Such programs can be quite expensive and involve paying for a teacher and materials, and if participants are undergoing face-to-face instruction, the

time and travel required in getting everyone to a central location. Additionally, everyone involved in the telecommuting effort, from top administrators to front-line supervisors to secretaries and accountants responsible for the administration, will need some sort of training.

However, if you train employees properly and they are loyal, you can actually save a lot of money down the road. If, for example, it costs $5,000 to train a customer service representative and you have a 60 percent annual turnover on 100 agents, that is 60 x 5,000 = $300,000. If your annual turnover falls to 10 percent, then you are only training 10 replacement workers a year. Therefore, 10 x $5,000 = $50,000, which results in a savings of a quarter of a million dollars in training costs.

3. *Continued.* These consist of expenses that the committee might normally not think of: subscription fees to expensive Internet databases (accessing a single journal article, for instance, can be prohibitive), wear and tear on hardware that might have to be replaced due to constant use, and travel. Ongoing bills, such as phone and Internet access and upgrades to software and equipment, should also be considered. If employees are to be located in an alternative arrangement, such as in a remote work center or a shared space, these costs should be factored in as well. Do you consider getting rid of the space or is the lease not up for a while? Also consider whether you will need to make temporary provisions involving these kinds of setups and estimate those expenses.

Once they've determined who will support the telecommuting effort and found the cost to be feasible, the committee's next step is to create a vision statement or team charter that conveys the company's telecommuting policy and mission: what the telecommuting team is about and what it hopes to accomplish. A cross between a business plan and a traditional mission statement, it will help everyone get clear on the objectives and goals of the program and its reason for being.

A vision statement should answer the following:

Why are we doing this? What are the achievable benefits in terms of employees, the company, and the community in general? As authors Margaret Tan-Solano and Brian Kleiner point out, telecommuting should be considered for the right reasons. "View it as a benefit and accommodation rather than a business strategy," they suggest. Other justifications may include "greater productivity, reduced need for office space, more contact with clients, and increased use of highly qualified people who aren't available or affordable on a traditional, full-time basis."

Which departments and employees will be telecommuting? Determining these factors will be discussed in the next sections, but you need to set forth who, what, and where so everyone knows exactly what's happening.

When will the first employees be starting? When will the program go "live"? Setting forth a timeline with plenty of advance notice can help eliminate the element of surprise and forestall resentment.

Everyone involved, including remote stakeholders, should have a chance to review the charter and provide input. To accomplish this, you may need one or more face-to-face or interactive web sessions with various parties to gather ideas.

The vision statement needn't be lengthy or go into great detail. However, since it covers a telecommuting or virtual environment, it is especially important that it be thorough yet concise, offering a starting point for the more detailed goals and work plans that will unfold as well as providing a baseline for performance evaluation. Often it is the single unifying factor for members of a diverse, physically separated team and any uncertainty or disagreement regarding its intent can result in dissention and undermine work efforts.

For example, on its website, ARO presents this statement of its corporate vision:

Cutting the Fat

Our business model is based on a unique framework of a distributed workforce. Some call it virtual, others may call it remote. We keep it simple and call it a work-at-home model. And this model goes beyond just being a virtual contact center. Instead, the virtual business model is a whole new way of thinking about how process flows within an organization. This allows us to implement new workflow solutions, cutting the fat, and delivering great customer experiences.

Programs such as Business Plan Pro (*www.bplans.com*) offer free examples of business plans, mission statements, and executive summaries. These should provide some basic ideas and general guidelines.

WHAT KIND OF JOBS AND WORKERS ARE NEEDED?

Before delving into who should telecommute, you need to make sure that they can; that is, that tasks are conductive to this type of arrangement. Several common telecommuting jobs were discussed in Chapter 1.

Aside from asking the obvious question of whether work can be done efficiently in a home environment and breaking down tasks into a percentage of home versus office, make sure that there are enough at-home tasks to justify a telecommuting position.

Other concepts to consider include:

- How much face-to-face time with other employees is required? You might want to schedule a phase-in period, where the telecommuter works part of the time at home and the rest in the office.

- How often do job incumbents need to drop what they are doing to deal with emergency situations?
- How often will workers need to access resources such as files, references, one-of-a-kind or secure or sensitive materials that can only be found in the office?
- How often will workers need to access special equipment that can only be found in the office?

If the answer to these questions is "more often than not," the job is likely unsuitable for telecommuting.

The next logical step, then, is determining selection criteria for team members. As with the "telecommuting personality" discussed in Chapter 3, the selection process should emphasize workers who are not only experienced in their jobs and familiar with the company but who also exhibit a high level of skill, flexibility, and self-reliance. This is especially important in the beginning, when things can and will go wrong, as the program is being fine-tuned. As any manager knows, planning and implementing can be vastly different universes.

Cookie-Cutter Telecommuters? Think Again!

ARO was approached by a large telecommunications company that wanted to take a third of their call center and send them home to work. Michael advised them to delve a little deeper into the situation before making a blanket decision. He knew from experience that not all employees are cut out for remote work or telecommuting, especially if they are entry-level and young, with much of their social life tied up in the office. They sometimes lack the discipline and drive needed to work at home. Sure enough, Michael's prediction came to pass: Shortly after the company instituted the program, many of the employees quit, saying the job had become "boring."

ORGANIZING THE PROGRAM

The committee will need to establish which type of telecommuting arrangement works best for the company and its requirements. Will workers be at home full-time, or dividing their days between office and home? What kind of equipment will be needed? Will you need to use hoteling, virtual offices, or other arrangements discussed in Chapter 2? The cost analysis should come in handy here.

Also, in setting up your program, consider the four basic kinds of telecommuting models:

1. **Departmental model:** Only one or two areas, such as data entry or the call center, offer telecommuting.
2. **Corporate-wide model:** Most, if not all, of the company participates in telecommuting.
3. **Individual model:** Telecommuting is arranged on a case-by-case basis, and is usually set up between the employee and the supervisor, with the support of the company.
4. **Contractor model:** Employees are moved out of the office and paid as if they were independent contractors. While saving money, this can result in scrutiny from the government if the company appears to be violating IRS regulations regarding full-time employees (see Chapter 2).

You can of course use one or several combinations of these arrangements and models. You may want to do a trial run—have a single department or a few employees telecommute for a short period of time, say six months, to see how things work out. That's the beauty of telecommuting—its very nature allows for such flexibility, and once you decide that it fits the needs of your organization, you will be able to mold the program according to your workflow and company goals.

OVERCOMING MANAGERIAL FEARS

Sometimes the greatest resistance to telecommuting can come from the manager—either you or someone who is managing you. Not only may the other employee feel threatened by a new idea and different methods of working but if he's a manager he may also feel he is losing control by allowing people to do their tasks off-site. Much of this depends on the manager's orientation; if you are used to walking around and physically supervising workers, how can you do this remotely without feeling nonessential or that your own job might be in jeopardy? Management cooperation with telecommuting can make or break the program.

Thus the evaluation committee should determine whether the current management style is compatible with the proposed telecommuting arrangement. The committee should consider such factors as the managers' flexibility and level of trust, as well as their communications skills. One solution may be retraining managers in how to supervise teleworkers. They need to be results-oriented instead of task- or time-oriented, not an easy change if managers are accustomed to working in a certain way.

For example, Michael encountered resistance from some of the more traditional managers during the early days when ARO was switching to remote workers. After identifying these managers, he attempted to work with them in changing their management style to a more results-focused orientation. Most were amenable to change, and although they may have been uncomfortable initially, eventually they came around to the new way of working. The one exception was let go early during the switchover so as not to undermine its effectiveness .

Workshops need to cover everything from new logistics and technologies to revised team and organizational protocols to different methods of evaluating and rewarding performance. For instance, since they can't holler over the cubicle or stop by for a chat, managers may need to brush up on their telephone and e-mail skills.

At least part of the program should consist of "team training" in which the telecommuter and manager come together. "The telecommuter has to understand what the supervisor's problems are going to be and vice versa," points out author George Piskurich. These joint sessions can include negotiating and planning basic issues, such as hours the employee will be available and how and how often he will communicate with the manager.

INTRODUCING AND IMPLEMENTING THE PROGRAM

Say the committee recommends telecommuting and top management is eager for implementation. Before telecommuting can begin, "team managers should meet with executive supervisors to establish working parameters," states the National Federation of Independent Business (NFIB). Among other things, such parameters should include:

1. Project schedules and deadlines, including ongoing stage-by-stage development benchmarks.
2. Establishment of specific tasks for individuals within the team, including management, in-house employees, and telecommuting employees.
3. Setting up channels of communication between team members and management.
4. Setting up schedules for reporting (daily, weekly, as needed).

Additionally, "be clear about why the organization is making changes in the process or environment: real estate costs, employee costs, organization change strategy, marketing and so on," advises Francis. She also suggests open and truthful disclosure about the business situation or factors driving the implementation, "at least three months prior to the proposed change."

Once the new program is introduced and the initial fanfare dies down, it needs continual support. This can be done through a telecommuting ombudsperson who oversees employee/management concerns or through periodic training to sustain interest and enthusiasm, or both. Teleworkers need to become a part of the corporate culture and be recognized as such through awards, in-house communications (such as the company newsletter), and other forms of communication. Such activities "remind employees that the changes are real and are here to stay," adds Francis.

Finally, the committee or outside consultants should periodically evaluate the success of the telecommuting effort. They can build upon existing information by measuring changes in performance and developing cost and benefit data.

Across the Pond: A UK Telecommuting Setup Success Story

In the five years that Coventry University Enterprises (CUE) has been running its Location Independent Working scheme, no one has been asked to leave the program for reasons of poor performance, according to head of homeworking, Jane Rawlings-Purcell. She puts that down to a formal, closely managed policy that introduces employees to flexible working in a structured manner and provides them with ongoing support. As a result, more than half of CUE'S 166-strong staff now work away from the office three days a week, and an average of ten more join the independent working scheme every three to six months. That's great for their work/life balance, but there's also a solid business case underpinning the program.

As the commercial arm of Coventry University, CUE is responsible for helping businesses to identify market opportunities and then providing them with the consultancy, applied research, and teaching support they need to take advantage of them. These clients tend to be small, dynamic start-up organizations that expect their CUE contacts to be mobile and accessible to them outside of usual working hours, so flexible working plays a key role in operational effectiveness.

What sets CUE's flexible-working policy apart from similar initiatives at other companies?

- Employees cannot opt for independent working until they have worked for CUE for at least three months. "By that time, we know them as individuals and are familiar with their preferred styles of working. Also, they've come to know us better and they understand the culture here," Rawlings-Purcell explains.
- All participants have a trial period of three months, so that they can "try before they buy" and see if working at home suits their work style and their personality.
- All staff who opt for independent working receive regular training on relevant work/life balance techniques and are briefed on health and safety regulations for the home office environment.
- Independent working participants are expected to meet regular targets and objectives, set for them by their manager. "As a participant myself, one of my objectives is to ensure that 65 percent of our workforce is signed up to it by July 2008, from today's figure of 58 percent," she says.
- Participants can be withdrawn from the scheme by their managers. If this action is taken because their performance is not up to standards, just one week's notice is required. If this action occurs because of operational reasons (for example, a particular project requires an employee's presence on-site) then one month's notice is given.

The results of this approach have been impressive. In a recent survey of independent working participants, more than two-thirds (70 percent) reported an increase in productivity between 40 and 100 percent over previous rates.

Costs per employee have been halved, from £6,000 (approximately $12K) per year to £3,000 (about $6K) for office-based workers who are now working remotely. The floor space freed up by employees working remotely has been leased to tenants, generating £68,000 (approximately $136K) a year in extra revenue.

SUMMARY

There is no single "right" way of establishing a telecommuting team, nor are there specific templates or plans to follow. Because telecommuting is constantly changing due to technology and virtual teams are a relatively new concept, you may find you have to make at least parts of it up as you go along. Hence it's a good idea to form a multidisciplinary telecommuting committee (or at the very least, use an experienced consultant) to get things started. Understand that every detail, from the budget to the types of work to the training program and methods, is subject to change.

However, general guidelines and common sense can go a long way in setting up a program. The following table provides an overall checklist for any committee or group involved in such an endeavor.

Factors to Consider: Telecommuting Evaluation Checklist

Support organization employees fall into the following categories:

- *Sponsors:* Determine type of work, and whether employees have the "telecommuting personality"
- *Stakeholders:* Design the telecommuting model, train managers and workers
- *Champions:* Help determine work setup (hoteling, etc) and related personnel

**Factors to Consider: Telecommuting
Evaluation Checklist—*continued***

"To Do" List:

- Schedule telecommuting committee meeting dates and dates of implementation
- Perform a cost analysis
- Develop a vision statement
- Disseminate information to all parties on a regular, ongoing basis

The next chapters will discuss hiring, training, equipping, performance, and other issues related to defining and implementing a successful telecommuting program.

CHAPTER 8

Hiring

INTRODUCTION

Hiring telecommuters has its own special challenges, which can affect locating and screening candidates, writing job descriptions and conducting interviews, and setting up work agreements and contracts. Managers need to ensure that they select someone who is up to the unique requirements of working independently, the characteristics of which are also elaborated further in this chapter. Also included are suggestions for making sure the new employee feels welcome and part of the team.

SCREENING CANDIDATES

Given the increasing number of people who want to at least try telecommuting, you should have no shortage of volunteers and applicants for your telecommuting effort. Whether you are in an existing organization switching over to telecommuting or a brand-new enterprise or are using existing employees or outside recruits (or any combination of these) you'll need specific and consistent standards of selecting workers.

The first question then is, who chooses the employee? As with regular office workers, it should be a collaborative effort: the immediate supervisor does the initial interviewing and screening—if applicable, with the help of human resources. If necessary, second or third interviews may require the presence of various higher levels of management and support groups; at the very least, they should get a chance to review the applications and provide input and approval.

A common and practical method of winnowing potential home-workers is through a workshop. Not only will it cover important aspects of telecommuting, and provide an overview of what the specific job will require, but you will also get a sense of whether the candidate has the "telecommuting personality" discussed in Chapter 3 and also whether they have a home office environment suitable for telecommuting.

The workshop can run from between a couple of hours to a full day and can include Microsoft PowerPoint and other presentations about the job, self-evaluation surveys and checklists, and group activities, such as simulations that provide real world challenges for telecommuting and the job itself. Unlike a training session or even a one-on-one interview, the workshop serves as a preliminary screening session and can save both employee and management valuable time and effort.

One Would-Be Telecommuter's Experience

One of Betsy's (not her real name) favorite job fantasies had been working in pharmaceutical sales. Not only would it get her away from the 9-to-5 cubicle humdrum of her administrative position in health insurance but it would, she felt, provide her with freedom to set her own schedule and additional income.

When Betsy saw an ad in the *Columbus Dispatch* for a regional representative for a well-known company, she willingly took the day off and drove two hours to Wheeling, West Virginia, where an orientation workshop was being held. When she walked into the room and saw the twenty-plus people who had applied for a mere two positions, she was a bit unsettled by all the competition. Betsy was good at her job, and she knew she was a quick learner and responsible, so she figured she had as good of a chance as anyone else.

Her intimidation returned when the representative began to explain the job, passing out descriptions and written requirements. Not only would she be driving all over Ohio, Indiana, and West

Virginia in all kinds of weather and traffic but she was required to call into the main office every day, providing specific sales numbers and contacts and filling out detailed reports of her activities, due every Monday. The job required meeting a weekly quota, both in terms of actual sales calls and places visited. Even though the salary was considerably more than Betsy was making, she knew it was well outside her comfort zone. So she left quietly during the break, before the work simulation exercise was to begin.

Several months later, Betsy's company offered some of its employees a chance to work from home. Although Betsy had to change jobs and get some additional training, she was selected for the pilot program for case managers. "Although the pharmaceutical sales workshop was ego-shattering, it opened my eyes to other possibilities," she says. "I realized my main desire was to work from home, although not necessarily switch careers." So the workshop was a win-win situation, for Betsy as well as her prospective and current employers.

However, some companies may lack the time, resources, and support to run workshops. If, like ARO, they are primarily searching for one type of position—customer service—it may be just as feasible and much more cost-effective to do preliminary screening through the *telephone interview*. ARO general manager Joye Moore looks for nonverbal cues such as tone of voice, background noise, and availability when she does her initial calls. "I have heard everything from a parrot chattering to the sound of children playing, when they were supposed to be at school," she says. The latter is especially important if work hours coincide with the times when kids are gone and it is supposed to be quiet. "The point being that the customers never know they are being contacted from the worker's home."

Whether or not the person is focused on her call and not distracted by the surrounding environment provides even more hints. "Presentation is the key. If the person's voice is squeaky or high-pitched, or if he uses improper grammar or slang or poor pronunciation, he's likely not a good candidate."

She uses the simple scoring system of image, attitude, and skill.

- *Image.* The first time you talk to the candidate during the phone interview, that's what the customer will likely encounter so it better be positive.
- *Attitude.* If the candidate states her last two bosses were jerks, then ARO will likely be the next one.
- *Skill.* This depends what is required of the job itself, as measured by assessment tests of typing, spelling, or other relevant knowledge.

Other screening instruments and activities can consist of *checklists* evaluating personal traits, feasibility of the workspace, and advantages and disadvantages of telecommuting. (Appendix A provides an example of a self-evaluation instrument that can be given to prospective telecommuters.) JALA (*www.jala.com*), which focuses on telework and virtual consulting for business and governments, offers a program known as Telepicker built around background questionnaires given to prospective teleworkers and their immediate supervisors. Along with determining the feasibility of business relationships, it measures such areas as job constraints (like location dependence), attitudes towards the work situation, and technology issues, among other things.

You can design your own evaluation instrument. Table 8.1 provides some suggestions.

Table 8.1

Example of Checklists

Personal Traits Checklist

- ❏ I'm good at organization
- ❏ I can set goals and meet them
- ❏ I can develop schedules and stick to them
- ❏ I can deal with the isolation of telecommuting
- ❏ I can deal well with distractions
- ❏ I can work well with a minimum of supervision
- ❏ I can communicate well using technologies such as phones, fax, and e-mail
- ❏ I'm self-motivated and don't tend toward procrastination
- ❏ I'm flexible
- ❏ I'm not a workaholic
- ❏ I'm good at meeting deadlines
- ❏ I'm a competent time manager
- ❏ Roadblocks do not unmotivate me
- ❏ I don't need other people's input to make decisions
- ❏ I'm a good stress manager
- ❏ I consider myself a good person and like myself

Workspace Checklist

- ❏ I have a private space in which to set up my home office
- ❏ It has the necessary space
- ❏ I meet the necessary power and lighting requirements
- ❏ I have the furniture I need
- ❏ There are one or more phone connections
- ❏ There is storage space in my office or near it
- ❏ I have a good comfortable chair
- ❏ Ventilation, heating, and cooling are good in my office space
- ❏ My computer screen can be positioned to minimize glare
- ❏ My office will pass a safety check

Table 8.1—*continued*

Personal Advantages and Disadvantages Checklist

Advantages	Disadvantages
❏ No commuting	❏ Isolation
❏ More time for my family	❏ Problems with those who live at home
❏ More flexibility for child or eldercare	❏ Loss of office opportunities because not there
❏ Freedom to work when most productive	❏ Always being at work
❏ Greater job satisfaction	❏ Poorer communications
❏ Dressing down	❏ Coworker jealousy
❏ Greater privacy	❏ Lost office services
❏ Fewer interruptions	❏ Loss of grapevine
❏ Fewer meetings	❏ Falling into bad habits at home
❏ Nicer working environment	❏ Never leaving the office environment
❏ Less stress	
❏ Savings on food, clothing, and gas	
❏ Can smoke at work ("advantage" may be relative)	

Other factors to consider are the quality and effect of telecommuting on home life, and a personal job analysis (evaluating chances for promotion, supervisory relationships, and requirements of the job itself).

You and HR can use such psychological instruments as the Myers-Briggs Type Indicator questionnaire, which provides insights as to whether the candidate has an adequate work/life balance for telecommuting (not too introverted or overly extroverted). Another method, behavioral interviewing, in which the applicant is asked to provide specific reasons behind a particular action, can also be effective in predicting job performance. Although most interviews have open-ended questions, behavioral interviewing takes it a step further by probing the reasons behind specific actions, thus making it more difficult for applicants to "fudge" information or gloss over answers. For example, asking the interviewee to describe a situation in which he had to deal with an angry customer will provide a greater understanding of how he may react in a future situation.

JOB ANALYSIS AND DESCRIPTIONS

Which comes first: hiring employees or setting specific criteria for the job? Although there are no clear-cut answers, and such decisions should be made on a case-by-case basis, job evaluation and definition for telecommuters should encompass content over specific processes. Employees should see a clear connection between job responsibilities and the company's mission.

When designing and setting up jobs, Jack Nilles recommends asking the following questions:

What really has to happen to make the job work? What sort of results does the job produce? Can you recognize the results easily—typed memos, reports, lines of debugged software codes . . . ? What is it, exactly that you use to evaluate the employee's work? How often are these discernable products produced?

From there, you can determine the skills and resources needed to get the job done as well as the channels, frequency, and content of communication required.

Chapter 7 discussed evaluating whether or not a particular job or department is appropriate for telecommuting. Once you make that determination, you can draft a job description, with the understanding that it will likely be more subject to change than traditional corporate jobs Managers should also re-evaluate telecommuters' job descriptions every six months, especially in the beginning.

Previous experience with traditional hiring practices can come in handy. For instance, you can use information from an existing description as a starting point or template and update or revise it if necessary. The description should provide an overview of the position and needs to concisely communicate the tasks and responsibilities, along with the qualifications, including the basic requirements, such as specific credentials or skills.

The following categories help make up an effective job description:

- Title of the position
- Department
- Reports to (to whom the person directly reports)
- Overall responsibility
- Key areas of responsibility
- Consults with (those whom the person works with on a regular basis)
- Term of employment
- Qualifications (necessary skills and experience required)

A gray area is educational and experience requirements. Especially with telecommuters, you can allow leeway for both, as job and telework experience may qualify an individual with less education who meets specific requirements.

Be specific in delineating the desired duties. For instance, describe the software programs in which the candidates should be proficient (e.g., Microsoft Word or Microsoft Excel) instead of merely saying the person needs to be computer literate. Specify that the candidate should to be able to clearly explain and interpret technical information to all types of audiences, rather than having good communications skills.

The following is an example of a full-time telecommuter job description.

Job Title: Information Architect
Publication or Company: Company X
Industry: Book Publishing, Online/New Media
Salary: Very Competitive
Job Duration Freelance: (Other)
Job Location: New York, NY USA
Job Requirements
Information Architect

We are currently seeking a temp-to-perm Information Architect for a publishing company in NYC. The Information Architect needs to be able to produce wire frames/storyboards as well as write use cases/functional requirements. Ideally this individual would have experience with e-commerce and have some educational design experience as our client develops a lot of applications for university students and professors.

If you are qualified, interested, and available please send us your resume and samples ASAP.

Hourly Freelance rate $40-$45 per hour.

Full-time salary up to $80K.

About Our Company: Company X, a division of specialized staffing leader Conglomerate Y, focuses on placing full-time and freelance professionals in the creative, advertising, marketing, web, and public relations fields. As companies develop short- and long-term strategies for building visibility in an increasingly competitive marketplace, they require immediate access to specialized professionals. They turn to Company X when supplementing their in-house creative and communications teams with employees who possess expertise in a range of areas, including Internet design, direct marketing, e-marketing, and media relations.

Contact Jane Doe

Email Address jane.doe@companyx.com

Address USA

Special Instructions: Please send salary requirements and samples along with resume. Cover letter preferred but not necessary.

The issues of having the necessary equipment and home office setup should be addressed in the job description (or at the very least, spelled out in a contract or other written correspondence). Make a list of what the home office needs and who will be responsible for equipment and upgrades, as well as repairs. In addition, ARO supervisors who work at home need a setup of printers, scanners, and speakerphones at minimum. Some supervisors may even need two phone lines and a cell phone so they can be reached at all times.

FINDING CANDIDATES

Given the geographic considerations behind telecommuting (cheaper salaries, a wider pool of available candidates, etc.), you may find recruiting from outside your company a feasible option. The Internet is an obvious source with reliable sites such as Monster.com and craigslist or recruiters specializing in a particular field. Many well-established independent contractors have websites that are easily uncovered through a routine Google search, or you can post job openings on your company website.

Other sources of applicants can include job fairs, on-site recruitment open houses or seminars, and referrals from colleagues and other employees. Another good source is a local search in the area where the desired workers are located (such as Silicon Valley for techies). Regardless of where you find potential candidates, you'll need to check references and previous work history, with an eye to the fact that this person will be working independently and off-site and should exhibit the "telecommuting personality" discussed in the next section and in Chapter 3.

INTERVIEWING AND SELECTION

ARO managers find that hiring employees through detailed and numerous telephone interviews works well in customer service and remote sales. The image in this job is a clear and good-sounding voice coupled with a pleasant speaking manner. However, if the employee is meeting customers directly and visiting their offices, dealing extensively with individual clients remotely (such as knowledge workers/consultants), or working in any major decision-making or influential capacity, a face-to-face interview is best, even if it means incurring additional travel and other expenses. You could visit the prospective worker's home office. Although this also might be costly and time-consuming, you get a clear picture of their situation, resulting in fewer hiring mistakes.

A good compromise is the video interview. Enhanced and improved web offerings and services such as Skype make this option increasingly feasible and cost effective. Videoconferencing offers the best of both worlds. Not only does it provide face-to-face contact, giving you an idea of the interviewee's mannerisms, personality, and dress, but you can also view her home office setup.

Along with the appropriate skill, experience, and "telecommuting personality," certain qualities—some of which were also mentioned in Chapter 3—are needed when making the final selection. They include:

Organization. Because you can't physically see the individual to supervise him, "communication and organization become incredibly important," observes Merrily Orsini, CEO of My Virtual Corp. "In working with a virtual team, you have meetings. You can't be late for the meeting, for instance, because it's on the telephone. In physical meetings, people often come in late and leave early. That . . . doesn't work virtually." Simply put, you need a person who gets the job done on time, no matter what other responsibilities she may have.

Multiple communication skills. You need to get an idea of how well a candidate handles situations on the phone, via e-mail, in writing, and in person. Virtual employees must be able to communicate effectively under a wide variety of circumstances—indicating, for example, understanding, disagreement, the need for clarification and so forth. During the interview, "pay careful attention to tone and how well candidates get their ideas across," in all modes of communication, suggests Jeanne Allert in *Training & Development* magazine.

Follow through and following directions. "If you say you're going to do something, you really do have to do it," adds Orsini. "We ask a question in our application process about whether they like to lead or follow. The leaders tend to be the best virtual workers. I think it's because they are used to setting individual goals and tasks and meeting those." Workers who need hand holding and constant contact are perhaps better left in the office.

On the other hand, they must also be able to follow directions and should be unafraid to ask questions. "It means clearly writing down what you need to have happen and . . . touching base with people along the way," she continues. "It is making very sure you understand what the task is, that the deliverable . . . is what the person had in mind before you go off and spend a week, a day, or even hours doing something . . . in the wrong direction."

Decision-making confidence. Therefore, rather than sitting around waiting for your help or for you to get back to them, they may need to take the initiative to solve a problem, even if it results in an occasional mistake. "Look for people who try—right or wrong—to fix their own problems," says Allert. Here is where behavioral interviewing can be helpful in uncovering how they handled past situations.

Values- or mission-based. Interviewees should see the "big picture" and share the team's enthusiasm for its goals. They'll need inner resources to keep them going, even if they work completely alone. "Ask candidates what motivates them," she goes on. "What internal rewards do they need? Look for signs that they are motivated from within."

Tech savvy. Many people can operate a computer and send and receive e-mails. But do they know how to download attachments and participate in web conferencing or IM? Are they familiar with scanning documents and Voice over Internet Protocol (VoIP)? Additionally, workers must be able to troubleshoot and have a backup plan should equipment malfunction. They should understand the steps that need to be taken (such as calling tech support) rather than waiting for you or someone else to get back to them. They also need to be willing to try new technologies and ways of working.

WORK AGREEMENTS AND CONTRACTS

Work agreements and contracts should be determined before hiring employees, so they will be ready and available for use. Every teleworker—if he's temporary or part-time, even if his job is the most routine and lowest in the hierarchy—should have a contract or formal written work arrangement. This will forestall any possible misunderstandings and will protect you and your company legally. Appendix B provides two very different examples of work agreements/contracts.

Information should include hours the employee is expected to be available by phone, e-mail, and elsewhere; if applicable, times he is expected to report to the office; who is going to be supplying what equipment and when; safety requirements; training schedules; and performance standards. The contract should also cover payment, whether the employee is an independent contractor or a salaried or hourly worker. If it's the latter, the person may be eligible for overtime and that should be included. Benefits are another issue; generally speaking, if the employee is full-time and not an IC, she receives the same benefits as on-site workers.

Specific assignments for each worker should be spelled out as well as the manager's role in the arrangement. Management responsibilities can range from determining work standards to the performance review schedule to establishing grounds for dismissal. Many times telecommuters are given a trial period, which can range anywhere from two weeks to several months depending upon the job. This time frame should be set forth, as well as the criteria used to evaluate the success or failure of the arrangement.

Other important points to be included are: insurance, both health and liability; the employer's right to inspect the workplace (for safety compliance reasons); privacy and confidentiality agreements; the fact that the teleworker must follow and abide by company policies and procedures; and conditions of termination. These can consist of: inability to perform duties, options for returning to office work should the telecommuting arrangement fail, and disposal of equipment.

Unless they are considered to be full-time, regular employees (see Chapter 2 for criteria), telecommuters should be aware that their jobs are considered by upper management to be the most expendable. Should they be let go for any reason, they have little recourse and will likely not even be eligible to receive unemployment. You need to emphasize this fact, especially when hiring former office workers who are making the transition to telecommuting or first-time, inexperienced employees. They may not realize that in the brave new world of virtual work, job security, in terms of being employed by the same company for an entire career, is a thing of the past. Of course, this is true for many office jobs these days as well.

INTRODUCING TELECOMMUTERS TO THE TEAM

The importance of recognizing telecommuters, many of whom are isolated, will be discussed in upcoming chapters. You can get things off to a good start by introducing new employees to the team, even if they are scattered throughout the globe.

Putting a picture and bio of the person on the company web-site—the new hire can supply the information—or sending around an e-mail to all employees, is effective. If your company's web-site supports the software, a short video in which the person talks briefly about himself and what he hopes to contribute can also go a long way in familiarizing him with the team.

Better yet, set up a video, telephone, or online conference, which gives all members of the team, new and old, a chance to interact and get to know each other. If employees are located within driving distance of one another, set up an informal luncheon or dinner so that the new teleworker gets to learn names and see faces, and the working relationship starts on a comfortable basis. For example, when the ARO worker base was mostly in Kansas City, Michael organized "Muffins with the Managers" for telecommuters.

SUMMARY

Hiring is one of the biggest challenges facing managers of tele-workers. Not only must you be careful in making sure that you've selected someone with the "telecommuter personality" but that individual needs to be aware that working from home comes with its own particular set of demands. Chief among these are:

- Self-starter and independent worker
- Follow instructions yet able to make decisions
- Tech savvy and open to new ways of working
- Enthusiastic about work and the company—sees the "big picture"
- Good communicator in all media
- Has a good work/life balance

This last point may be harder for managers to discern in initial interviews, so you may be called upon to deal with it after the employee is hired.

Additionally, you'll need to be innovative in your process of selection and in job descriptions. If you are choosing from employees within the organization, they should be educated as to the requirements and pitfalls of telecommuting, and also the possibility that they might fail if they've never done it before. If you're using an outside pool, you'll need to interview and screen applicants carefully, checking references and past work history. Job descriptions must similarly be flexible. Although you can outline and anticipate duties, often they will change and evolve as situations or the project unfolds.

No matter for what position you hire or under what circumstances, it's necessary to have a contract. It should outline the "who, what, when, and where" of duties, payment, equipment, benefits, and circumstances of termination, among other things.

Telecommuters also need to be aware that their position may be more expendable than office jobs, simply because they are still considered "outside" or "extra" employees, at least in most situations. On the other hand, many have skills that can easily translate into new positions or companies.

However, that doesn't mean that they can't—or shouldn't—be an integral part of the team. As with any regular new hire corralled into the cubicle farm, telecommuters should be introduced through various available media, meeting their coworkers face-to-face if possible. This is an important and positive step in creating what should be a long and successful working relationship.

CHAPTER 9

Training

INTRODUCTION

If it was easy to train for a job at home, everyone would do it. But as anyone who has worked on either or both sides of the worker/ manager telecommuting fence knows, all parties need to know what to expect and what is expected of them. No matter which method you use to train—on-site, remote, or virtual—workers and managers require specific guidance, not only regarding job duties and performance, but also on ergonomics, home safety, time management, and communications skills. This chapter covers these topics, and the importance of mentoring and evaluating learning.

WHY TRAIN?

You get what you pay for. Companies that fail to invest in training sessions for managers and employees will likely have to deal with an array of problems.

Lack of face time: Managers need to learn new and different ways of measuring productivity and dealing with trust. Also, how do you forestall resentment from other workers who are still in the office?

Absence from the workplace: Out of sight, out of mind . . . Teleworkers need to learn ways of communicating to remain visible and productive.

Lost creativity: Family interruptions and procrastination issues can become major roadblocks if workers don't know how to handle them. How do you compensate for the lack of motivation when you're not around your coworkers on a day-to-day basis?

Unmet expectations: One might imagine working all day in pajamas, uninterrupted by phone calls and other noise. The reality of telecommuting can be fraught with complications including frequent interruptions and demands by family members, equipment failures, and other unexpected emergencies.

Yet an effective training program—one that sets objectives and measures productivity, fosters performance management skills, and provides a list of requirements, such as what comprises a safe and comfortable home office—can go a very long way in ensuring that the telecommuting program is a success. The needs and concerns of managers must also be anticipated and met; thus they should be trained at least part of the time in the same class as employees so they hear what is being said to their workers and can resolve potential problems through open discussion and questions. Both positive and negative experiences of telecommuting employees and managers should be incorporated into the program to provide continuity and a basis to address ongoing issues.

TYPES OF TRAINING

Three types of training methods or platforms are commonly used: On-site "old school" where students meet in a traditional classroom setting; distance learning, in which training materials are sent to the employees who study them and take tests and return their answers via mail or email; and online computer-based learning (CBL), in which the classroom is connected virtually and students and teachers interact in a web or satellite conferencing mode. ARO uses the latter via a "virtual whiteboard" type setting with a webinar-type conference (a "webinar" is an interactive web-based, lecture, meeting, or presentation). Sometimes it is more realistic and cost-effective to use a combination of these techniques: for example, a half-day or day face-to-face session, with the remainder of the training being done via CBL.

Under the right circumstances, all of these types of training can be effective. However, nothing takes the place of face-to-face training—either in a classroom or through a web seminar involving the entire group—in developing social skills like providing and receiving feedback, conflict resolution, and effective communication. Although they may be located in different places, it's key that team members interact directly, in real-time, even if only virtually.

However, for certain other types of jobs, such as the customer call centers at ARO, virtual training may be more effective. Not only is it more focused by honing in on specific skills rather than social interaction between participants but it takes less time. So, when the skills required are more remote and more routine, virtual training not only fills the bill, it may even reduce it!

On-Site

In the 1990s, before the Internet came into general use for businesses, this was basically the most feasible method. In his book *Managing Telework*, Jack M. Nilles recommends group sessions of fifteen to twenty-five students in a traditional, daylong lecture format. He suggests a teleworker's workshop, a manager's workshop, and then a joint workshop for both. Topics covered in the first would be a list of concerns, company guidelines, breakdown of job duties, communications skills, developing telecommuting skills and the home work environment, and crisis management. The manager's workshop would encompass what is expected of a telemanager and related concerns, selecting telecommuters and structuring jobs, analyzing flow of information, and establishing performance measures and evaluation results. The joint workshop would include a review of the contract/agreement, communication patterns and requirements for telecommuters and managers, setting goals and expectations, dealing with change, and any other related issues. Along with preparing employees/managers for telecommuting the goal of such training is "to produce agreements—of whatever formality and length of term—between teleworkers and their supervisors" to increase confidence and ease transitional concerns.

Remote—Distance Learning

Today most reputable colleges and instructional institutions have some sort of distance-based program. As Sandra has pointed out in her own writings on the subject, nowhere does it say "distance learning" on your resume or degree.

Distance learning involves taking classes via audio or video tapes, the Internet, study guides, CD-ROMs, and traditional textbooks. It covers the same topics as classroom training—traditional syllabus or agenda—only it is done via e-mail and Internet discussion groups. What is missing of course is the face-to-face interaction, but by its very nature distance learning provides a taste of what real world telecommuting is like, perhaps even more so than the interactive online CBL in which trainees are closely monitored. Distance learning simulates the telecommuting environment "by having the participants conference call . . . manipulate files, and basically perform many of the activities that they would do in a normal day of telecommuting," observes author George Piskurich.

Along with being cost effective—especially for geographically disbursed companies—distance learning allows for large groups of telecommuters to start work simultaneously. However, Piskurich also recommends teacher-student interaction during training, even if it's only virtually and if only to stimulate "responses . . . to off-the-wall questions, and the human feeling that these technologies can't deliver. Real time . . . contact must be part of your program."

Online/Virtual Computer-Based Learning (CBL)/ Computer-Based Training (CBT)

The newest wrinkle in telecommuting and other types of training is Computer-Based Learning (CBL) or Computer-Based Training (CBT) in which computers are integral to teaching, testing, and evaluation. Often the format is similar to the step-by-step tutorials used in learning how to operate PCs and other electronic equipment. In ARO's CBT programs, students keep their modules to review. As they are updated, they can go back over the modules to refresh and relearn processes.

Closely interrelated (and some say interchangeable) is web-based training, which is delivered over the Internet and integrates blogs, chat rooms, bulletin boards, Instant Messaging (IM), video-conferencing, and other technologies.

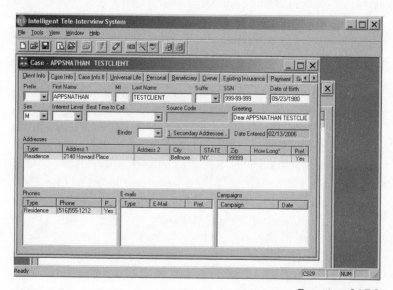

Courtesy of ARO

Web/CBL training can involve both asynchronous and syn-chronous communications technologies. Using such formats as blogs, discussion boards, and e-mail, *asynchronous* technologies allow for the exchange of knowledge and information by partici-pants at different times. In contrast, *synchronous* activities involve the exchange of ideas and information with participants during the same period of time, with the low-tech version being face-to-face discussion and the electronic format including online chat sessions, videoconferencing, and the virtual classroom.

A discussion of specific programs and applications using CBL/ web training would probably be outdated by the time this book goes to press, but certain requirements are always necessary .The instructor and all participants will need a computer and Internet access with DSL, wireless, or cable connection (dial-up may prove too slow,) and a land line telephone or cell phone that accommodates a headset or has a speakerphone so the student can easily type in information and take notes.

Additionally, instructors will need a method of *polling*—that is, making sure that the students are actually physically present during the synchronous session. Rhonda "R.J." Johnson, training manager of ARO, does a roll call at the beginning of each virtual training session in addition to periodically taking attendance and asking pointed questions throughout. "I have a pretty good idea when they put their headsets down and go do something else," she says. She also gives quizzes, further ensuring students are paying attention. If the session is asynchronous, the instructor can ask students to e-mail questions that will be responded to in a short period of time, which allows for at least some immediate interaction. Other virtual training tips include:

Limit sessions to two hours each. If they must be longer, include a short break so students can stretch, get a snack, and go to the restroom. "Two hours is the maximum span that almost anyone can be effective working remotely," observe authors Fisher and Fisher.

As with telecommuting itself, focus on results not activities. Training—no matter what the platform—should be specifically geared to the organizational goals, performance standards, and the job at hand.

Make sure employees know in advance what they'll need to participate in training—uninterrupted "quiet time" and the proper equipment if training is remote or CBL, for example.

Understand that as with any training activity, people learn differently. It is important to use graphics, sound, and written materials to accommodate a variety of learning styles.

Virtual Training—A Good Thing

R.J. Johnson, training manager of ARO, found the use of a remote webinar in training call center employees to be far more efficient than the real-time, face-to-face group setting originally used when she started with the company. Meeting virtually "eliminates the clique-building that can take place in-house," she observes. "It also helps the workers stay more on task and on the subject. Sometimes in a traditional training situation, there can be distractions. You can get into discussions that have nothing to do with the matter at hand." Even innocuous topics, such as the weather or the rising price of groceries, can take away from time designated for learning.

Johnson estimates that not only has the webinar reduced the training time by as much as a third, but employees are much more knowledgeable when they complete the program. "You are putting more responsibility on the trainee to learn. It helps them step up to the plate and be more focused."

JOB SKILLS TRAINING

Training for job skills is probably the most straightforward part of telecommuting training. You have specific duties that need to be accomplished and the employee needs to be taught how to complete them as well as meet the standards for performance. You should establish measurable goals so the employee knows what is expected of him. These can range from X phone calls per hour using a designated script to a long-term project that can take several months but must be finished by a certain date (the latter being a situation requiring considerable managerial trust). Employees also have to get a sense of the "big picture," that is, where their job fits into the overall scheme and company's mission and goals.

ARO trains for a wide cross-section of telecommuting jobs: scheduling and insurance certification, billing, and collection in medical and healthcare; customer service and support for brokerage and financial services; sales, underwriting, auditing, and claims in insurance; technical support for original equipment manufacturers (OEMs), wireless vendors, independent software suppliers, retail, entertainment, hospitality, real estate, and many other kinds of businesses. Each type of telecommuting job has an online training manual specific to the work requirements. The manual also provides step-by-step information so the employee can review what was covered after the training class is completed.

Many telework arrangements rely heavily on technology; therefore, training for this should be incorporated as well. At ARO the host or client system usually has a testing or "demo" module that can also be used for training or practice. By following the visual through a set of logical steps or screen shots, trainees can practice the keystrokes and maneuvers required for their job, giving them hands-on experience.

Also, depending on the worker's skill and familiarity with technology, they may need to learn everything from the basics—how to access a remote network and send/receive e-mails—to troubleshooting equipment used in job performance to the ins and outs of application-specific software. For example, if VoIP technology is used, employees will need to learn an entirely different way of dealing with telephone features and problems, such as how to send and receive faxes, which can be extremely problematical depending upon the speed and quality of the Internet connection and type of fax machine.

As with office work, training relies heavily on the requirements set forth in the job description. Human Resources and professional trainers in your company should help develop content if training programs aren't already in place for similar positions within the organization. At ARO, customer service and care is taught to all employees whether they are working in underwriting or retail, as they use the same skill sets in dealing with clients.

TIME MANAGEMENT TRAINING

Newbie telecommuters often think, Gee, look at all the time I'll save—no more commute or long lunches out or putting on makeup/shaving/getting into work clothes and so on. What they often don't realize is that nature abhors a vacuum and just as many precious minutes/hours can be wasted dawdling over the newspaper with a cup of coffee, or running errands: At last! Time to get that replacement faucet!

So the first thing they'll need to learn is how to compartmentalize: Certain hours are to be devoted exclusively to work, while others should be off-duty. Division of hours may be easier for jobs involving service, support, and sales when workers are expected to be available and in touch—you will likely be checking on them, especially in the beginning. However, all workers—even creative ones in the arts—must set aside certain times of the day and stick to those hours, no matter what. This discipline is reinforced by having a specific workspace devoted exclusively to the job, which will be discussed further in the chapter.

Other time management suggestions to emphasize:

Make a list with duties and priorities. This can be a diary, either electronic or paper, or a chart/wipe-off bulletin board placed prominently in the workspace. Either way, it should be something that workers see daily enabling them to keep track of various projects as well as the order in which they must be accomplished.

Understand that each person has her own way of organizing work. No device or method applies to every task, even the most routine. It goes back to focusing on results—employees need to find the best and most effective methods of doing their job. Some people can require electronics for every minute detail while others prefer low-tech paper and pencil. Micromanaging their every move can actually be counterproductive, creating unnecessary work and an atmosphere of resentment. What's important is they get the job done and provide the information you need in the required format.

Share "best practices" with the teleworking team. Two (or more) heads are better than one, and brainstorming and idea sharing in the training session can get things off to a positive start. As mentioned earlier, bringing in experienced teleworkers can go a long way in providing helpful hints and initial encouragement.

Another—and potentially bigger—threat to telecommuters "is not working too little but working too much," observes author Jeanne Allert. "Because work is only a couple steps away, it's easy to start at 6:30 A.M. and find yourself still at the keyboard at 11 P.M. I've . . . logged on to the network late at night and sent 'Stop working and get some sleep!' messages to employees who were still logged on." Keeping in touch with fellow workers virtually is also helpful in overcoming isolation, which will be discussed in Chapter 13.

Sandra's Tips for Self-Starting (and Stopping)

As someone who has had a home office for nearly three decades, Sandra knows (almost) every trick to get going. Others may disagree, but that is the beauty of virtual work.

- Get dressed, at the very least as if you're going to have a "casual Friday." This means putting on clothes that actually match and looking presentable. Okay, it's only you but if you feel like a slob, it can show up in your work.
- Be at your desk at the appointed hour, no matter what. This may not be as easy as it sounds, as you may find reasons to avoid facing the computer or other work by doing nonessential tasks, such as brushing the cat.
- Know your most productive hours and work then, no matter what. This is true of any job, but it's especially important with

telecommuting when you have specific deadlines and less structure.

- Take breaks. Time frames and conditions can be discussed during orientation and/or mutual training sessions. If all parties know what's expected beforehand and if workers are taught that they need to inform management of any deviations in the agreed upon schedule, this will become a non-issue and will help build trust.

- If it's 10 P.M. and you've been working nonstop for several hours and your significant other/child/pet start to bug you and demand attention, it's time to quit. The work will be there tomorrow and a good night's rest is crucial.

- Make it clear that you are not available for babysitting, informal psychiatric consults, or whatever interruptions friends and family may come up with during work hours. This should be emphasized during training as well.

Dealing with Interruptions, Temptations, and Crises

Which leads into the next point—how do you train workers to say "no" to family and friends? This can be the biggest challenge faced by those new to telecommuting. Establishing an office environment in your home—where you and your family normally eat, sleep, and relax requires setting new precedents and rules. And as anyone who's tried it knows, change can be difficult. Managers and trainers need to encourage workers to get their family's support and should provide suggestions for setting boundaries, such as mutually agreed upon times when workers should not be interrupted.

Temptations such as excessive snacking, shopping, and television watching are other issues beginning teleworkers must deal with. These behaviors can be countered by helping the employee develop a system of positive rewards for not giving in ("If I work until 4, then I can watch *Judge Mathis*"); avoiding the source of temptation (such as the refrigerator, or pets, which can be especially distracting—tell yourself that they have "clocked in" by sleeping and you shouldn't disturb them), and the creation of strict break schedules.

Of course, there will be the occasional emergency and/or crisis on either or both ends. Such things are often out of everyone's control. For example, snow and electrical storms in Kansas City cause periodic outages with ARO's Virtual Private Network (VPN) making it difficult if not impossible for the main control center to route incoming calls to customer service teleworkers. "We can't see what they're doing virtually so we don't know whether they're sitting there, waiting to speak to a new customer, or are still talking on the line," observes call center manager David Beighley. However ARO has backup (redundant) power, so this doesn't happen often. If the host computer connection is down, and workers are unable to access the host client system for account lookup, depending upon the client's needs, they are given instructions during orientation as to how to handle such situations.

Whether the emergency is personal, family, or equipment related, instruct employees to notify you immediately so you can provide help. This will go a long way in preventing a sense of isolation and helplessness.

COMMUNICATIONS SKILLS TRAINING

The ability to communicate may be the biggest factor in a successful telecommuting venture. Although it's obvious that good communication must take place within all teams, whether office-based or virtual, telecommuter training needs to hone in on effective and specific methods of communication.

Trainers can start by having employees analyze their current communication modes and patterns: Do they like to talk on the phone? Are they comfortable with going on the Internet and/or using email? They can then explore what kinds of communications will be needed on the job—will workers need to "check in" via e-mail or phone at scheduled intervals? What kind of meetings will be held, and when, and how long are they anticipated to take? Should the worker expect frequent contact from the supervisor and how quickly should he respond? The fact that the worker should remain "visible"—attend company meetings and gatherings, be in regular contact with the supervisor, and submit periodic status/progress reports—should be emphasized.

Additionally, teleworkers need to understand that they must *always* be reachable during business hours. If for some reason their Internet server goes down or there is a power failure, it is the employee's responsibility to immediately contact the supervisor, even if it means borrowing a friend's cell phone. Employers won't see any worker who "disappears" in a favorable light.

Conversely, managers and, if necessary, coworkers should also be accessible, letting callers know if they are out of the office and providing an alternate contact (this can also be done with auto-response via e-mail). Nothing erodes trust more quickly than not being able to get in touch with someone when you need him.

Most important, teleworkers should be coached to "speak up." In face-to-face office meetings, visual cues and body language can reveal who may not be quite on board with your proposals and ideas. With telephone conferencing and less-sophisticated visual web programs, you can miss these important signals, although tone of voice and the reaction of the other individuals (silence, an intake of breath) can provide clues.

The most difficult media for discerning intent are e-mail and text and instant messaging. Their short and informal nature some-times makes it almost impossible to figure out exactly what the other party means. Responses can be misinterpreted as indiffer-ence or rudeness—when in fact the writer may be distracted or in a hurry—resulting in "flames," angry, impulsive retorts dashed off without a review or cooling-off period. A quick refresher course in business communication etiquette ("Don't push 'send' until you have an idea how it would look in your local paper") can help forestall this as can emphasizing the fact that the worker should call you with any questions or concerns. If, during any part of the work process, either party feels that they may not be able to adequately express their feelings virtually they should PICK UP THE PHONE (written in caps = the equivalent of shouting over the Internet).

Depending upon the requirements of the job, you may need to emphasize other aspects of communication, such as developing a pleasant phone voice and verbal mannerisms, how to write effective messages on electronic bulletin boards and other virtual meeting spaces, and ways of communicating effectively with coworkers and other individuals in the organization, whether they are located remotely or in the home office.

During training, convey methods of communication as a team collaboration rather than set them forth as "rules" that must be obeyed. "For example, the team may identify team-specific meanings for the use of certain e-mail symbols or phrases; team members may discuss and agree on the types of situations in which they will use face-to-face, phone, and e-mail communications," suggest Diane Moody and Ingrid Steinberg. "The ground rules can be extended to form a group contract for working together. Such contracts have been found to be invaluable within virtual working groups where distance, silence, and limited communication cues can provide a breeding ground for suspicion, perceived exclusion, and demotivation. Simple things like committing to a fixed-time telephone conference, agreeing to let colleagues know you need support, or contracting to acknowledge others' work when it's posted online (because nobody knows if you've seen it if you don't say so) go a long way in preventing problems."

ERGONOMICS AND HOME SAFETY TRAINING

Like many companies, ARO has developed a detailed and extensive program on home office safety and ergonomics, which is the applied science of equipment design to maximize productivity along with operator safety and comfort. In addition to videos that the worker can view at leisure, ARO provides detailed, written instructions on every issue from the proper use of electrical cords and outlets to selecting the best chair and desk, organizing files and other paperwork, reducing clutter, air quality considerations, and fire safety, among many other aspects. (See Appendix C for a safety checklist and Appendix D for ergonomics information and guidelines.)

During this portion of the training, the company's policies and procedures regarding how the office should be set up should be covered. This includes, but is not limited to, the type and amount of space required; security, furniture, and equipment needed; work storage and surfaces to be used. Employees can then design their own "mock office" and compare notes and brainstorm ideas. Chapter 10 will go into detail about setting up a home office and ensuring its safety.

MANAGERS TRAINING MANAGERS

If you are managing others and need to train them, that will have its own set of challenges. Especially if they are new to telecommuting, they will need to be included in setting up the program so they don't feel as if they're being "put out to pasture" so to speak.

In the late 1970s, when computers were just beginning to become part of the workscape, employees worried that their jobs would be phased out and they would become obsolete. To an extent, the same fears have surfaced among some managers regarding telecommuting. However, once they recognize it is an efficient and cost effective way of doing business that will enhance rather than take away from their workload, it will be accepted.

The biggest shift managers face is the switch from activity-based to results-based management. "How do you manage people you can't see?" they may wonder. "How do you manage performance if not by hours worked?"

The solution revolves around many of the basic issues faced by the telecommuters themselves: communication, organization, time management, and performance standards. Particularly with the latter, they must be clear-cut, whether you are measuring the output of customer service employees or the effectiveness of your web design team.

You can't holler at them over the cubicle or corner them in the break room, but you can get in touch with them by e-mail or phone. In many ways companies like ARO monitor their workers more closely than many traditional offices. ARO's virtual network allows management to see exactly who employees are calling and when; what they are discussing and for how long; as well as making sure they're not idle. The company knows when its employees go on break, how many calls they fielded that day, and when they go to the bathroom. However, the most important measure of telecommuting workers is not what activities they perform but what results they achieve.

In his training program for managers, telecommuting expert and consultant Gil Gordon emphasizes five points:

1. Managing by results instead of by observation
2. Fine-tuning skills for setting performance standards and giving ongoing performance feedback
3. Keeping telecommuters linked to the office
4. Career management issues for telecommuters
5. Spotting problems and dealing with them effectively

The following checklist can be adapted to cover most if not all concerns and make sure that all parties clearly understand what is expected of them.

Table 9.1

Human Resources Supervisor's Checklist for Telecommuters
This checklist from the University of California, San Francisco (UCSF) provides general guidance and orientation to department managers and telecommuting candidates.

Name of Telecommuter: _____
Name of Supervisor: _____
Date Completed: _____

❏ Employee has read the UCSF's telecommuting guidelines.
❏ Employee has been provided with a schedule of assigned work hours or guidelines for flexing work hours.
❏ Equipment issued by UCSF is documented.
❏ Performance expectations have been discussed and are clearly understood. Assignments and due dates are documented.
❏ Requirements for adequate and safe office space at home have been reviewed with the employee and the employee certifies that those requirements have been met.
❏ Requirements for the care of equipment assigned to the employee have been discussed and are clearly understood.
❏ Requirements for establishing or for suspending telecommuting have been discussed and are clearly understood.
❏ The employee is familiar with UCSF's requirements and techniques for computer information security.
❏ Phone contact procedures have been clearly defined and unit assistants and receptionists have received training.
❏ The employee has read and signed the Telecommuter's Agreement prior to actual participation in the program.
❏ The responsibility for understanding the tax and insurance implications for telecommuting rests with the employee.

I have read, understood, and complied with the above terms:

_____
(Signed/dated by both employee and supervisor)

Along with attending classes with telecommuters where all parties can brainstorm and roleplay to simulate real-world situations, managers should have their own sessions to address supervisory issues, concerns, and questions, as well as be provided with guidelines for employee performance, discipline, and evaluation. It's also a good idea to have at least a brief overview session for all departments, such as support, administration, and HR, which are peripheral to the telecommuting effort. This will go a long way towards alleviating resentment and fostering understanding of how telecommuting fits into overall company goals and mission.

IMPORTANCE OF MENTORING

Rather than the manager, it's often more practical to have experienced telecommuting employees mentor the newcomers. You can help foster these kinds of relationships by matching up people with similar experiences, job responsibilities, and work situations. For example, observes Jeanne Allert, "In our company, only two of us are parents. There's an unspoken fraternity among people who have to deal with carpools and sick kids and snow days; it's a different level of peer support. Similarly, I can't relate to the twenty-two-year-old whose distractions might be dating or planning the weekend." Such relationships can also develop naturally during the training period when workers start to form their own network of friends and advisors. Either way, they help strengthen morale and keep up team motivation.

Whether in or out of this office, with managers or more experienced employees, mentoring should be done with an eye to the following:

- Provide guidance based on past business experiences
- Create a positive counseling relationship and climate of open communication
- Help the mentee identify problems and solutions
- Lead the mentee through problem-solving processes

- Offer constructive criticism in a supportive way
- Share stories, including mistakes
- Assign "homework" if applicable
- Refer the mentee to other business associates
- Be honest about business expertise
- Solicit feedback from the mentee

EVALUATING LEARNING

Training should be completed as close as possible to the actual start date of the job. If too much time elapses, the worker may lose his initial enthusiasm and begin to forget small but important details. Additionally, along with the quizzes, exercises, and other work simulations during training, you may want to have periodic refresher courses or focus groups. These not only help keep employees' skills sharp but also help check how well the program is working and whether training was effective.

Such gatherings can be informal and virtual or even be held asynchronously. The more people from different areas are involved, the more helpful feedback may result. Not only might you find and correct common patterns that occur across the organization but you can develop a list of actions and remedies that need to be taken as well as further refining scheduling and future training. Generally speaking, follow-up sessions should be more frequent at the beginning of the telecommuting program and then occur at regular intervals once it is underway.

SUMMARY

Because you are dealing with time management, communications skills, and ergonomics and home safety issues, training telecommuters is more complicated than training office workers. Also, along with learning job skills, telecommuters must be resourceful and technically savvy enough to troubleshoot problems and know where to go for help, as well as be prepared to fight isolation, procrastination, and the interruptions and temptations of working at home.

Managers need to be trained as well, both alongside their employees and separately. This is especially important in addressing and resolving issues and questions that can normally be taken care of right away in an office environment, but not so much virtually, where people can hide behind telephone calls and e-mails. Additionally managers need to learn a new way of evaluating work and monitoring employees by focusing on results rather than actual processes.

If the organization uses teleworkers at all, it's a good idea to give the entire team an orientation of how and why they fit into the big picture, even if the session is only for a couple of hours. This will go a long way in alleviating the conception that they're "sitting at home and collecting a paycheck." In fact, having an experienced teleworker share his daily efforts—and challenges—would provide much needed insight for all parties concerned.

Although initial training may be completed, learning and refining is far from over, especially with a new telecommuting program. Refresher courses and focus groups that include different departments or teams go a long way in identifying organizational patterns, correcting problems, and planning future actions.

CHAPTER 10

Equipping

INTRODUCTION

This chapter will help you set up home offices for your workers that are productive and comfortable work environments.

Employees must also be educated about what constitutes a safe workplace. Although there are no clear-cut laws regulating safety in the office home environment, this chapter can help you as a manager to monitor workers and help avoid accidents and injury.

THE IDEAL HOME OFFICE

Like traditional employees, those working from home will require certain equipment. After all, their workspace is their office, so you need to make sure it meets the specific requirements of your business. At ARO this means a computer with appropriate software and peripherals that in some cases allows workers to enter clients' responses from the designated script; Internet access to the ARO infrastructure for monitoring and transmission of information; e-mail and messaging capabilities; and a phone headset and land line. This is opposed to just having a cell phone, although an Internet-based VoIP line may be acceptable provided the service is consistent and reliable with good sound quality.

Depending upon the type of work and duties involved, employees may also require a fax machine, a photocopier, and a personal digital assistant (PDA) or BlackBerry. However, these may not be necessary if support functions are available nearby at the company's administrative office or a telework/satellite center. The worker will need—in addition to a room that is *not* the kitchen or dining room table—an office-quality desk and chair, filing cabinets, storage space, and supplies.

Table 10.1

Equipping the Home/Virtual Office

For each worker
Personal computer with:
E-mail
Browser software
Internet access
Intranet access
Telephone with voice mail

Optional:
Camera for web videoconferencing

For each "road warrior"
Laptop with:
Fax capabilities
E-mail
Software
Internet access
Intranet access
Cell phone with voice mail
Scanning capabilities

Optional:
Portable printer

For each telework site:
Network
Printer(s)
Server
Fax
Teleconference equipment
Internet connection

Optional:
Broadband connection and firewall
Videoconferencing equipment

Table 10.1—*continued*

Equipping the Home/Virtual Office

For each business
Intranet (a private, secure network for communication within the company)

Optional:
Extranet (an Intranet that's partially accessible to authorized outsiders, such as clients or remote workers)

Much care and thought needs to be put into planning and designing workers' space (see Appendixes C and D for information and guidelines). Since you will not be there physically to see them perform their jobs it's important that they have all necessary components handy and organized in an efficient, safe, and productive way. As mentioned in Chapter 9, this can be put into motion during training sessions by having employees do mock-ups of their proposed office or supplying a suggested layout. In addition to in-class learning modules, ARO gives its workers complete information on ergonomics and safety to take home with them for future reference. ARO was also a test site for a government program that developed various ergonomic and safety training sessions on CD for remote employees.

Planning their office will also help acclimate employees to telecommuting and get them comfortable with the idea of having a designated workspace in their home. As ergonomics expert Lisa Kanarek advises them: "Think of your desk like an airplane cockpit where a pilot needs to have everything in easy reach without having to stand up." She also recommends that they look around their desks/work area, and envision how it could be more efficient. "Start by reflecting on each and every item . . . then ask yourself:

- How often do I use this item?
- Is this item something I rarely use? If so, move it as far away from your primary workspace as is feasible.

- If not, then ask: Is this item something that I use only sporadically?
- If this situation is true, then move it away from your primary workspace, but to an area still accessible.
- Anything left over should be something you use all or nearly all of the time. These items go within your reach in the valuable real estate of your primary workspace."

Additionally Kanarek suggests regular re-evaluation of workspace, as workers' activities may change over time.

At some point, you may want to inspect their office, either by going there physically, through a web cam or other virtual method, or by hiring a safety consultant to check out the premises. The purpose of the visit is to examine the workspace, not critique the décor or make sure the toilets are sparkling (although if the home appears unsafe, you might want to reconsider allowing the individual to work there).

"Look for things such as ergonomically friendly furniture, properly maintained and taped-down extension cords, outlet safety (surge protectors, proper grounding, and no overloads), clear rooms and hallways, and general structural and organizational safety," observes author William Atkinson in *Risk & Insurance* magazine. If you are doing it yourself, or accompanying the consultant, take the worker out for a meal or coffee before or after the inspection.

WHO PAYS FOR EQUIPMENT AND HOME OFFICE SETUP?

If the person is a regular (W-2) employee, whether full- or part-time, the employer covers equipment costs. If the worker is an independent contractor, chances are he or she will already have most if not all of the equipment on hand, so the employer usually does not pay. However, if specialized software or other materials are needed, the employer may cover the expenses, regardless of the employee's status.

In other cases, the employee and the company may split the bill, or the company may work with the employee in getting a discount; for example, academic rates for expensive software if the company is a nonprofit or learning institution. Non-reimbursing employers can also point their workers in the direction of where to get the safest and most ergonomically correct office equipment at a reasonable price,

The argument for the company paying is straightforward: If you own the equipment then the employee must use it for your business only. It also allows for better control of access to customer service or sensitive information. Additionally you can dictate the type of hardware, software, and peripherals workers will use, thus allowing for constancy across the organization and making it easier to support equipment should it break down.

Use of equipment can be defined through an agreement similar to the following equipment receipt form previously used by ARO and should specify how equipment will be maintained, who can use it and what it will be used for, who owns the equipment and furniture, who is responsible for insuring the equipment, and so on.

ARO Equipment Receipt Form

By signing this receipt form, I willingly acknowledge that I have received the items listed below in good working condition. They are the property of ARO, Inc. and they are to be used solely for the purpose of performing work for ARO, Inc.

I understand and agree in advance that upon termination of my employment relationship with ARO Inc., I will return the following items in good working condition or be subject to my final paycheck being withheld pending return of said items, and that if said items are not returned or are returned in a damaged condition, that I am subject to deductions from my final paycheck and/or billing by ARO for the cost of replacement or repair of said items:

- Plantronics Headset Model #H51 _____
- Plantronics M12 Box _____
- Plantronics cable P/N 40974-01 _____
- Plantronics A/C adapter _____
- ARO Training Manual _____
- Lucent 146 Analog phone _____
- Shredder _____
- Other equipment_____

Employee Signature:_____Date:_____

Employee Name (Print):_____

Social Security Number: _____

However, ARO no longer purchases equipment for employees, although it does pay for some of it. Early on, the company supplied workers with computers to be used only for business, only to receive worker complaints about having two PCs on their desktops—it was too crowded, especially if they needed a router or hub for each computer. At one point ARO also supplied workers with a headset, amp box, and phone, but those were impractical as employees had their particular preferences and comfort level about the kinds of models they favored. Now the company allows employees to choose their own headsets; even if they quit they can keep them, and employees are much happier using their own computers. Still, this situation would not be feasible if the information was confidential or presented a security risk.

WHAT'S NEEDED TO GET THE JOB DONE

The requirements of furniture, lighting, electricity and storage are mostly dictated by safety issues to be discussed on page 128. An investment in ergonomically correct equipment, as well as a private, well-lit, and ventilated space will pay off for both employer and telecommuter. Along with being private and kept away from family activity especially if there are young children (see list on page 131), the room should be an enclosed space with a door, rather than opening into the family room or main living area.

Telecommuters, like any other worker, need to take frequent breaks. Sitting at the computer for hours on end can result in eye-strain, back problems, and carpel-tunnel syndrome, among other work-related injuries. In order to get the job done, you need to emphasize not only a safe work environment but healthy work habits, whether it be socializing with family members or pets or a seventh-inning stretch for breaks. (See Appendix D for some simple exercises that can be done several times daily.)

Frequency and length of these breaks depends upon company policy and the specific requirements of the job. ARO's software monitors their time to make sure they are keeping correct hours and taking appropriate breaks. Everyone who works an eight-hour shift must take a half-hour lunch, and they get one fifteen-minute break every four hours. Some companies forbid work in certain areas (such as the kitchen) or during specific hours.

Equipment and software must be consistent across the board. For example, if faxing is important to the job, the worker will likely need a regular land line, since VoIP and other Internet or broadband connections are notoriously unreliable when it comes to sending and receiving faxes.

Everyone needs the same or compatible operating systems powerful enough to perform the tasks and synchronize with each other's software—this is true of all software bundles as well. Will workers just need Microsoft Word or will they also require Microsoft Excel, Microsoft Powerpoint, and Microsoft Sharepoint?

What about the specific platforms bundled with "professional" editions, such as networking support, Virtual Private Networks (VPNs), and Windows Meeting Space? Many times employers get caught up in the "gee-whiz" factor and purchase features they don't need.

When purchasing software and other equipment, ask yourself these questions:

1. How will technology fit into the system? It's not enough that it be stand-alone. Just because it works well by itself doesn't mean it will mesh with everything else.
2. Do employees have a reliable telephone system, including voice mail?
3. Does the telecommuter have dependable DSL, cable, or other broadband communications that will link in with your network? This will enable participants to share data files and peripherals like printers as well as allow for security, IM, and web conferencing. It can be simple or complex, from a local area network (LAN) with a few linked computers to an Ethernet using a private server to a complex, multifunctional Intranet. Your IT department can offer guidelines and suggestions; independent web consultants can also help set up networks.

Don't skimp on equipment. Purchase teleconference equipment with good speakerphones for meetings and conferences and clients, as well as high-quality headsets so team members can walk around and use the computer without head and neck strain. Hands-free cell phone systems are also advisable if the employees are on the road; accidents are more frequent while driving when talking on a handheld cell phone—it is distracting and dangerous. Several states, cities, and municipalities have declared driving while talking on a handheld cell phone illegal, and many others have legislation pending (it is also illegal in many countries overseas).

Pick your software before purchasing hardware. If for example, you do video or graphics work, you'll need much more memory than word processing.

When purchasing computers, let the job dictate whether it's a desktop or a laptop. Although desktops are less expensive than laptops, the latter are essential if the worker does any kind of travel. In some cases he may need both. Regardless of what you select, the computers should be easily upgradeable with both wireless and broadband capability and plenty of memory. You can add on, but it's almost impossible to "delete" to make room for more memory or new programs.

Thirty Years of "Home Officing"

Sandra has seen it all, from her first Atari (circa 1984) whose word processing program was operated by a plug-in (remember Pac-Man?) and used floppy disks that stored about 200 pages (264 KB) on a good day to the latest iteration, a fully loaded Dell 1330 laptop that's so slim that CDs slip right into the side with a 2G plug in zip drive smaller than a stick of chewing gum and everything in-between.

One thing she's found in her three decades of purchasing equipment is that cutting corners does not pay. For example, in the 1990s when DOS was doing battle with Windows, she purchased a slightly older model DOS computer with less memory, which of course was replaced by a Windows-based system much sooner than anticipated because everyone she wrote for had switched to Windows-based software. So she tightens her belt each time she buys new equipment. This saves money in the long run, because it lasts much longer and stays current with clients' needs.

On the other hand, Sandra has seen home-based businesses fail because they overextend themselves with the latest bells and whistles. Whether it be a loaded PDA or twenty-two-inch monitor with a huge video capacity, the question is, "Do I really need that?"

She sometimes holds onto equipment longer than necessary, but once it starts interfering with her productivity or ability to deliver books and articles on time, then it's out the door.

SAFETY ISSUES AND REQUIREMENTS

In November 1999, in response to an inquiry from a Houston-based company that employed telecommuters, the Occupational Safety and Health Administration (OSHA) released an advisory stating that employers were responsible for the safety of their home-based workers. The ensuing firestorm of controversy from lawmakers, businesses, and workers resulted in the withdrawal of the letter in January 2000. However, a debate had begun and representatives from business, government, and labor were called upon by the Department of Labor to review the needs of the growing segment of telecommuters. It has been several years, and nothing has been forthcoming from the government, but many employers now have a policy regarding safety requirements for at-home workers.

For safety training ARO uses a program from Harrington Software Associates (teleworkersafety.com; *www.hsainc.net*). As part of an OSHA grant, the Virginia-based company has developed an interactive web-based training program that includes modules on ergonomics, fire safety, electrical safety, indoor air quality, and general office safety. They also include information on how to configure your home office work area; how to adjust your chair, desk, keyboard tray, and computer monitor to fit your body; how to protect electrical equipment from power surges; how to test and maintain fire safety devices; how to protect a home office from theft; and how to improve air quality. Appendixes C and D provide information and checklists regarding these and other aspects.

Additional needs include a comfortable and ergonomically correct chair and desk of appropriate height, sturdiness, and design so employees can comfortably reach and work with computers, phones, and other equipment. The keyboard needs to be placed so wrists are in neutral position (to avoid carpal tunnel and other repetitive injuries) and the monitor should be at eye level with lighting to eliminate glare.

The Telecommuting Safety Checklist developed by the General Services Administration (GSA) and disseminated by U.S. Office of Personnel Management (OPM) (see Table 10.2) can serve as a basic guide. Each employee can fill it out, sign it, and return it to the supervisor.

TABLE 10.2
TELECOMMUTING SAFETY CHECKLIST

Name: _____

Organization: _____

Address: _____

City/State: _____

Business Telephone: _____

Telecommuting Coordinator: _____

Alternative Worksite Location: _____

(Describe the designated work area in the alternative worksite.)

A. Workplace Environment
1. Are temperature, noise, ventilation and lighting levels adequate for maintaining your normal level of job performance? Yes _____ No _____
2. Are all stairs with four or more steps equipped with handrails? Yes _____ No _____
3. Are all circuit breakers and/or fuses in the electrical panel labeled as to intended service? Yes _____ No _____

4. Do circuit breakers clearly indicate if they are in the open or closed position? Yes _____ No _____
5. Is all electrical equipment free of recognized hazards that would cause physical harm (frayed wires, bare conductors, loose wires, flexible wires running through walls, exposed wires to the ceiling)? Yes _____ No _____
6. Will the building's electrical system permit the grounding of electrical equipment? Yes _____ No _____
7. Are aisles, doorways, and corners free of obstructions to permit visibility and movement? Yes _____ No _____
8. Are file cabinets and storage closets arranged so drawers and doors do not open into walkways? Yes _____ No _____
9. Do chairs have any loose casters (wheels) and are the rungs and legs of the chairs sturdy? Yes _____ No _____
10. Are the phone lines, electrical cords, and extension wires secured under a desk or alongside a baseboard? Yes _____ No _____
11. Is the office space neat, clean, and free of excessive amounts of combustibles? Yes _____ No _____
12. Are floor surfaces clean, dry, level, and free of worn or frayed seams? Yes _____ No _____
13. Are carpets well secured to the floor and free of frayed or worn seams? Yes _____ No _____
14. Is there enough light for reading? Yes _____ No _____

B. Computer Workstation (if applicable)
15. Is your chair adjustable? Yes _____ No _____
16. Do you know how to adjust your chair? Yes _____ No _____
17. Is your back adequately supported by a backrest? Yes _____ No _____
18. Are your feet on the floor or fully supported by a footrest? Yes _____ No _____
19. Are you satisfied with the placement of your monitor and keyboard? Yes _____ No _____

20. Is it easy to read the text on your screen?
    Yes _____ No _____
21. Do you need a document holder? Yes _____ No _____
22. Do you have enough leg room at your desk?
    Yes _____ No _____
23. Is the screen free from noticeable glare?
    Yes _____ No _____
24. Is the top of the screen eye level? Yes _____ No _____
25. Is there space to rest the arms while not keying?
    Yes _____ No _____
26. When keying, are your forearms close to parallel with
    the floor? Yes _____ No _____
27. Are your wrists fairly straight when keying?
    Yes _____ No _____

Employee's Signature and Date: _____

Immediate Supervisor's Signature and Date: _____

Approved _____ Disapproved _____

Workers with young children also need to take special care. Along with watching them closely at all times, the nonprofit Home Safety Council (HSC) suggests several steps to ensure their safety:

- Be aware of workspace hazards and control them.
- Keep your workspace off-limits to children unless a grown-up is with them.
- If you work and care for young children, set aside one area of your workspace for the playpen or mark out a play area with a blanket. Make sure these areas are in your direct line of vision, and away from equipment and office supplies.
- If you have an entire room devoted to workspace, consider installing a door lock and keeping it locked when not in use.

- When you establish a work area, look at it from a child's point of view and take steps to make it safer.
- Install all home office equipment so it is out of children's reach. Place desktop equipment away from the edges of tables and desks so children cannot reach it.
- When purchasing a paper shredder, look for one that comes with safety features to protect children and larger pets from injury.
- Be aware that shredders, paper cutters, hole punches, electric pencil sharpeners, and other home office equipment can be tempting for children. These should be placed well out of children's sight and reach.
- Make sure taller bookcases are bolted to the wall so that they cannot tip. Don't permit children to climb on any furniture.
- Keep file cabinet drawers closed when not in use.
- Locate the trash barrel away from children's reach.
- If your workspace is in its own room, install a smoke alarm and test it regularly.
- Only an adult should use office equipment.
- Unplug shredders and other office equipment when it is not in use.
- If you smoke in your workspace, use a large ashtray and empty it frequently.
- Keep matches, lighters, and cigarettes out of children's sight and reach. It is safest to keep these dangerous materials locked.
- Thumbtacks, paper clips, and other small objects are choking hazards. Keep these where young children cannot see or reach them.
- Keep power strips and electrical cords out of walkways and out of children's reach.
- Install safety covers on unused electrical outlets.
- Keep scissors, letter openers, and all sharp office supplies away from the edges of the desk. Ideally, these should be kept in a drawer, out of children's sight and reach.
- Keep emergency numbers posted by the telephone.

ANOTHER ALTERNATIVE: TELEWORK CENTERS

In some cases, the workload dictates that employees divide their time (or supervisors divide their employees) between home and telework centers. Such centers can be established with an eye to flexibility of office design and work arrangements, and close to the majority of workers, preferably in a quiet area. For example, the site can be located in a suburb that's opposite of the flow of rush-hour traffic but with plenty of free parking and/or places to eat within walking distance. The "green"—and green with envy—arrangement would be that workers could walk or bike to the center.

Office sharing is acceptable, with the understanding that the other workers' papers and possessions are not to be disturbed, and if they need to be moved for some reason they are to be put back in their original spot. The center should include plenty of conference space.

Since it is an extension of the original office, the center needs amenities to make it attractive to workers—operational and up-to-date equipment and sophisticated software to facilitate performance of duties.

Given the increased prevalence of home-based working, establishing telework centers seems like an expensive alternative. A more practical choice may be to reimburse employees for mileage and equipment usage at a service center like FedEx Office, which offers support such as direct mail, printing and graphics, video-conferencing, and more. Even WiFi coffee shops can be used for small-group, informal meetings.

SUMMARY

The home office needs to be a safe, comfortable environment, free of distractions and productive for the worker. Therefore you need to be acquainted with the various safety rules and regulations as well as the importance of ergonomics. Although you do not see your employees on a day-to-day basis you are still responsible for their workplace well-being.

Wise choices regarding equipment and software are essential. Often it is easy to get sidetracked by what everyone else is doing in regards to the latest work fad, without considering how it will help *your* business. A good rule of thumb is to make sure it's what you really need (even if it involves experimenting with several different solutions for a trial period) and then sparing no expense on a quality product that will last and provides room for growth.

Finally, another issue is *where* will the employee work? Sometimes they need access to specialized equipment or conference rooms. Although establishing telework or satellite centers is a possibility, business service centers or even coffee shops can be more cost-effective and fill the gaps. Results and products, not processes, are what count here.

CHAPTER 11

Insurance, Benefits, and Tax Issues

INTRODUCTION

Not only can insurance, benefits, and taxes for telecommuters be vague but they are ever-changing so it's often quite challenging to find a solution.

This chapter will cover what to look for and potential pitfalls, as well as exploring areas needing further growth and research. Specifics are still being hammered out in Congress and state legislatures, especially regarding taxes.

PROPERTY INSURANCE: WHO IS LIABLE?

As the advertisement for the large insurance company says, "Life comes at you fast." So, who's responsible if your worker trips over his cat and falls down the stairs while brainstorming a new project? What about if her laptop is stolen from her home or briefcase while traveling? If you're pointing at yourself, it's in the right direction. The home office is equivalent to the main office—at least for insurance purposes. Employers need to provide replacement equipment when necessary. However, workers should also consider their personal insurance needs. Most homeowner's policies provide a minimum of coverage, usually only for the business equipment in the residence itself. However if the loss or accident pertains to your business, the employee should only file one claim—with your insurance company. The procedure for doing this needs to be set forth in the telecommuting agreement and during the underwriting process.

What if a client comes to your worker's home office and sprains an ankle on the employee's child's skateboard? As farfetched as this may sound, this did happen to Sandra a few years ago when her son was a teenager. In these cases, the employee should exempt your company from injuries claimed by third parties in their home and other damages unrelated to the business and should be required to have insurance for these types of claims.

There is no way to cover all contingencies of course. The terms of who is responsible for what liabilities should be as detailed as possible in the telecommuting contract. Also, you should educate employees in various options regarding insurance, depending upon what the job requires. For example, there are specific automobile add-ons for those using their vehicles for business; business interruption, which will cover salary, utilities, etc.; and an umbrella policy, which can help with larger claims, as long as initial expenses are taken care of under basic insurance. However, these extras can increase the cost of premiums.

WHO PAYS FOR HEALTH INSURANCE?

Given the current healthcare crisis in the U.S., offering full or even partial coverage for health insurance premiums can be attractive to potential employees. You have only to look at the retirees employed by Wal-Mart or those with PhDs and Masters degrees who work at Starbucks. Although they may be making close to minimum wage, at least they have health insurance coverage.

However, health insurance costs have become so exorbitant that even full-time employees are paying partial or a la carte coverage for certain services, such as dental or vision. Depending upon your company's policy towards W-2 and part-time workers, you may not have much of a choice. The bottom line is that teleworkers should be treated the same as office-based workers if they have the same duties. For example, if health insurance is provided to part-timers in the office, it should be provided to those part-timers who work at home or on the road. However, contract workers will likely be responsible for their own health insurance.

You can also assist employees in getting the best deal possible. Often companies employ consultants or in-house specialists whose job it is to provide information about the most comprehensive and cost-effective health insurance for their workers. Suggest contract employees check out a group plan from their trade or professional association or even a local Chamber of Commerce. Many associations of independent contractors—such as writer's organizations, for example—offer reduced-cost health coverage to qualifying members.

A relatively new wrinkle in health insurance is the Health Savings Account (HSA)—also known as a medical savings account (MSA)—which allows workers to allot pretax dollars to cover out-of-pocket expenses. Employees can set aside as much as $2,900 for singles and $5,800 for families, which can be used to reimburse medical, dental, and vision expenses not covered by health insurance. These figures are for 2008 and generally go up every year to cover cost-of-living increases. Employers can also make HSA contributions for workers, which are also excluded from income and not subject to any income tax or Federal Insurance Contributions Act (FICA). Most states also allow state income tax deductions for HSA contributions.

Accompanied by a High Deductible Health Plan (HDHP), HSA funds are not subject to federal income tax at the time of deposit. They can be used to pay for qualified medical expenses at any time without federal tax liability. However, should an employee decide to make a withdrawal for non-medical expenses he would be subject to the same penalties as if it were an Individual Retirement Account (IRA) account, unless he was retirement age. The savings accounts can be used to help pay smaller covered medical expenses until the deductible is met; the high deductible insurance policy then takes care of covered medical expenses exceeding the deductible.

HSAs are useful because they help keep down health care costs while providing an opportunity to accrue a tax-free financial nest egg in event of an illness. A health savings plan also allows employees to choose their own physician (typically from an extensive preferred provider organization (PPO) directory) without the restrictions imposed by health management organization (HMO) plans. However, it may not be viable or practical if the worker has pre-existing conditions or healthcare coverage from another source.

WORKERS COMP

Chapter 10 discussed safety requirements and OSHA's failed attempt to regulate safety for telecommuters. A related issue is workers compensation. Generally, if they are considered W-2 workers (as opposed to independent contractors), in most states telecommuters are covered under the same WC regulations as office employees. However, most common WC-covered injuries such as slips, trips, falls, lacerations, and so forth "tend to be few and far between on the telecommuting front," observes William Atkinson in *Risk & Insurance* magazine. Since they are working at home, which is for most a safe and comfortable environment, the chances of these kinds of accidents are less.

This is another instance where defining workers as W-2 employees or independent contractors raises its head. If the worker is an independent contractor, then he or she may not be entitled to workers compensation. However, the burden is on the employer to make sure he is *truly* an IC. In many instances, courts strictly apply the twenty IRS guidelines (see next page) to determine whether the worker fits the definition of a W-2 employee. Check with your state's Workers Compensation office for specific regulations and guidance.

Yet even if the person is an IC, your company may still be liable for injuries suffered on the job. W-2 employees covered by workers comp insurance, "in exchange for the benefits they receive for their injuries . . . give up the right to sue their employer for damages," points out Forbes.com. However, "ICs are not covered by workers compensation, which means that they can sue you for damages if they are injured on the job . . ."

Either way, it is the responsibility of the employer to ensure an environment is as safe and risk-free as possible, whether it be in the home, the office, or even the employee's car if it is used for business purposes.

IRS Twenty Factor Test on Employment Status

1. **Instructions.** A worker who must comply with other persons' instructions about when, where and how he or she is to work is ordinarily an employee. This factor is present when the person for whom the services are performed has the right to require compliance.

2. **Training.** Requiring an experienced employee to work with the worker, corresponding with the worker, requiring the worker to attend meetings or using other training methods indicates the person for whom the services are performed wants them done in a particular method or manner.

3. **Integration.** Integrating the worker's services into the business operations generally shows that he or she is subject to direction and control. When the success or continuation of a business depends to an appreciable degree on the performance of certain services, the workers who do them must necessarily be subject to a certain amount of control by the business owner.

4. **Services rendered personally.** If the worker must render the services personally, presumably the person for whom they are performed is interested in the methods used to accomplish the work as well as in the results.

5. **Hiring, supervising, and paying assistants.** If the person for whom the services are performed hires, supervises, and

pays assistants, that generally shows control over the workers on the job. However, if one worker hires, supervises, and pays the other assistants under a contract in which the worker agrees to provide materials and labor and is responsible only for attaining a result, this indicates independent contractor status.

6. **Continuing relationship.** A continuing relationship between the worker and the person for whom the services are performed indicates an employer-employee relationship exists. This may occur when work is performed at frequently recurring although irregular intervals.

7. **Set hours of work.** If the person for whom the services are performed establishes set work hours, this indicates control.

8. **Full-time required.** If the worker must devote himself or herself substantially full-time to the business of the person for whom the services are performed, the latter has control over the amount of time the worker spends working and implicitly restricts the worker from doing other gainful work. An independent contractor, on the other hand, is free to work when and for whom he or she chooses.

9. **Doing work on employer's premises.** If the individual performs the work on the premises of the person for whom the services are performed, this suggests control over the worker, especially if the work could be done elsewhere. Work done off the premises, such as at the worker's office, indicates some freedom from control. However, this fact by itself does not mean the worker is not an employee. The importance of this factor depends on the nature of the service involved and the extent to which an employer generally would require that employees perform such services on the premises. Control over the place of work is indicated when the person for whom the services are performed has the

right to compel the worker to travel a designated route, to canvass a territory within a certain time frame, or work at specific places.

10. **Order or sequence set.** If a worker must perform services in the order or sequence set by the person for whom the services are performed, that factor shows the worker is not free to follow his or her own pattern of work but must follow the established routines and schedules of the employer. Often, because of the nature of an occupation, the person or persons for whom the services are performed do not set the order of the services or set it infrequently. Retaining the right to do so is sufficient to show control.

11. **Oral or written reports.** A requirement that the worker submit regular or written reports to the person or persons for whom the services are performed indicates a certain degree of control.

12. **Payment by hour, week, or month.** Payment by one of these three methods generally points to an employer-employee relationship, provided this method is not just a convenient way of paying a lump sum agreed upon as the cost of a job. Payment made by the job or on a straight commission basis generally indicates the worker is an independent contractor.

13. **Payment of business or travel expenses.** If the person for whom the services are performed generally pays the worker's business and travel expenses, he or she is ordinarily an employee. To control expenses, an employer usually retains the right to regulate and direct the worker's business activities.

14. **Tools and materials.** The fact the person for whom the services are performed furnishes significant tools, materials, and other equipment tends to show the existence of an employer-employee relationship.

15. **Significant investment.** If the worker invests in facilities not typically maintained by employees (such as an office rented at fair value from an unrelated party) and uses them to perform services, that tends to indicate the worker is an independent contractor. On the other hand, lack of investment in facilities indicates dependence on the person for whom the services are performed for such facilities. Accordingly, an employer-employee relationship exists.

16. **Realization of profit or loss.** A worker who can realize a profit or suffer a loss as a result of his or her services (in addition to the profit or loss ordinarily realized by employees) is generally an independent contractor. The worker who cannot is an employee. For example, if a worker is subject to a real risk of economic loss due to a significant investment or a bona fide liability for expenses, such as salary payments to unrelated employees, that indicates the worker is an independent contractor. The risk a worker will not receive payment for his or her services, however, is common to both independent contractors and employees and thus is not sufficient to support independent contractor treatment.

17. **Working for more than one entity.** If a worker performs more than de minimis services for multiple unrelated persons or companies at the same time, that factor generally indicates the worker is an independent contractor. However, a worker who performs services for more than one person may be an employee of each, especially where the two are connected.

18. **Making services available to the general public.** The fact a worker makes his or her services available to the general public on a regular and consistent basis indicates an independent contractor relationship.

19. **Right to discharge.** The right to fire a worker is a factor indicating the worker is an employee and the person with the right is an employer. An employer exercises control through the threat of dismissal, which causes the worker to obey the

employer's instructions. An independent contractor, on the other hand, cannot be fired so long as he or she produces a result that meets the agreed contract specifications.

20. **Right to terminate.** If the worker has the right to end his or her relationship with the person for whom the services are performed at any time without incurring liability, this indicates an employer-employee relationship.

RETIREMENT ALTERNATIVES

Some companies offer pension plans to telecommuters; most do not. The equitable rule—the same benefits apply to all employees, whether they're working at home or in office—often isn't applied to pension plans. While telecommuters may have leverage when it comes to full-coverage health insurance and workers compensation, they are pretty much on their own for pension plans. However, you can provide telecommuters some basic information about the various retirement fund alternatives and if possible, make arrangements for them to participate in the company plan.

The following is an overview of the most common pension plans:

401(k) Plan. Here the employee defers part of his current income, with a limit of 25 percent or $30,000, into a tax shelter where it grows tax-free until he withdraws it. In some cases, the employer matches the employee's contributions. The beauty of this plan is that it allows an employee to save for retirement and simultaneously reduce her current income tax bill. Employees can also make decisions as to the investment of these funds.

Defined Benefit Pension Plan: This traditional pension plan pays workers a specific monthly benefit at retirement, either by stating it as an exact dollar amount or a specific formula that calculates the benefit. Generally, the company funds the pension plan, and a professional money manager invests the assets of the fund.

Qualified Retirement Plan: A qualified retirement plan is established by a business and includes profit sharing, defined benefits, and money purchase pensions. Employees' contributions to a qualified plan are not taxed until they withdraw the money. In addition, any contributions made to the plan on the worker's behalf by the employer are tax deductible.

Regardless of their status, all employee contributions to retirement plans are subject to protection under law (see sidebar).

There's Something about ERISA

The Employee Retirement Income Security Act of 1974, or ERISA, protects the assets of millions of Americans so that funds placed in retirement plans during their working lives will be there when they retire. ERISA is a federal law that sets minimum standards for pension plans in private industry. Most of the provisions of ERISA are effective for plan years beginning on or after January 1, 1975.

However, ERISA does not require any employer to establish a pension plan. It only requires that those who do establish plans must meet certain minimum standards. The law generally does not specify how much money a participant must be paid as a benefit.

TAXES: WHO PAYS AND WHO FILES (IC VS. W-2)

Taxes for telecommuters can be complicated for both worker and employer. Let's face it: Most of us don't even want to think about taxes.

For the workers themselves, and this applies whether they are W-2 workers or independent contractors, along with keeping records on monies received and reimbursed expenses (backed up with check stubs and receipts), they should keep and maintain thorough records of all expenditures, even if it means throwing them in a box and handing them over to an accountant on April 14. They must also fill W-2 forms or, if they're independent contractors, 1099s, of which there may be several if they are working for different companies. You, as an employer, are responsible for making sure contractors receive 1099s if they earn over $600 a year.

Another issue facing telecommuters is whether their home office qualifies for a deduction. If the primary place where they conduct business is the company office or a telework center, they may not meet the criteria. The business part of the home must be the principal place where workers meet or deal with patients, clients, or customers. However, even if the worker's home office does not qualify, she can still deduct all legitimate business expenses. Point them to websites (e.g., *www.irs.gov/newsroom/article/0,,id=108138,00.html*) and written information (often found in the public library) from the IRS as to what is and what is not deductible.

The tax issues facing companies are even more confusing. Not surprisingly, most of the confusion arises from intrastate (and by extension intra-county and city) taxes. Telecommuters often work in one state and live in another, where they also work part of the time. Obviously, this has huge and conflicting consequences in terms of state unemployment insurance and state income taxes. Each state has its rules for enforcing state unemployment insurance. Usually an employer tax, this is more commonly known as the State Unemployment Tax Act (SUTA). What remains up in the air is the definition of "employee" and which wages are subject to the tax. "At the federal level, the Federal Unemployment Tax Act (FUTA) provides some common rules that all states must follow," explains the *Institute of Management & Administration Payroll Manager's Report*. The goal is for each employee to have a single state for SUTA purposes.

Therefore all states, except for Minnesota, adopted the following rules for determining which state gets to collect SUTA:

- Where the work physically is done
- Base of operations
- Place of direction and control
- Place of residence

For example, if your company is in California and you hire someone in Oregon who works from home, Oregon SUTA tax applies to this employee. "The employer has just created a tax nexus, or legal business presence, in Oregon and is subject not only to all Oregon state and local payroll taxes, but other taxes as well, including sales tax and state corporate income taxes," continues the report.

What about state income tax (SIT)? "Each state has different rules concerning residency, and all states start with the assumption that the state in which the employee is physically doing the work is subject to SIT withholding," points out the report. Basically, most states want the taxes of their residents working in other states as well as taxes of residents working in their state. "Unfortunately for payroll, states agree on little regarding SIT, and when employees live and work in different states, payroll challenges are compounded. In addition, there are local taxes that present analogous and equally complex problems."

Some states have also developed the "convenience of the employer rule," whereby a nonresident employee may allocate income between two states (assuming the employer is in a different state) but only if it is for the employer's convenience. A question arises, however, between the words "convenience" and "necessity."

Two Landmark Teleworker Cases

What is "Convenience of Employer"? The Cardozo Law School of New York in New York City employed Edward Zelinsky, a Connecticut resident, as a law professor. Zelinsky worked at the law school several days a week, lecturing and meeting with students.

The rest of the time, he worked in his Connecticut home, grading student assignments and conducting work-related legal research.

Connecticut regards the work done in state to be taxable in Connecticut based on the point-of-presence test. New York, however, regards all work done by Zelinsky as taxable in New York because Cardozo Law School could have instructed its employee to work in New York. Taxed in both states on the same income, Zelinsky took his case to court.

The New York Court of Appeals found against him [citing] "convenience of the employer" when an employee's work location was not required by the employer for hard business reasons. In another case, Thomas L. Huckaby, a computer programmer, lived and worked mainly in Tennessee. His Tennessee-based employer went out of business in 1991. In 1994, Huckaby was hired by a New York–based company to support software purchased from his former employer. Huckaby, who never lived in New York, spent 75 percent of the time between 1994 and 1995 working in Tennessee and 25 percent working in New York. He reported as New York wages only those wages earned while on visits to the corporate office. Since his employer could have relocated him, but did not, New York claimed that Huckaby's working in Tennessee was "for the convenience of the employer," and all wages earned were subject to New York taxes.

In a four-to-three decision, the New York Court of Appeals found in favor of New York. However, out of lemons occasionally emerges something resembling lemonade.

The adverse ruling in the Zelinsky case led to the introduction of the Telecommuter Tax Fairness Act of 2004 by Connecticut senators Christopher Dodd and Joseph Lieberman and U.S. Representative Christopher Shay. No action was taken on the bill in 2004; it was reintroduced in May of 2005 and then again in May 2007 by Shay. As of this writing it has still not passed.

No doubt as a result of the controversy generated by the Huckaby case, New York issued a memorandum that said effective retroactively to January 1, 2006, income for any day worked at home will not be subject to New York state income tax for nonresidents with a primary office in New York and office at home. A 2006 law passed in Georgia rewards employers who implement teleworking programs by giving them a tax credit of up to $1,200 per employee for a percentage of their telework expenses in calendar years 2008 and 2009. The program's success will be evaluated by the Department of Revenue in 2010.

SUMMARY

Insurance, benefits, and taxes are complex and often confusing, even with full-time office workers. When dealing with telecommuters, they take even more of a toll. Questions arise such as: Who is liable if a visitor to your worker's home office slips on the front porch and breaks his arm? What kind of insurance will teleworkers need and can your company supply it? Can you help them take advantage of the pension plan available to full-time office workers?

If that's not enough to think about, there is workers compensation. Whether or not the teleworker even receives it depends upon whether he is a W-2 (regular employee) or an independent contractor. If it's the latter, the burden of proof is on you, the employer, to ensure that their job is outside of the court's definition of a "basic employee." If the employee actually is an IC not covered by workers compensation, your company can still be sued for damages if negligence can be proven.

Then there are taxes to consider. Employees—especially former office workers who may have little or no knowledge of such things—need to be educated as to the finer points of home office deductions and keeping track of receipts, mileage, and related expenses. Their days of zipping through the simplified 1040EZ tax form may be gone forever. If your employees work in different states, you are faced with figuring out who pays what, and to whom.

Unfortunately, as of this writing, much legislation, both at the federal, state, and even at the local level is either pending or non-existent. Until such time as laws like the Telecommuter Tax Act and the Georgia telework tax initiative become a permanent part of the national and local firmament, managers are left hanging.

As manager, you are primarily responsible for the safety, benefits, and well-being of your workers. It behooves you to become acquainted with the various options mentioned in this chapter and explore them more thoroughly as fits your particular situation. Some issues, such as Health Savings Accounts if workers are covered by traditional health insurance plans, may not apply at all. A good resource would be your company's legal department or federal or state informational websites.

CHAPTER 12

Managing Workers and Workload

INTRODUCTION

Let's face it: Managing is not for the faint of heart. If you're dealing with the additional challenge of working with telecommuters—whether they be your entire staff or only a few people—it may seem even more daunting. However, as this chapter will reveal, along with improving morale, working effectively with telecommuters can help enhance efficiency and increase productivity for the entire team.

QUALITIES NEEDED IN MANAGING WORKERS

Before setting goals and measuring milestones, consider your feelings towards working with telecommuters. Are you frustrated with the idea of getting the job done from a distance—with little or limited control over workers' schedules—and not actually being able to walk around and see them perform their tasks? Do you feel employees are not responsible enough to work on their own? There are two halves of telemanagement: quality communications and establishing trust.

One way to develop confidence in your leadership is to focus on outcomes rather than processes. When looked at that way, managing telecommuters is not really that much different from office workers. Managers who communicate clearly and offer direct feedback, along with providing well-designed and measurable objectives, are generally effective and successful, no matter how their employees get the job done. When asked how they measured productivity for their telecommuters as opposed to their office workers, managers at the National Center for Transportation and Industrial Productivity at the New Jersey Institute of Technology (NJIT) replied they used similar processes for both. This is how things are done at ARO as well; in-house and remote employees are managed in the exact same manner, using identical performance and evaluation standards.

Author Lin Grensing-Pophal lists additional qualities important in managing telecommuters:

Comfort with supervising a remote workforce. This is a threshold issue. Many managers simply cannot overcome their perceived need to keep employees in their sight.

Understanding what is required of the position. The manager must clearly know the requirements of the position and be able to quantify or measure the output expected from the position.

Ability to clearly articulate goals and objectives. Telecommuters must know what is expected of them. Management must be able to specifically outline the expectations and job standards that the telecommuter will be expected to meet.

Effective interpersonal communication. Communication is key to a successful telecommuting relationship. Managers must establish means of interacting with the telecommuter, and allowing the telecommuter to interact with the rest of the staff through both face-to-face and technological methods.

Ability to provide clear and consistent feedback. Managers must be willing and able to provide telecommuters with frequent and specific feedback. At any sign that the relationship is not working, or that objectives are not being met, the manager must immediately address the situation and, if necessary, rethink the approach.

Understanding these characteristics and being comfortable with management by results can provide a basis or starting point for effective workload planning.

SETTING CLEAR PERFORMANCE STANDARDS

When formulating the performance standards, focus on the final product rather than the processes used to achieve it. For example, ARO requires that its employees make a certain number of sales calls a day. Although they need to follow a script and are required to work certain hours, they have some leeway as to how they can perform their jobs. It is of no concern to Michael how they're dressed, whether they snack at their desks while working (as long as the client/customer doesn't hear them eating), or whether they're walking around instead of sitting down. The point is, as long as they fill their quotas, which result in satisfied customers and increased sales, they're doing their jobs.

Successful teleworking programs require consistent performance standards for *all* employees, whether they are on-site or offsite, telecommuters or office-based. So when designing goals and objectives, make sure you are clear on:

- What must be done
- Why it must be done
- How well it must be done
- By when it must be done
- What constitutes a job that is complete

Ask yourself, what elements of the position will provide the most effective and efficient operations, and what is the desired end result? It could be anything from X number of sales to Y number of claims filed to an aesthetically pleasing website or ad campaign that fulfills a client's needs. You also need to communicate to employees how these goals tie into the business plan of the overall department and company. This provides a sense of ownership as well as a feeling that they are part of the overall team.

Measures should be objective and focus on four factors: *quality, quantity, timeliness,* and *cost efficiency.* Quality concerns the amount of errors, omissions, and complaints tolerated over a specific amount of time. Quantity is the measurable unit of production. Timeliness focuses on deadlines for tasks and amount of turnaround time required. Cost efficiency deals with staying within the constraints of a budget and being accountable for monies spent.

Make sure telecommuters don't waste time and resources pursuing wrong objectives but instead complete specified goals. The more clearly you describe objectives, the less time you will need to spend explaining them.

Some goals are easier to define than others. Goals are clear-cut and easily quantifiable for production-oriented jobs such as sales, customer service, and forms or file processing whereas it is more difficult to pinpoint goals for jobs like web design and project management.

GOAL POSTS

Supervisors and telecommuters need to agree upon goals, which should have the following characteristics:

Clearly defined and measurable. For example, make twenty calls for every four-hour workday or sell six policies a month, rather than "increase sales." That way the person will know what he is achieving and how far he has progressed. ARO does random sampling of its calls for quality purposes; the worker needs to score an average of 94 out of 100 to pass muster.

Challenging, yet doable. One person's challenge can be another person's impossibility. If the worker knows the task up front, then she will know whether she can accomplish it. By its very nature, challenge allows more variation in the range of outcomes, so it may not always work for all aspects of routine jobs.

Results-oriented and clear. The worker knows the end result and understands what is expected.

If there is more than one goal, you may need to help workers prioritize; that is, rate their importance as high, medium, or low.

Telecommuters in particular may need guidance with this, especially in the beginning.

ESTABLISHING RULES AND BOUNDARIES

Another important aspect of workload management is developing work plans and task schedules. Whenever you make an assignment, clearly define what is to be accomplished and the schedule for completing the task. Telecommuters should acknowledge the assignment, agree to the schedule, and take responsibility for finishing it in the appropriate manner. Work plans ensure that the worker remains on course as well as providing clear and measurable results. It should also be made apparent that the worker's performance evaluation is based upon the plan. It also allows for helpful one-on-one coaching time, since you are both involved in developing the plan and can make modifications if necessary.

Work plans should include the following:

- The objective(s) that will be met
- Tasks to be accomplished
- The product to be developed as necessary
- The time frame for completing tasks
- A schedule for accomplishing interim milestones (for longer-term assignments)
- Who else needs to be involved, and what resources may be needed
- Criteria or standards for evaluating performance

SCHEDULING

In an ideal world—at least for the telecommuter—the worker establishes his own schedule. However, real life is quite different and you may be called upon to provide parameters as to when duties should be performed. This is for the convenience of all concerned—the company's goals; the other team members, some of whom may be office workers or on a different time schedule or zone; and of course, you own workload needs. It is important to sit down with the employee and develop a schedule that will work for everyone, with a minimum of inconvenience. What you don't want is to have the teleworker absent or unavailable when you need him the most. So communicate this at the beginning of the arrangement.

Consider the following guidelines when scheduling:

- What are the core hours that you'll need telecommuters to be available?
- Is there any flexibility in these hours?
- How often do they need to call in or check their voice and e-mails?
- How quickly do they need to return messages?
- How often will they need to communicate with you or other members of the team?

Depending upon the job and its requirements, workers may need to come into the office or be available for extra hours. If this is the case, mentiont it when doing scheduling.

An example of a standard scheduling agreement is on the following page.

Flexiplace Work Schedule

Employee: _____

Date: _____

Type of Flexiplace Schedule _____ Fixed _____ As Needed

Type of Alternative Work Schedule*

_____ Flexitour _____ Gliding Schedule _____ Compressed

Schedule: _____ 5-4-9 _____ 4-10

Week 1: Office Alt Worksite	**Start Time**	**Finish Time**
Mon:	_____	_____
Tue:	_____	_____
Wed:	_____	_____
Thu:	_____	_____
Fri:	_____	_____

* If you select the flexitour or compressed schedule, indicate your proposed start and finish times in the space provided. It is not necessary to indicate start and finish times if you select the gliding schedule.

At ARO, workers are scheduled at different times of the day in shifts to meet the needs of clients. This is made clear during the interview process, and managers work with them to find the shift that best meets their needs. For example, if a call center employee has children in school, a 9 A.M.–3 P.M. schedule may best accommodate their lifestyle.

COMMUNICATION PROCEDURES

As mentioned earlier in this chapter, communication is key—both in establishing trust and in making sure all parties understand the meaning and intent of what is being said.

Of course, the gold standard in communication is face-to-face contact, but even that doesn't always do the job. In telecommuting you may be missing out on important visual cues like facial expression and body language as well as verbal hints such as tone of voice. On the other hand, what may be lost in personal charisma and office schmoozing might be gained in increased productivity and alternative communication skills. In other words, the distance may actually help you verbalize exactly what you want and need from your employees through e-mails, videoconferencing, and other limited methods of communication. It will require more effort initially, but in the end, it may make you a more effective manager, one who is able to clearly and concisely state what you want, no matter what the mode of communication.

Some employees may need more one-on-one communication than others. Especially in the beginning, those new to telecommuting might appreciate a daily call or e-mail, while more experienced telecommuters may operate under the "no news is good news" principle.

However, in some cases, daily feedback is not only positive but necessary. For example, an insurance client of ARO requires that the manager provide a daily summary of production. Not only is this sent to the client but it goes to all the remote members of the team. The report details who did what and the accomplishments, and team members are cited for special efforts. Problems are dealt with on a private level between manager and employee.

When establishing communication guidelines with telecommuters, consider the following:

- What needs to be communicated?
- How will the teleworker communicate (e.g., when is e-mail sufficient or when is a phone call warranted)?

- What type of communication should be used for what situation?
- How can "predictable access" be established; that is, a method of reaching the person within a set amount of time?

For example, when working with various clients, Sandra always lets them know how she can be reached—leaving her cell phone number on her land line voice mail, for example. You can make these and other suggestions regarding accessibility, such as providing an incentive or reimbursement for BlackBerries or other Internet-based cell phones, so workers can be in touch when you need them.

Also determine which mode of communication best fits the situation. Leaving a complex message with statistics and figures on voice mail can be downright frustrating, not to mention increasing the possibility of errors as the worker frantically tries to jot down the information. Sending an e-mail with the same information may be more effective. Trying to train employees in a new procedure or explain a complicated methodology through a conference call can be equally confusing. These situations generally require either virtual or in-person training, preferably with visuals.

On the other hand, a routine matter may only require the briefest of e-mails or even a text message. It might even be more efficient to wait until several minor matters accumulate and then provide a list to the worker via phone or e-mail. A major difference between working at home and the office is the latter provides an immediate and convenient venue for frequent interruptions. Such small intrusions on a telecommuter's concentration may be counterproductive.

Of course, any situation dealing with communication is rarely black and white, and depends upon the demands of the workload as well as the personalities involved. Some prefer speaking on the phone, while others prefer e-mail or face-to-face videoconferencing. Through trial-and-error and perhaps even a few blunders, you and your team will eventually get a sense of which communication tool fits the right time and circumstances.

MEASURING PRODUCTIVITY

What exactly is "productivity" anyway? In some cases, the answer is simple—X sales calls during Y period; Z medical claims filed within a week. At ARO, for example, the remote worker fills out production electronic forms that provide managers with a quick view of what he has accomplished if these are not automatically available via computer systems.

But how can you measure the effectiveness of say, a legal consultation, computer program, or video graphics design? It may take months, or even in some cases years, to make a fair and equitable evaluation of its success. Even if someone appears to be productive, meeting their quota of phone calls and audits may not tell the whole story. What if the customer service representative takes or makes fewer calls but is highly successful in resolving problems and instituting goodwill and faith in the company? At the opposite end of the spectrum, a representative with a high call turnover may be abrupt or less willing to give customers the information they need. What if a site inspector assigned to audit various companies completes the assignments on time but does a poor job of evaluating important elements and neglects to pinpoint problem areas? How then can you measure quality and task completion?

A rule of thumb is to compare the productivity of office workers with that of telecommuters. That is, they should do the same amount of work within the same time constraints. Often, with fewer distractions, the telecommuter can be even more productive. Once again, quality may be an issue. Depending upon the nature of the work, the office employee might just be working by rote—or overworked and pulled in too many directions—while the telecommuter can focus on the task at hand due to his work-at-home environment, increased morale, and motivation to maintain the arrangement.

An Employee Newsletter

Along with responsibility for several satellite hospitals, a big-city medical center had an overworked communications department. The person assigned to the employee newsletter and the monthly physician's report of one of the smaller but important satellite healthcare facilities was juggling six other publications, and was unable to devote the time needed to work on them effectively. They were often late and publication was intermittent.

The communications manager decided to hire a freelance writer on a trial basis. Although no one was sure how well it would work, the writer took "ownership" of the two publications, personalizing articles and adding design elements and color to the employee newsletter and making sure that the physician's report was published on a timely and regular basis. Both physicians and staff members began to regularly contribute to the publications and they became part of the culture of the hospital.

Although these results can't be quantitatively measured in the conventional sense, the reduction in workload for the office workers and quality and creativity invested in the publications by the telecommuter made it a win-win situation for everyone.

You can establish procedures to help measure productivity; that is specific objectives for employees to meet, individually and as a group. You can then judge the group's performance and the performances of individual employees, according to how well they meet these objectives. The procedures can be used as general guidelines for both office workers and telecommuters.

The following are some elements of productivity measurement for knowledge workers. Rather than looking at a single measure, they should be evaluated cumulatively, with an eye toward the end product or results.

- Quantity of work produced
- Timeliness of work products submitted
- Timely and appropriate communication with managers and coworkers
- Timely and appropriate responses to e-mail, phone calls, and requests from managers and coworkers
- Written or verbal progress reports or reviews
- Ability to "juggle" multiple tasks simultaneously

Another way to determine productivity is to solicit feedback from customers or coworkers. You can do this through surveys; monitoring, such as recording customer service calls or having the supervisor listen in at periodic intervals; or follow-up phone calls, letters, or e-mails.

RECOGNIZING AND IDENTIFYING PROBLEMS

Perhaps you've tried everything: listened to concerns and ideas, shared information, been available, provided encouragement and recognition, and the telecommuting arrangement doesn't seem to be working out. This could be due to several factors.

1. The job responsibilities are not suited to telework. If the employee finds she is needed in the office more often than not and spends much less time working at home than in the office, the arrangement needs to be re-evaluated.
2. The employee is not familiar enough with the organization or the job to work independently from home. He may need an adjustment period under the more close supervision of the office, and you may also need to become more acquainted with the type and quality of his work to see if telecommuting is feasible. The telecommuting arrangement can be put on hold until the desired

level of competence and confidence is reached by all concerned.

3. The employee lacks the so-called "telecommuting personality" discussed in earlier chapters. Not everyone is suited for telecommuting—in fact once they get into it, they may find it lonely and counterproductive. The worker may need to return to the office or may not be suited to the job at all.

Regardless of the cause, if productivity or customer service starts to suffer at any point during the telecommuting arrangement then you as a manager need to take immediate action. The longer you wait, the worse it will get.

As mentioned in the beginning of this chapter, management is not for the faint of heart. It requires fairness and objectivity as well as an ability to communicate effectively, analyze causes, and determine workable solutions. Very few people enjoy telling someone he is not performing to standard. In fact, some managers go to great length to avoid such discussions. In an office, this usually manifests itself when the unsuspecting worker finds he has fewer assignments, is excluded from meetings, or his desk has been moved to a less pleasant area.

If telecommuting issues aren't dealt with directly, not only will the burden of work fall more heavily on the rest of the team, creating an unfair situation and setup for resentment, but the telecommuter will be paid the same for doing less, draining the resources of the company.

Instead, look at the situation as an opportunity for coaching the worker and helping him improve, even if he has to return to the office or receive additional training. If a problem becomes apparent—or even hints at surfacing—deal with it immediately and directly (see Chapter 14 on evaluation and counseling).

GETTING AND GIVING FEEDBACK

Since they are not physically present, you need to establish regularly scheduled feedback sessions with your telecommuters. These should be a matter of course, and not related to punishment or reward. Although such sessions may seem like more work, you'll be spending more time involved in communicating while also establishing a solid and honest relationship that will motivate and inspire employees to do their best. Most teleworkers want and in fact may cherish this arrangement, and regular feedback will only strengthen their commitment.

Managers should also do the following:

Make sure employees understand how, when, and under what circumstances feedback will take place. Criteria used for measuring performance should be included.

Ensure employees know the door is always open and they can come to you at any time with questions and problems. You can also contact them regularly to solicit their feedback.

Give feedback throughout the year so there are no unpleasant "surprises." Also regularly reinforce positive behaviors and tell them what they are doing well.

- Be open and honest, along with being constructive. Discussion should revolve around the job criteria or the work situation, rather than personalities.
- Make every minute count—since employees are working remotely you don't see them much, if at all. Make sure you use all the tools (phone, e-mail, fax) at your disposal to communicate effectively, quickly, and in as much detail as possible.
- Praise in public, criticize in private. Certain kinds of feedback—especially constructive criticism or information of a sensitive and personal nature—must be kept between the manager and employee. This will also be discussed in Chapter 14.

"Intelligence Gathering"

In his book *An Organizational Guide to Telecommuting*, George M. Piskurich recommends regularly surveying employees and their managers by asking a combination of support and evaluation questions.

Questions for telecommuters can include the following:

- What do you think of the telecommuting arrangement? What types of problems are you experiencing? What are the benefits?
- How well is the equipment working in your home office? Is it meeting the needs and requirements of the job? Do you find that you're more productive?
- Are you more satisfied with your job? Why or why not?

Questions for managers can be:

- How well is the teleworker meeting the goals and objectives of the job?
- Are there problems or communications issues between telecommuters and office workers? What are they? Does one group appear to resent the other?

SUMMARY

In many ways, managing telecommuters is the same as managing office workers. You will likely find that you're calling upon the same skills and experience when setting performance standards, assigning workload, doing scheduling, and so forth.

However, there are important—and challenging—differences. By focusing on results instead of processes you must become an effective communicator, one who is versatile and well-versed in the different methods of exchanging information: phone or e-mail, real-time videoconferencing, or use of Intranets and electronic bulletin boards. This may require a considerable investment of time and effort, especially when it comes to setting up channels of contact with virtual employees, each of whom has their own preferred methods and personal communication strengths. Still, if they don't know exactly what you mean, how can they be expected to perform the job?

An added complexity in dealing with telecommuters is measuring productivity. So much more than the traditional counting of widgets produced each hour, many factors come into play: Is the person doing the job better, even if it takes more time? What are the long-term results? How do you measure customer satisfaction? Of course, there are issues raised by technology. Is it helping or hindering your organization's goals and how does it affect worker performance?

Finally, you'll need to set a schedule for regular feedback with you, your employees, and the team in general. This can take the form of face-to-face meetings, conference calls, or the various modes of virtual communication. In addition to soliciting their comments and opinions, as well as making sure that everyone (office, support, and remote workers) is apprised of what's currently happening with projects and processes, you must address problems immediately and directly.

The next chapter will discuss effective methods of dealing with telecommuters, which will help handle and circumvent this and other issues.

CHAPTER 13

Keeping Track and in Touch

INTRODUCTION

This chapter will address the softer side of telecommuting—establishing and maintaining trust, training employees to deal with family issues, and showing them how to compartmentalize to avoid overwork and isolation. It will also discuss monitoring employee satisfaction and what red flags to look for. Matters of confidentiality and how to maintain a secure network are also covered.

Especially in the beginning, managers need to work closely with telecommuters to make sure they stay on track. Once they actually start working at home or remotely, they will be confronting unexpected challenges. This chapter will provide guidance on how to facilitate a smooth and effective transition.

THE IMPORTANCE OF TRUST

Trust is the core of every relationship, be it business, love, or friendship. It is especially important in telecommuting, because there is so much physical distance between you and your workers. This is true of every job, from call center employees at ARO to high-level executives who manage dozens of virtual teams around the globe. As Michael's decades of working with telecommuters has shown, if you believe your employees are doing their job properly—and if they think you are providing competent and fair guidance and direction—then things will move along smoothly most of the time.

However, if you *don't* trust them for any reason, then it's time to take stock. Either you are buying into the Big Brother mentality that they are children and must be watched every minute—which doesn't make for a healthy work environment under any conditions—or certain red flags have popped up causing an undermining of trust.

When working with employees who have been with your organization for a while and with whom you have a rapport you will find a high level of trust between you. The same is true of workers experienced in their field who can provide references or have a proven track record. However, circumstances may dictate that you have to look outside your company and hire someone completely new. In that case, networking can come in handy; for example, a colleague or peer can recommend a worker. Local colleges or trade schools can be especially helpful in supplying recent graduates or leads, especially if you are looking for teleworkers in a geographic area with which you're unfamiliar. Likewise, personnel or temp agencies can be a source of reliable clerical or customer-support referrals although, of course, most charge for this service. Additional methods of finding potential employees are discussed in Chapter 8.

Many times your instincts will tell you whom to trust. Does the worker appear to learn quickly and display enthusiasm during training and in your communications? Does he express an interest in the company and its goals along with a willingness to learn new things? Does she make that extra effort to satisfy the customer or end user rather than shrugging and saying, "It's not my job"? Is he willing to participate in meetings, either on-site or remotely, to get to know members of the team and share information? During training, if a new hire seems unresponsive or disengaged, watch him closely to make sure he's actually capable and willing to do the job.

Most of us have an internal alarm that goes off whenever we encounter someone who may not be trustworthy. Often this is triggered by such cues as a lack of eye contact or a bored tone of voice or just a sense that their personality may not mesh well with the team. Because you are not seeing the individual or probably even speaking with him daily, telecommuting adds an extra layer of distance, so it's especially important to have a positive gut feeling about this person, whether you're meeting him face-to-face or over the phone. When it comes to establishing trust there's no substitute for direct contact during the interview process.

Once the person is hired, you can take specific steps to foster trust among team members.

Open and honest communication. The only way employees will know what you're thinking is if you tell them directly.

Give trust to get trust. Leading by example sets the stage for an atmosphere of mutual trust and encourages others to trust you back. Especially at the beginning, if you communicate mistrust, then it may very well condemn the team—and the project—to an atmosphere of negativity and suspicion.

Honesty is always the best policy. Although they are physically removed from the rumor mill and corporate politics, telecommuters hear things as well. However, if you are upfront with them about the good, the bad, and the not so certain, they will feel they can come to you with questions and concerns. If you are bound by confidentiality not to reveal specific information—say, a corporate takeover or layoffs that are imminent but not confirmed—tell them you do not yet have concrete answers (the truth) and you will get back with them as soon as you know something for sure.

If you make a mistake or don't know something, it's better to admit that than try to cover it up or talk your way around the topic. Most people can sense when they are being stonewalled, and nothing undermines trust faster than that.

Establish a core set of business ethics. These basic standards of honesty, decency, and behavior should be set forth as part of the company culture and work plan and agreed upon, understood, and internalized by all team members. Ethics are the glue that hold teams together, and are especially important to those separated by time and space, allowing them to operate under common beliefs and the same principles.

Follow through. If you say you're going to do something, do it, and do it out loud. Team members should know that for better or worse, you are true to your word.

Be consistent. If your team members know you're going to react logically and fairly to mistakes and problems, they will be more willing to approach you. Unpredictable reactions however, elicit the opposite response and can set the stage for cover-ups and misunderstandings.

Be responsive and available. No matter how you implement the system of communication, employees need to know you'll get back to them within a reasonable amount of time.

Ask questions. Diverse teams may use different cultural slang and points of reference. Be sensitive to these, and ask for clarification to avoid confusion and misunderstandings. This is true whether you're dealing with face-to-face meetings, teleconferences, or written communications such as e-mails.

Be trustworthy. Sometimes employees will come to you with personal information or express concerns about work-related matters or even personality conflicts. Keep this confidential, even if the employees are scattered around the globe. The best way to keep a secret is to keep it to yourself.

Be generous with praise and include everyone. Take the time to get to know your team members, and ask about their families and hobbies (make sure not to get too personal or break any confidences). For example, workers bond during ARO virtual training seminars by sharing their hobbies and interests with the group.

SECURITY AND CONFIDENTIALITY

Many telecommuters worry less than they should about confidentiality. They may take it upon themselves to disable annoying firewalls and other software that seem to slow down the computer or prevent them from gaining access to certain websites. They may not think twice about allowing family members access to company laptops and PCs. "That's why it's essential to educate your home-based telecommuters about proper security measures," states Michael J. DeMaria of networkcomputing.com. Confidentiality agreements and adherence to security procedures should be part of the telecommuting contract. "Let them know that disabling a virus scanner or firewall is reason for termination."

This may sound extreme until confidential or valuable data is destroyed, lost, or stolen by a hacker. This could be anything from medical records, to credit card and Social Security numbers, to scientific and military research that could fall into the wrong hands.

Computer crimes are becoming more prevalent and sophisticated in a knowledge-based culture where information is currency. Consider the fact that hackers are now stealing personal data from wireless routers. At one point the computer culture was such that users were willing to share unsecured networks—no longer!

Laptops should be guarded carefully. If misplaced or stolen, they represent a double loss for the company in terms of actual hardware and information contained.

Employers can take certain steps to protect valuable data, such as installing VPNs (Virtual Private Networks), and supplying their workers with security packages that include everything from antivirus programs to firewalls, spyware, and passwords. A data network that makes use of the public telephone infrastructure, the VPN maintains privacy through the use of a tunneling protocol, encryption, and other security features. "A VPN connection is required for remote access," states DeMaria. He also recommends a virus scanner to ensure the safety of data sent to the corporate Local Area Network (LAN). "The desktop machine should be loaded with VPN client software, and all policy files centrally managed from the corporate LAN." Companies also need to make sure the connection to the corporate network is secure; any breach can result in the spread of viruses or malicious code.

Depending upon the circumstances and requirements of the job, business and personal computers may need to be kept separate. If this is the case, "No personal programs, e-mail, web browsing, or game playing should be done on the home office computer," advises DeMaria. "In addition, the computer should be password protected" using an encrypted program. "Let's say a home user's personal machine is infected with a virus. That virus can migrate onto a floppy disk, and the user can put that floppy in the work-machine drive. The old-fashioned method of spreading viruses via floppy disks still works just as well today."

Of course, some companies require tighter security than others. At the very least, educate your workers about the importance of keeping antivirus and other measures in place, not using the company computer for anything other than business purposes, and not allowing family members to use the company computer. Along with creating procedures and processes for securing documents and other critical material, provide information on how to duplicate, back up, and store data or other work-related materials in the event of a crash or other computer or home office disaster.

DEALING WITH THE "MOMMY (OR DADDY) SYNDROME"

The telecommuter is hired, trained, and eager to get started in the home office. There's a little problem: three-year-old Johnny, and Grandma, who needs to be taken to her many doctor's appointments, and the parrot, which keeps chattering when the worker is on a business call. What about the next-door neighbor who expects your new teleworker to provide daycare for her toddler daughter while she goes to the office? Suddenly your worker's not so promising anymore—she's frazzled, pulled in many different directions, and not getting the job done.

You may have tried to explain these and other challenges in advance, but until the employee is actually in the situation, she may not realize how daunting and counterproductive the many demands of home/work life can be. The following are some suggestions to help workers through the transition:

Insist that the worker have his own space, preferably a room with a door in a quiet area of the home. This can be a condition of even getting the job. A separate workspace lends itself to fewer distractions and interruptions. Investing time and effort to establish a private area also sets the stage for a higher level of discipline and organization. In addition to having a door with a lock that partitions off the workspace, the ARO worker's setup must be such that the bathroom door is far away enough from the office so the caller can't hear the sound of running water or a flushing toilet.

Set ground rules for interruptions. The teleworker needs to sit down with friends, neighbors, and family members and let them know the specific hours that she is working and that interruptions should only be in the case of an emergency. This will likely mean hiring a babysitter to watch children or elderly parents and to take them to daycare or school. When friends call or drop by, the telecommuter can gently but firmly tell them she will get back to them after work.

Gain support. At first families and significant others may feel that the telecommuter's presence is license to interrupt or ask for favors or additional help. Children may resent having to be quiet and leave Mommy or Daddy alone. At the beginning of the arrangement, the telecommuter needs to explain that the condition of the job is that he be solely dedicated to performing the assigned work and that he needs their help and support in this endeavor. Without it, he will be unable to telecommute.

Keep children, pets, and personal life away from professional contacts. There is nothing more annoying than calling a business number and hearing a young child's babble on the voice mail. Kids do answer the phone, and most people understand this, but the message on the answering machine is within the parents' control. As much as workers may love their dogs or cats, they need to make sure that barking, meowing, and other noises can't be heard over the phone. This is most important if they are in customer service or call center positions. More than one promising employee at ARO has put their job in jeopardy because of an inability to control background noise.

COMPARTMENTALIZING

A major difficulty faced by beginning telecommuters is the need to separate home from work life. One of Sandra's writer colleagues recalls feeding her infant daughter while interviewing a judge over the phone and taking notes with her free hand.

Although some people can make this work, Sandra has always found that dividing work and home life into two compartments is the best way to ensure long-term telecommuting success. For her, it meant paying extra for a babysitter and sometimes leaving the house to work at a library or coffee shop when her family was at home. Now that the kids are grown, Sandra still compartmentalizes by closing the door of her home office suite and only going inside it during business hours.

Experts have found that under certain circumstances telecommuting can be even more stressful than office work, especially for those who have families. According to a Michigan State University study of ninety-five supervisors and 300 employees, home workers and those with flexible schedules actually reported more conflicts between family and work. However, those who set firm boundaries were able to handle the nontraditional work arrangement, even if it meant not picking up the phone after certain hours or staying away from the work e-mail account on weekends. The study also found that women were less able to set limits than men and that female managers had greater conflicts with family and work than those in less responsible jobs.

Telecommuters—especially those who are at the office part-time—can also suffer from the two-briefcase syndrome. This means that they must deal with maintaining two workplaces, carrying files from one office to another or even having separate briefcases for each.

Compartmentalizing can help alleviate this as well. Decide which records belong where, make copies for reference in both places, and plan for what you will require. Soon there may be no need for a briefcase at all—or only a small one. On a similar note, suggest that workers group like tasks together—for example, making all phone calls at once or sending faxes and e-mails at a specific time.

AVOIDING OVERWORK AND PROCRASTINATION

Compartmentalizing also helps avoid overworking and procrastination, which are two sides of the same coin. Especially if the worker lives alone or is partial to pulling all-nighters, it's easy to get lost in overwork. In the long run, this does not benefit anyone. Not only can it create health problems for the worker, such as repetitive stress injuries and exhaustion, but it can affect the quality of the output.

Studies have found that telecommuters work longer hours and even take assignments on vacation, and some experts believe that their dedication may be in part due to gratitude over the fact that they can work at home, even if only part-time. However, as a manager, you need to reinforce the need for a balance between work and life because in the long run employees will get more done if she is well rested and healthy.

Some suggestions for avoiding overwork:

Encourage frequent stretch breaks, at least once every hour or two. Not only does it ease the strain on muscles from repetitive motions, but it also clears the brain.

Just because they are working at home doesn't mean employees are under house arrest. Encourage your workers to get out at least once a day—for example, go to the park for lunch or to the gym for a workout.

If possible, suggest that they take their personal clock into account when planning their workday. We all have times of day when we're most alert, so they should do more difficult projects then. Conversely, easier tasks such as phone calls and e-mails can be accomplished during periods of lower energy.

Teach them to prioritize by labeling tasks on a scale from one to three. First priorities should be accomplished as soon as possible; priority-two duties can be completed if time permits; and third-tier items can be delegated or postponed, but not indefinitely.

Encourage the employee to ask for help. If the job takes more time than initially planned, then he should be comfortable requesting an extended deadline or additional workers to help ease the burden. Make sure you're available and receptive to these requests.

On the other side is procrastination. In a way it's almost worse, because once people fall into that mode, they will do almost anything to avoid work. Temptations include the television, family and neighbors, the refrigerator, and even—though this may seem hard to believe—the cat box and the laundry. The thought of work becomes so overwhelming that an employee will do almost anything to avoid it. Not all people are able to overcome procrastination—some are simply not self-starters and need the stimulus of the office and coworkers to get the job done. However, there are some tools that can help nudge telecommuters into work mode:

Treat their home office as a standard office. That is: get up at a certain time, get dressed, and be at their desk at set hours. Take a regular lunch and stretch break and make a commitment to doing this the days they're supposed to be working. They can even dress business casual at home to get into office mode.

Have teleworkers come into the office part-time. Along with keeping them motivated and in the loop, they will have social interactions and contact with coworkers, which in and of itself can be motivating. It also helps overcome the dreaded sense of isolation common to beginning telecommuters.

Set deadlines. Even small ones can provide incentive. Breaking a large project into smaller, more manageable chunks can overcome the intimidation factor. Detailed work plans and schedules can be especially helpful.

Provide rewards. If the employee knows she will be getting a promotion or even praise by accomplishing tasks in a timely manner, it can serve as a motivator.

Overcoming Isolation

"Mary Ellen," a video editor and a new mother, thought working from home would be the ideal arrangement, allowing her to be close to her son all day. However, once she began, she found it frustrating and lonely, and it was difficult to concentrate. "I missed the atmosphere of the office and my coworkers," she admitted. "I'm an extrovert who gets energy from people around me; they help start the ideas flowing. . . . Working from home basically turned off my creative faucet."

Although this may not be true for teleworkers at a company like ARO when they are constantly on the phone, some people simply cannot work alone. They may not discover this until they are actually in the situation, alone with only the same four walls, day in and day out.

However, there are steps you can take to help them overcome a sense of isolation.

Keep them in the loop. "Telecommuters have a heightened need to feel included," observes author Lin Grensing-Pophal. "When you share information with them, they will feel more involved in what's happening at the company." This can take the form of an informal luncheon, fellow worker's going away party, or something as simple as informing them about the organization's long-range plans.

Create an atmosphere where the team can connect regularly, be it virtually, through conference calls, or even meeting face-to-face. Consistent contact and a sense of camaraderie with peers help eliminate feelings of isolation.

Encourage the telecommuter to pursue professional development and training. Depending upon the company's policies, you might provide partial or full reimbursement. New knowledge and brainstorming with colleagues help inspire and motivate workers.

Suggest that the telecommuter network with professional or social organizations related to the job or even his hobbies. This can be anything from meeting regularly for lunch with those in the same field to taking up a social sport such as tennis or softball.

Provide the option of working part-time in the office, or returning full-time for a designated period. If the sense of isolation continues or worsens, office time might need to be increased or perhaps be made permanent.

RED FLAGS FOR POTENTIAL PROBLEMS

Many telecommuting arrangements are hybrid; that is, workers are in the office some of the time and at home the rest. Often this depends on the nature of the work—solo tasks can be performed at home, while those requiring interaction and contact are more easily accomplished in the office. The ratio of home to office time varies depending upon the situation and demands of the job. Sometimes it can be challenging to spot potential problems.

However, certain red flags may indicate the arrangement may not be working as well as it should.

- Job performance starts to suffer either in quantity or quality of results.
- Absenteeism starts to increase.

- You or coworkers start having communication problems: either decreased or poor communication.
- The teleworker shows less interest in attending department meetings or otherwise shows signs of becoming a loner. (Don't confuse this with signs of irritation at ill-organized and rambling meetings. Teleworkers tend to become more time-conscious and agenda-oriented as they gain experience.)

Before jumping to conclusions, however, your next step is to get more information from the teleworker. Sit down with the employee and have an open discussion, asking how he feels about the work and being objective about your various concerns. "The teleworker might be having problems adjusting to the new routine, or still be trying to work out the fine points of scheduling his or her time," suggests author Jack Nilles. "Sometimes the relative independence [of teleworking] can be overwhelming and more detailed supervision can help." If things continue to worsen, you may need to take disciplinary or corrective action.

How can you tell if telecommuting is working for the *organization?* This is a far more difficult and complex question, which depends upon productivity and performance, telecommuter and supervisor satisfaction with the program, achievement of corporate internal and external goals, and cost benefit and analysis. Factors can range from decreased turnover, sick leave, and absenteeism to time and money spent on commuting and gasoline to quality of work and productivity. Chapter 17 will discuss these factors in more detail.

MONITORING EMPLOYEE SATISFACTION

Researchers have finally acknowledged what telecommuters and their supervisors have known for years: Telecommuting is a win-win situation for almost everyone involved, "resulting in higher morale and job satisfaction and lower employee stress and turnover," according to a 2007 study released by the American Psychological Association (APA).

The findings were based on twenty years of research and a meta-analysis of forty-six studies of telecommuting involving 12,833 employees. Scientists found that by allowing more autonomy and control, telecommuting not only increased job satisfaction but it resulted in less worker stress. Employees remained loyal to the company and had higher performance ratings. It also appeared to improve the work/life balance, allowing for better management of the often-conflicting demands of work and family. Once workers get used to telecommuting and adjust to it, things can run pretty smoothly.

The only way to know if your employees are really satisfied is to ask. Here are some sample questions.

- How has telecommuting contributed to your personal goals?
- Are you more satisfied or less satisfied with work now that you're telecommuting?
- How has telecommuting affected your home life and family relationships?
- Has it increased or decreased your job stress?
- Do you feel you're working longer/harder than your office counterparts?
- Do you feel isolated from your coworkers?
- Do you feel they resent your telecommuting arrangement?
- How do you feel telecommuting has affected your relationship with your manager?
- Do you feel being a telecommuter will hold you back in your career? Why or why not?
- What are your work habits? Do you have trouble concentrating? Or are you working nonstop?
- Overall, do you think telecommuting has been a success for you personally? Why or why not?

Getting and soliciting regular feedback will not only help solidify and improve work operations but will also boost morale, increase and improve communication, as well as facilitate trust and strengthen relationships.

SUMMARY

Your telecommuting workers will be dealing with the job in the context of demands of family members, friends, and neighbors. They may find it isolating or hard to get started or they may discover that they're working all the time.

Any or a combination of these scenarios can result in resentment, anger, and discouragement, culminating in failure of the telecommuting arrangement. However, by training and working closely with employees—especially in the beginning—managers can help them learn to anticipate and cope with these challenges. Many of these obstacles can be overcome by fostering and developing a sense of trust with your team—among the members both in and out of the office.

Another increasingly important aspect of telecommuting is maintaining security and confidentiality. As more people join the ranks of home workers, companies need to enforce measures that will ensure the safety of work products. As technology evolves, information becomes more valuable—and vulnerable—to theft.

Finally, you need to be on the lookout for potential problems and red flags regarding your telecommuters. The earlier these are spotted the better; direct communication can resolve most issues before they result in major misunderstandings.

The good news is that once it's in place and employees have adjusted, telecommuting is a win-win situation. Along with increased satisfaction and productivity, employees are more loyal to the organization and entrenched in ensuring its success. The next chapters will focus on evaluating goals and recognizing employees' efforts.

CHAPTER 14

Evaluating and Strengthening Performance

INTRODUCTION

This chapter will describe methods of assessing telecommuters, from coaching to performance appraisals to discipline to providing rewards. It will discuss additional skills that virtual managers need to make sure that issues, accomplishments, and shortcomings are clearly and fairly communicated to the employee.

As with any employee, telecommuters need specific guidance in their careers. This chapter will provide suggestions as to how to keep them in the loop and help them develop and expand their skills for both their benefit and the company's.

Most people dislike confrontation, and managers are no exception. Direct and effective ways of counseling employees, as well as solutions for correcting performance problems and revising or terminating the telecommuting arrangement, will also be included.

CAREER PATHS FOR TELEWORKERS

Being out of sight and out of mind is a primary concern of telecommuters. Though conventional wisdom holds that face time at the office is essential to upward mobility, the 2007 American Psychological Association (APA) study discussed in the last chapter revealed that teleworkers' relationships remained strong provided they spent at least two days a week in the office. These statistics only deal with relationships with coworkers. Managers reported that working from home had no negative impact, nor did teleworkers believe their careers were suffering.

Women may derive even greater benefits from telecommuting, continues the study. In contrast to their male counterparts, a larger proportion of women received higher performance ratings from their supervisors and their career prospects improved. "Contrary to expectations in both academic and practitioner literatures, telecommuting has no straightforward, damaging effects on the quality of workplace relationships or perceived career prospects," concluded the authors.

There are certain steps managers can take to help the teleworker stay on track with his career:

Make sure he receives "the same credit or attention for work done remotely as if it had been done in the office," advises author Jack Nilles. This may involve some extra effort, such as sending out a broadcast e-mail announcing work results to the entire team whereas in an office, such recognitions are informal or ad hoc.

On the other hand, a disproportionate amount of recognition can result in a backlash or resentment from office workers. So telecommuters and office personnel should be honored or praised in exactly the same way.

Assign the telecommuter a variety of tasks so she doesn't stagnate or get pigeonholed. "Again, the goal is to mirror the job or task mix that would have happened in the office," Nilles goes on. Such diversity will build skills and enhance creativity. To forestall resentment, both telecommuters and office workers should receive the same proportion of creative and routine assignments.

Cross-train. This works well for both physical exercise and in the world of work—the more skills and muscles you use, the fitter and stronger you become in terms of competencies and strengths. For example, although Sandra is primarily a writer, she has picked up some photography skills throughout the years, especially since the advent of the digital camera. This comes in extremely handy when she's writing travel or entertainment articles and books and editors ask for photos. By allowing workers to stretch and expand their skills into a field that may only be tangential to their jobs, not only do you have someone to cover for an area when needed but you are increasing their overall marketability and value to the company.

Understand that teleworkers "do their own thing" and give them credit for it. You may find that telecommuters use different methods to achieve the same or better end product. This may require some thinking out of the box—after all, you've been used to doing things by following X and it can be disconcerting to learn that Y is the same or better (and after you think about it, you even may recommend Y to the entire team). But in the end, what counts is results.

DISTANCE COACHING

It's best for all concerned to regularly evaluate team members monthly or every six weeks. Yes, it takes more time, especially in the beginning but once again the payoff will be worth it in terms of improved communication and performance. Instead of wondering what they did wrong when they are called on the carpet either physically or virtually, employees will hopefully approach such conversations with at least a neutral mindset.

Current management lingo has replaced the word "counseling" with the more user-friendly and objective term "coaching." Rather than trying to counsel by fixing bad behavior or solving a problem, coaching implies enhancing or developing performance, which sets a more positive stage for improvement. For example, call center employees at ARO are evaluated using a squeaky wheel approach, that is, those making the most noise in terms of poor performance ratings on their monitored calls get the most grease or personal attention to improve their work performance and habits. They need to improve to a certain score to get to maintenance mode. Managers must be able to work with employees in this manner, as each quarter they are also assessed on the success of these efforts.

Coaching from a distance has its own challenges. Coaching implies the need for specifying goals and measurement of performance, and if you're doing it virtually these should be crystal clear since telecommuters are working independently, making many of their own decisions and solving problems.

Authors Kimball Fisher and Mareen Duncan Fisher suggest a *proactive* approach to coaching. By coaching proactively, you are dealing with situations throughout the entire project and not just when a problem arises. Proactive coaching involves what is called on-the-spot coaching during telephone and videoconferences or through e-mails. By asking open-ended questions, team members can "think through all aspects of the project and its outcome," observe the authors.

Similarly a postmortem at the end of the project "provides a good opportunity to reflect on well-dones and opportunities for improvements" for future efforts. However, if the situation calls for corrective feedback, then one-on-one coaching should take place privately with the team member to avoid shaming or embarrassing him in front of his peers.

The following are some tips for distance coaching.

Listen carefully to subtleties and nuances. How do workers react to your suggestions over the phone? Is there a stone cold silence or murmurs of agreement? If coaching is done by e-mail is the tone of their response defensive or appreciative? Even if you sense there's a problem or the employee seems to be struggling with a certain aspect of the job, asking an up-front question can head it off at the pass and provide a quick resolution. Coaching by email can be almost impossible as tone and wordage can often be misinterpreted. So if you get even a sense of dissention from an email, pick up the phone.

Implement a peer feedback process. This can be especially helpful if the manager is far removed from the employees. Often team members work more closely with one another and are therefore more familiar with processes and problems. However, such a system needs to be implemented equally for everyone, using what Fisher and Fisher describe as a "stop/start/continue" method that specifies behaviors that need to be changed (stopped), modified (started), and praised (continued). "Having peers give input provides a more balanced and accurate picture," say the authors. However, it must take place in a supportive, constructive, and non-threatening atmosphere.

Use one-on-one coaching. As mentioned earlier this does require more time, but it allows you to catch problems at the beginning, stay informed as to exactly what's happening, and maintain a positive and open relationship with workers. It also builds loyalty and can "move the coaching process in the arena of developmental conversations versus coaching only when problems arise." The following provides a suggested format for individual coaching sessions.

TELECOMMUTER ONE-ON-ONE COACHING FORMAT

Team Member Name:_____ Date: _____

1. Update on personal development plan
2. Discussion of key projects (deadlines, issues, etc.)
3. Business information for team member
4. Feedback on team member performance (accomplishments, areas for improvement, etc.)

Develop a structured improvement plan when the situation warrants. The employee can put it together, but as manager you need to set expectations. By investing effort in his own success, the employee is more likely to internalize improvements and changes.

CONDUCTING PERFORMANCE APPRAISALS

Office managers have the advantage of sitting down with employees face-to-face and evaluating their performance. This gives them the benefit of softening criticism with cues such as an apologetic smile or an encouraging tap on the arm. Such body language goes a long way in helping the worker internalize and understand what you are trying to say. Facing someone directly through one-on-one conversation facilitates a deeper and more comfortable discussion. Even the act of handing someone a Kleenex invites confidences.

Distance managers have no such luxury. Often when you evaluate performance it's over the phone or via e-mail, two media that by their very limitations can facilitate misunderstanding, hurt feelings, and resentment. So how do you overcome these obstacles, resulting in a positive and objective learning experience for both you and the employee?

Chapter 12 discussed setting and establishing clear and unbiased performance standards and boundaries. Defining key measures and areas of responsibility are also essential in evaluating performance. Thus, each team member is aware of his "arena of power" and how well he is performing at any given time. Given that atmosphere, the performance appraisal should theoretically hold no surprises.

It also helps to do the following:

Reinforce the fact that the appraisal is about looking forward, not a rehash of what they've done wrong. This is where having the employee develop a structured improvement plan for future behavior comes in handy.

Be descriptive about what the person did. For example: "You made three mistakes in the budget and they are A, B, and C."

Avoid subjective labels: "This is sloppy work." Keep the tone objective, consistent, and constructive.

Limit feedback to priority changes. Begin with the changes that will allow for the most improvement and value, rather than fixing everything at once.

Give feedback sooner rather than later. Don't wait for the right time because the employee may continue to make the same mistake over and over again, not knowing she's doing anything wrong.

Give positive and negative feedback. It's best to begin by describing what the person did right, before detailing what needs to be changed. At each stage of the process, ask for their input.

At the end of the discussion, jointly agree on performance objectives and continue with a plan of action. Periodically follow up with the employee and see how well she is doing.

DISCIPLINING EMPLOYEES FROM A DISTANCE

Despite your best intentions and careful planning, sometimes problems arise. The teleworker may decide to return to the office because she misses the camaraderie of the office or you may find that productivity or customer service is suffering.

Whatever the cause, act immediately. Deal directly with problems, rather than avoiding them. However, make sure the method of communication you use fits the situation.

For example, if the issue is minor—the employee fails to turn in a report or makes a small error in documentation, a simple e-mail in the form of a gentle reminder will suffice. However, if the infraction is more serious and persistent—being rude to customers or failing to follow up on an important lead, then further action may be necessary, such as a face-to-face meeting or, barring that, a one-on-one video or telephone conference. Under no circumstances should managers hide behind technology to circumvent confrontation, such as firing someone by e-mail when no previous discipline was attempted or texting them that they have made mistakes. At ARO, all employees are treated equally; they are given written warnings and if they don't improve, they are fired. The same standards apply to all workers; and most realize that a steady job—especially one from home—is desirable in an economy where unemployment is becoming rampant, so they try to do their best.

To avoid creating an adversarial atmosphere, keep the conversation to the facts—the who, what, when, and where of the problem—then ask to hear the employee's side of the story.

During such a discussion, managers should do the following:

- Have notes and make use of them. Sometimes it may be more difficult to document occurrences, but keep records as detailed as possible.
- Explain facts thoroughly and objectively.
- Pay close attention to the employee's perspective and reactions.
- Expect and allow emotional venting.
- Be specific about consequences if problems continue.
- Provide a system for follow-up that is both solution- and results-oriented.

Generally, discipline should be handled in a progressive manner. When the problem first starts manifesting itself, it is time for an informal chat, as soon as or immediately after the incident occurs. Often that does the trick but if repeated reminders fail to have any effect, then you must move on to the next level. Some misconduct may be governed by more stringent disciplinary action as dictated by company policy. The manager is responsible for knowing the company's procedures for investigation and disciplinary action.

Whenever possible, put a positive spin on discipline. Deem it a "call to improvement" rather than a punitive action. Also always make sure to follow company policy to the letter regarding discipline. As a manager, you're responsible for making sure all your actions are fully and correctly documented.

TELECOMMUTER TERMINATION—MAYBE NOT "THE END"

Unlike office employees, telecommuters are held to different standards of discipline. Because the arrangement is voluntary in nearly all cases and considered a privilege for the employee, the protocol of action—reprimands, probation, demotion or reassignment, and suspension—may not be followed as closely.

Rather, solutions are more immediate and may include:

- Rescinding the telework arrangement
- Modifying the telework agreement to better define your expectations
- Setting a time frame for the employee to demonstrate a significant improvement
- Resolving other circumstances that may have contributed to the unsatisfactory performance

Often telecommuting problems deal with circumstances surrounding the work-at-home arrangement, such as childcare or eldercare. The worker may need additional training or may have equipment difficulties. Sometimes these issues can be resolved; on other occasions, not. Regardless, you need to document times, dates, and any other information that may lead up to your decision, being very specific about what transpired, what was discussed, and when the various conversations and problems occurred.

The worker needs to know about each infraction and understand what will happen if she fails to improve. This information should be documented and signed by all parties as well.

Finally, the end of the telecommuting arrangement doesn't necessarily mean the worker needs to leave the company. If he is productive and valuable, he may be better suited to the office, particularly if he succeeded there before telecommuting. However, whether working from their basement or a cubicle in the middle of headquarters, employees need to be held to the same standards of performance. This should be made clear regardless of the final outcome or decision (see Chapter 16 for information on employee termination).

CELEBRATING FROM A DISTANCE

Just as important—and a lot more pleasant—is celebrating the accomplishments of and honoring your workers. Although telecommuting can be a reward in itself, it's not enough; even the most far-flung virtual worker in Antarctica wants to celebrate with his team when a project is successfully completed.

There are of course the more conventional rewards like bonuses, raises, time off, honorary awards (for example, a plaque or certificate), and informal recognitions such as after-work cocktails "on the company." But these are based on the traditional office structure. Telecommuting has widened the playing field in terms of time, space, and culture, so organizations might want to retool their incentives.

If possible, bring in all employees for the event, and if they're so remote that this is impractical, provide a comparable incentive. For example, if the home office is participating in a training session, then make sure the employee is scheduled for a similar class in his home town. If the office has box seats to a sporting event or theatre to recognize the team effort, then all distant employees should receive tickets for something equitable in their locale. The point is that distance should be no barrier for providing either coaching or rewards and the telecommuters are a valuable and recognized member of the team, regardless of where they live.

ARO sends vouchers for movie tickets or gift cards to chain restaurants, which are valid almost anywhere, as well as promotional items with the client's logo, such as T-shirts or mugs. They also provide bonuses on certain projects that require extra effort or overtime. The following are some suggestions for instituting rewards from a distance.

Use e-cards, gift certificates, and other virtual forms of recognition. Electronic rewards can be sent anywhere. These can celebrate milestones and specific goals throughout the project, and they are always good for keeping people motivated and interest high. They can also be used to remember birthdays, anniversaries, and other personal celebrations as well as for individual and group thanks. However, be consistent in determining under what circumstances and when they should be furnished.

Plan a group gathering so everyone can meet face-to-face. This can be done at the beginning or end of the project, preferably both. Along with helping team members bond initially, a farewell party provides a sense of completion and job well done.

Take the time to visit individual or group teleworkers. Nothing is a substitute for a face-to-face encounter. Even in the scattershot world of freelance writing, editors travel to meet with regular contributors. Conversely, writers regularly go to New York, Chicago, or other publishing locations to network with their clients. When ARO executives travel, sometimes they meet with employees in different cities. For example, if Michael is in a city where several of his teleworkers are located, he'll arrange for an informal gathering and give them promotional items or buy them a drink.

Create an electronic bulletin board or web page for "best practices." "The opportunity to share your learnings or have your process or approach posted . . . is a subtle but effective way to celebrate accomplishments," observe authors Kimball Fisher and Mareen Duncan Fisher. "Not only does the team or individual receive recognition, but team members are able to learn from one another."

Recognize personal differences in providing rewards. Cultural variances can have an impact on virtual teams. For example, sending a ham to Orthodox Jewish members in Israel would likely not be appreciated, so do your homework when selecting a gift; e-certificates are usually a good idea. Also, some people are particular about recognition and don't like to be singled out. Telecommuters can be an independent lot, so check first with the individual before announcing a reward.

Finally, ask team members how *they* would like to celebrate. You might come up with something even better after you get their input and ideas.

SUMMARY

As with office workers, telecommuters need regular and consistent evaluation to improve performance and grow their careers. A popular method is through coaching, which can assume the form of manager-to-employee or between various team members. No matter how or when it takes place, it should be done in an objective manner, in an atmosphere of mutual support and encouragement.

Because telecommuters tend to think more autonomously and work on their own, cross-training and assigning them a variety of tasks will strengthen their overall job skills. Having someone to cover specific areas also adds to your organization's or department's efficiency. Additionally, pay attention to the different methods telecommuters use to get the job done; not only may these be more efficient and cost-effective, but the techniques might make work easier for some or all team members.

Dealing with performance appraisals, discipline, and especially termination can be difficult for most managers. However, by communicating regularly and frequently with teleworkers, you can help make at least the first two relatively painless. Discussing problems as soon as they arise and providing immediate feedback go a long way in eliminating many difficulties. Most teleworkers are there because they want to be and cherish their arrangements and thus are willing to go that extra mile to make sure they—and the project—succeed.

While discipline may be inevitable, it doesn't necessarily signal the end of the employer-worker relationship. The telecommuter can return to the office or take a short hiatus until he (and you) feel he's more capable of working at home. At the opposite end of the performance spectrum is praise—it should be even-handed and fair for both telecommuters and office workers. Using a variety of innovative methods, recognition can provide added incentive for even the most isolated virtual employee.

PART THREE

LEADER OF THE PACK

How to Effectively Guide and Manage Your Telecommuting Team

CHAPTER 15

Handling Different Types of Jobs

INTRODUCTION

Although there are certain requirements for dealing with tele-commuters in general, each field has its own specifications and demands. This chapter will discuss basic differences in work methods and skill sets in common telecommuting jobs. Understanding the distinctiveness of each job type will also help you in the selection process; for example, you might want to look for someone with a bubbly personality in customer service whereas this might not be as important when hiring a creative individual or someone in information technology (IT).

While many of the requirements may be the same as for office jobs, telecommuting has its own particular demands. These will also be addressed.

DATA AND INFORMATION PROCESSING

Since they are mostly routine and can be performed independently, many data and information processing jobs lend themselves to telecommuting. Along with being well defined, results are fairly simple to check. For example, you could give a transcriptionist an assignment, have her return it by a certain date, and easily review it for accuracy. The most basic issue is how fast she can produce the material. Other factors in determining the workflow would be the size of the operation and the needed turnaround time.

Depending upon confidentiality and scope, you may need a private Intranet or electronic bulletin board for electronic drop-off and delivery of work. Other traditional methods such as fax, messenger services, and especially snail-mail are being used much less frequently. Privacy might also be a major concern if workers are processing medical, insurance, or financial information. Depending upon the requirements of the job, employees must follow security measures and use the computer only for designated purposes, as was discussed in Chapter 13. If the worker is an independent contractor with several clients, you might have him sign a confidentiality agreement that also guarantees that antivirus and firewall programs are in place.

Many companies use teleworkers for their order entry systems. These are often outsourced to countries such as Mexico and India where labor is cheaper and workers don't necessarily have to be conversant in English. They do, however, need to understand how to fill out the forms and process the data. However, given the current state of the economy, managers and executives might want to consider keeping the workflow within U.S. borders.

Because they are so repetitive and offer very little career advancement, information and data processing jobs can have a high turnover. However, you can improve your chances of retaining employees if you hire from the right demographic, including those who need to stay at home due to eldercare or childcare responsibilities, the physically disabled, or retirees or others looking for a secondary income.

CUSTOMER SERVICE

Here is where many companies have actually gone back to hiring American workers. (There's nothing more frustrating than calling a toll-free number, only to find that the person on the other end barely understands what you are trying to tell them!) It's also a boon for employees because, depending upon their circumstances and the job requirements, they might be able to use their office for tax deductions, which also can boost their net pay.

At ARO, workers in *general customer service jobs* answer inbound and outbound calls. To qualify for this position, they must have a customer service background and skills and be able to type efficiently and accurately. There is no cold calling or telemarketing (see "Sales" below). ARO's *technical support* people provide detailed information and guidance in troubleshooting the various products sold by the company's different clients. Along with knowing how to deal with the public, they need extensive knowledge of the product along with problem-solving skills and the ability to think independently and somewhat creatively.

The challenge with customer service, as Michael can attest, is not in filling positions but in locating the right kind of individual. Finding someone with good communication and interpersonal skills is even more important than extensive knowledge of the field. It's easier to learn information about a product or service than try to change a person's personality and ways of dealing with others. Desirable traits may include:

- Excellent customer service and problem-solving skills
- A positive, friendly attitude with the willingness and ability to help customers
- Ability to learn and share information with others
- Ability to work independently with minimum supervision in a fast-paced environment, while effectively managing multiple tasks

Along with full technical support for basic PC problems, connectivity issues, and company applications, ARO team members are available at all times to answer workers' questions. Additionally, employees are made aware of ARO's workload monitoring system. Along with tracking productivity and keeping them "on task" the software serves as an effective deterrent in unauthorized use of the computer, such as sending e-mails or surfing the web while on the company clock. Additionally, when employees log onto ARO's web center, the desktop is specific to the profile of that particular employee. This makes the information secure and encrypted.

AUDITING AND INTERVIEWING

Other telecommuting jobs involve calling or visiting people to obtain specific information or for other investigative purposes. Building inspectors, property assessors, and similarly focused workers are increasingly based in their homes or at other remote locations. At ARO, phone auditors conduct audits for clients that evaluate general liability and workers compensation cases, with all documents and materials entered into ARO websites. ARO also uses physical auditors, who although they do most interviewing over the phone, actually visit and inspect the site(s).

Although they may require additional specialized training or education in a particular field, many of the same traits discussed in the customer service sector apply to these jobs as well. However, individuals hired to do physical audits or have any direct contact with a customer or client should come in for a personal interview to make sure they are presentable and personable, with the skills necessary to perform the face-to-face portion of the job. They might also need to be trained on how to use electronic tablets to input information on-site or a similar configuration that meets the company's needs.

SALES/SERVICE

Another fertile field for telecommuters is sales and service. Many of these jobs have been home-based for a long time. ARO uses two different types of sales positions. The overall responsibility of the sales representative is to maximize sales and growth of the insurance and finance service division and requires travel approximately 10 percent of the time. Duties include making presentations on ARO's outsourcing offerings and managing and promoting relationships with clients in targeted areas of the U.S. B2B marketing/telesales representatives sell products for ARO clients to their customer base. Along with sales experience, customer service skills are needed here,

Telecommuting has extended to all aspects of sales and service. Representatives in textbook and pharmaceutical sales use laptops and other accoutrements to create portable offices that provide sophisticated demonstrations and generate paperwork or electronic forms to close deals wherever needed. Real estate agents have computerized listings that can immediately call up clients' specific requirements. Looking for a 3BR 2½ bath in suburb X with a dog run? Just type in the information and several addresses pop up! While many sales individuals are affiliated with a particular company, they work from home, often longer and odder hours than their office brethren. Even home repair workers use their truck as their office thanks to the advent of cell phones and other forms of electronic communication.

In general, people in sales and service are motivated self-starters and already have many of the requirements of the telecommuting personality mentioned in Chapter 3. Of course it depends on what they're selling and whom they're selling to. If they are new to the field, they should be watched closely to make sure they don't get off track.

PROFESSIONALS: CREATIVE AND KNOWLEDGE WORKERS

In a sense, teleworker qualities in professionals are the opposite of customer service: You need someone with specialized knowledge and expertise, with perhaps not as many people skills, especially if she is working autonomously. For example, when hiring a writer or an engineer, the ability to answer the phone in a cheerful manner and field customer complaints take a back seat to technical ability and subject matter knowledge.

Generally professionals fall into two categories. *Creative workers* consist of artists, writers, musicians, videographers, and anyone who generates new material in a variety of art forms. *Knowledge workers* deal primarily with information and include those in the information technology fields—systems analysts, programmers, technical writers—as well as more general disciplines like researchers, scientists, and lawyers. Along with computers, cell phones, and Internet access they may need additional equipment and software, such as fax machines and scanners as well as access to specialized subscription databases and programs that require them to create a particular product.

Although they do vastly different kinds of work, creative and knowledge workers can be managed in somewhat the same way. As primarily self-motivated, independent, and creative individuals, they can be especially effective and successful as telecommuters. However, take special steps with them:

- *Ask them whether they are more productive in isolation or as part of a group.* Although some professionals work very well alone, others require the presence of others in an office to keep them motivated and inspired.
- *Along with freedom, provide some structure.* Offer general guidance as to deadlines and schedules. Gently remind them when routine work, such as reports and other paperwork, is due.
- *Understand that creative and knowledge people need time to think.* They may not seem like they're doing much, but they're actually processing information and figuring out designs. Again, it's an issue of measuring results instead of methods; what's important is that they meet deadlines and do their work correctly. Have a system in place so they can periodically update you on the status of a project or piece of work.
- *Also provide them with full knowledge of the end result.* Creative and knowledge workers can get off track and hung up

on smaller details. But if you give them a full view of the problem or issue, they can come up with surprising and innovative solutions.

- *Praise them.* They need recognition, along with feeling like they're an integral part of the team and that their career is on track. Otherwise, they may begin to experience that dreaded sense of isolation and begin to look elsewhere for employment.

EXECUTIVES AND MANAGERS

These are the smallest group of full-time telecommuters. However, this is beginning to change, as virtual teams separated by time, space, and culture are managed from a distance. Still, most executives and upper-level managers are at the other "home office"— that is, corporate headquarters—at least part of the work week. Their days are generally spent in meetings, dealing with crises, or in other planning activities.

However, thanks to utilities such as LiveMeeting and web conferencing, even these are becoming virtual—and visual—eliminating some of the need for travel and frequent face-to-face meetings, saving money and, at least theoretically, increasing productivity. Be aware, executives are notoriously unwilling to take the time to use complex software and learn new technology.

Nevertheless, at some point most managers will need to deal with telecommuters or may possibly have to telecommute themselves. Chapter 9 offers suggestions on how to cope and adjust.

SUMMARY

There are no hard and fast rules in selecting and dealing with various telecommuting jobs. Certain fields such as routine data and information processing, customer service, sales and support, and those requiring the use of creative and knowledge skills, among others, can lend themselves to working at home. However, determining whether the team should work at home or in the office should be decided on a case-by-case basis, dependent upon many factors. Depending on the project and its requirements, finding the group of people in the same city can be next to impossible, so virtual may be the only way to go.

The next chapters will discuss evaluating the overall telecommuting effort as well as how to run various types of meetings for optimum workload effectiveness.

CHAPTER 16

Managing Real-Time and Virtual Meetings

INTRODUCTION

To paraphrase the late, great humorist James Thurber, "Are meetings necessary?" The answer, whether your team is completely virtual or partially office-based, is probably yes. However the good news is that you have a number of alternatives to choose from, ranging from conference calls and face-to-face meetings to cutting-edge virtual conferencing and more.

This chapter will discuss the various options as well as how to use the right tools for the right situation. Many variables come into play—the urgency of the message, the complexity of the information, and what you're trying to achieve. The latter also relates to whom you are talking to: You might use a different mode of communication for a potential client or a distant collaborator than for members of a close-knit team.

TELEPHONE

In spite of technology, the telephone remains the basic form of communication. Just look at the iPhone—underneath its touch screen and video capabilities, including software that can give the impression that you're drinking champagne from it, it serves the same purpose as the device invented by Alexander Graham Bell in 1876.

With the advent of the cell phone you can reach out and touch anyone, anywhere, at any time. This can be both a good and bad thing but is mostly beneficial to telecommuters who need to be reached from a distance whether they are based in a foreign country or en route to a child's ballet lesson. Such contact, however, should be limited to the mutually agreed upon boundaries set by the job. There's no excuse for calling someone when they're off duty unless it's an emergency.

The most common form of telephone meeting is a *teleconference*. This allows several users to dial into a single number and is either hosted internally or through a third-party service provider. Along with connecting everyone simultaneously, it offers real-time interaction and is fairly inexpensive.

However, there are disadvantages. You are "not always clear who's talking," states author Kelly Pate Dwyer of Bnet.com. Also, "time lags result in people talking at the same time. Callers often multitask, so their attention is divided. If most of the group is in one location, people calling in feel left out of the conversation." Additionally, it's "hard to show people what you're talking about or give visual presentations."

Therefore, teleconferences work best with smaller groups or teams who know each other, for shorter meetings and planning sessions. Dwyer recommends sending out an agenda or a visual aid beforehand and being very specific during the meeting as to the item referenced and its actual location.

All team members need to have the proper equipment so they can clearly hear what's being said. They should also be trained in the technical side of teleconferencing so they can to join in and add others, if necessary.

Etiquette is another important area. Assign meeting roles and make sure participants identify themselves when talking. Allowing everyone a chance to speak, even if it means taking an informal roll call when decisions are being made, is also vital; silence does not necessarily indicate agreement. Team members need to weigh in with their opinion. Also, when someone is inadvertently interrupted or two people start talking at the same time, the person who interrupts should apologize and allow the other party to complete her thoughts before giving his.

Background noise can create major embarrassments, particularly if the conference is taking place over speakerphone or microphone. Depending upon the sensitivity of the equipment, even the most ambient sounds of shuffling papers, personal noises such as sneezing, or a neighbor's loud music can be heard by all. Participants should be made aware of this beforehand so they can put the speakerphone on mute when they're not talking.

Keep conversation to the subject at hand. A drifting topic can happen more frequently when people know each other and start chatting about mutual interests and unrelated subjects. This can add unnecessary time to the meeting and be counterproductive to completing the agenda.

Meeting Roles for Teleconferences

Leader. Organizes and facilitates the meeting, making sure the agenda is covered in the allotted amount of time. This can be the manager or preferably a team member who has a vested interest in the topic.

Gatekeeper. Makes sure that everyone participates as equally as possible. Along with encouraging reticent members to speak up, this may mean squelching those who talk too much. "Thanks for the information, John. Lisa, what do you think about this?"

Scribe. Takes notes during the meeting and distributes them afterwards. This person is responsible for making sure that all important information is included, such as key decisions and action items.

Participant. Although this may seem obvious, participants should understand their importance in the meeting. They need to honestly express opinions, stay on track with the agenda, and follow teleconferencing etiquette.

These roles can be rotated, so everyone gets a chance to experience the different responsibilities. Acting in the different capacities provides team members with a sense of ownership, as well as building communications and leadership skills.

E-MAIL

It's easy, quick, and can be the ultimate time waster. Who hasn't gotten an e-mail from a friend or colleague about a strange or hilarious website, only to click onto it and several minutes or maybe an hour later realized he is wasting time? E-mail distractions are especially seductive to telecommuters whose web surfing habits, in some cases, aren't monitored at all.

How do you prevent e-mail from taking over your life? A good spam filter helps, as does having separate addresses for work and personal accounts. The latter isn't always effective, especially if you are e-mailing with a friend or significant other via the personal account and can't resist checking to see if they've responded.

Certain guidelines can be followed in conducting business or making decisions via e-mail. Some of these may be obvious, but it's wise to review even the basics with your team to prevent costly mistakes and professionally harmful situations.

Keep correspondence to one page or less. By its very nature, e-mail is intended to be brief and focused. Anything longer is best discussed using a different method of communication, such as a phone call. Lengthy written text can be sent as an attachment.

Think twice before you hit the send button. Everyone has a story about e-mails they've composed to an individual and then accidentally hit "reply to all." Additionally if you're forwarding an e-mail and it has numerous names of people who received copies, delete the list, as long as it has no relevance to the context. If you're sending or replying to an e-mail and it's urgent, say so in the header; some e-mail programs allow for "priority" e-mails. Only do so when it is necessary.

Be judicious in quotebacks. Some e-mail programs automatically copy the full text of the e-mail in the response. While this can provide useful information, it can also be very tedious to plow through.

Keep a lean and mean Inbox. This means getting rid of outdated addresses, deleting unnecessary e-mails, and organizing e-mail topics into specific folders. It also means checking your e-mails on a regular (but not constant) basis to avoid a major backlog.

Be careful about opening attachments—only open those from a known source—and never click onto a website from an e-mail from an unknown or unfamiliar recipient. Such sites are a breeding ground for hackers, viruses, and spyware.

Finally, both managers and team members should understand that e-mail never actually is erased. You can delete something, but hackers and other experts might still be able to exhume it from the bowels of your computer if they want to badly enough. Therefore, think twice about sending any e-mail with emotional, confidential, or sexual content—it can come back to haunt you.

Also, as mentioned in earlier chapters, e-mail should never be used to address performance or personal issues. If you feel compelled to shoot someone an angry e-mail, also known as a flame, write it out and let it sit in the Draft folder of your Inbox for twenty-four hours. Almost every time, you will find that you'll delete it or at least revise it heavily the next day.

A variant of e-mail is known as *instant messaging* (IM). Here participants send and receive messages in a single pop-up screen. It's faster and more personal than e-mail and, along with providing a list of who's online, gives the feel of being part of an immediate group, a boon for isolated or remote workers. However, IMs can be even more distracting than e-mail. Not only do you instantly see who is online, but it notifies you the moment you receive an e-mail or IM, increasing the temptation to procrastinate even more.

If you want to appear offline and not be bothered you can select an invisible or busy status.

IMs are particularly useful when you want a quick answer or need to locate someone for a meeting or phone call. Managers and trainers at ARO use IM to communicate with employees on a real-time basis, whether to reply to a question or provide immediate feedback. It's also good for sending reminders and alerts, and if it has video capacity, you can also check in to see who's available for a meeting. However, IMs should be used judiciously and with a secure network.

VIDEOCONFERENCING

Remember *The Jetsons*? Perhaps not, but in the 1960s when that TV show was in its heyday, George Jetson and his family communicated by videophones and other virtual technology. While videophones haven't quite yet reached the average American household, their first cousin, videoconferencing, has. Although the equipment and technology have a way to go and can be clumsy and awkward, it has become somewhat cost effective. All you need is a video camera or webcam; computer monitor, television, or projector; microphones; loudspeakers hooked up to the monitor or telephone; and a data transfer system—and you can communicate live! The data transfer system can be either an analog or digital telephone network, LAN, or Internet.

Another, more expensive videoconferencing option is a dedicated system, where all the components are combined in a single piece of equipment. This consists of a remote control video camera, which can zoom in and pan wherever needed. It provides better overall quality of communications but is more expensive. Systems can be large, small, or even portable. Cameras can also be posted in conference rooms or workstations, and voice activation allows the camera to focus on whoever is speaking.

Videoconferences are particularly helpful in that you can see a person's expressions, gestures, and general body language—as long as the images remain sharp and clear and there are no delays in transmission. It can be especially useful when hiring and interviewing, and is a good alternative in introducing team members who are geographically dispersed. It can also take the place of some time-consuming and expensive travel.

It still has a ways to go in terms of sound and video quality, which, depending upon the setup, can be erratic. Another major issue in many videoconferences is the lack of direct eye contact. If participants look straight at the camera, they can't pay attention to what's taking place on the screen, thus defeating its purpose. So there is a disconcerting sense of talking to someone without looking him in the eye.

If you're willing to spend $500,000 or more you can purchase *telepresence*, a high-definition, high-bandwidth version of videoconferencing that uses multiple oversized plasma screens and speakers and real-time audio, not only allowing for clarity of expression and eye contact, but eliminating audio delay. However, it requires dedicated conference rooms, high bandwidth audio, and a modern Voice over IP (VoIP) switching infrastructure. Because many systems operate on proprietary networks, this usually only works for meetings within the company.

Even telepresence doesn't overcome the fact that many people are uncomfortable in front of a live camera and may not perform at their best.

Still videoconferencing can be useful if all team members are trained in equipment and presentation, time limits are observed, and the "mute" features are used when participants aren't talking, as microphones pick up all sound. Encourage participants to be creative in their use of the media, allowing team members, for example, to zoom in on the individual who is speaking and use show-and-tell video clips. "When people have more control over the technology, they are more likely to use it effectively," say Fisher and Fisher.

INTERNET CONFERENCING

The Internet is expanding and evolving, as are the ways of using it for conferences and meetings. However, the same rules of etiquette and methods of organizing meetings discussed earlier in this chapter apply here too.

For a web conference, users log on to a real-time website or software program such as Microsoft Office Live Meeting (an earlier version of NetMeeting) or Windows Meeting Space. Various media can be used, from slides to live video to text chat to audio VoIP to whiteboard annotation. The electronic equivalent of a chalk and blackboard, whiteboard systems enable participants to simultaneously view one or more users drawing with an on-screen blackboard or running an application that provides a visual of the same. Whiteboards are especially helpful in documenting the results or action decisions of the meeting. The scribe usually jots them down, enabling all to see and agree or disagree with various points while the meeting is taking place.

Although web conferencing allows team members to troubleshoot, share documents, and collaborate remotely across time, space, and even cultures, technical difficulties frequently occur. Often this is due to the incompatibilities of the various technologies or the fact that one vital feature isn't working, such as a microphone, or a team member unintentionally downloaded a program that disabled certain web meeting functions. A quick run through before the meeting gets underway can alleviate many of these issues.

Additionally, complicated discussions can get bogged down, so it's important to keep visuals interesting and use the polling and messaging functions. When polling—an electronic form of taking attendance—the main computer interrogates its connected terminals in a round robin sequence. Users then send a response. Regardless of what method you use, make sure participants stay engaged by typing e-mail comments or using the audio portion to indicate their opinions and involvement.

As with all meetings, set an agenda and time limit, along with providing sufficient advance notice. This is especially important with a far-flung team that is engaged in complex tasks. Team members need time to prepare, especially for the complicated and in-depth discussions that often take place during these types of meetings. Although this may seem a small thing, make sure to have the right time and a specific date: for example, March 23, 2010 at 1:30 P.M., Eastern Standard Time. Even saying "Tuesday" might cause confusion for someone in Australia or Asia who is twenty-four hours ahead or behind.

Chapter 9 discussed synchronous or asynchronous communications technologies. In contrast to synchronous web conferencing is the Wiki or FTP site, which allows for the exchange of knowledge and information by participants at different times. Basically online archives of large, linked files for team and clients' access, the Wiki allows participants to add, modify, and update information. Wikipedia, the definitive but often controversial encyclopedia of information on the Internet, is an example of this.

File transfer protocols (FTP) are more stagnant but allow users to download information at their leisure. Both formats can be helpful in gathering feedback from all users and for project planning, although maintenance and implementation can be time-consuming and difficult. It's also best to designate a gatekeeper who will make sure that updates don't override each other in the Wiki and information stays current in both.

Internet conferencing also uses collaboration technology, a project-specific online workspace that allows colleagues to exchange and modify information. It is especially useful for brainstorming, customer presentations, and storing company and client information in a central location, and it works well with small, tech-savvy groups.

Programs such as Microsoft SharePoint provide a single workspace for teams to coordinate schedules, organize documents, and participate in discussions—within the organization and over the Extranet. This can be done asynchronously, a benefit to team members in different time zones.

WHEN TO MEET FACE-TO-FACE

Chapter 14 and earlier chapters discussed the importance of face-to-face meetings. If at all possible these meetings should occur during these circumstances:

Initial Interview. While not always necessary—depending upon the situation, phone interviews may be equally if not more effective, as discussed in earlier chapters—the initial interview should be in person, especially if the potential employee is in a customer-facing role.

Project Kickoff. Getting off to a good start is important to a team's success and sets the tone for the entire project. Along with building a common understanding and purpose and helping the team coalesce into a solid unit, this meeting can "define the team's charter, set goals, establish operating guidelines, describe communication preferences, and review boundaries," observe authors Kimball Fisher and Mareen Duncan Fisher.

Mileposts. Especially if it's a long-term project it can be difficult to stay focused. Periodically bringing the team together provides an added boost and impetus to complete the task. In addition, teams can stay current on problems and maintain a sense of connection and trust. If possible teams should meet regularly, ideally once a quarter.

Wrap-ups or Celebrations. Along with celebrating project completion, these can "prepare the team to be more effective in future assignments," continue the authors. By meeting face-to-face, workers can build upon each other's ideas and review and analyze problems, decisions, and other issues. Such in-person meetings also provide much needed recognition and networking opportunities.

Conflict Resolution, Performance Reviews, and Discussions. As mentioned in Chapter 14, anything relating to performance is best discussed in person to establish rapport and eliminate confusion and misinterpretations. If there is a conflict among team members, this is likely best resolved face-to-face as well, if possible.

EMPLOYEE TERMINATION

In the brick-and-mortar world, employee termination usually takes place face-to-face. Few things are more indicative of weak management than hiding behind e-mails, faxes, or other technology to avoid the unpleasantness of letting someone go. However, in the universe of telecommuting, workers can be far-flung and very removed from their managers, such as at ARO, where they are located all over the country. There may be no choice other than to fire an employee over the phone. Regardless of how it's done, termination needs to be accomplished in a fair, equitable, and calm manner.

Circumstances for firing may vary: It could be because every avenue has been tried and exhausted to improve performance or behavior; the job itself has evolved and the person is unable to adapt; or the worker has committed an act or misconduct—such as sexual harassment or drug use—and the only choice is to let him go.

Regardless of how or when you fire, make sure that the time and place is private. Only those who are directly involved—managerial personnel, witnesses—should be told in advance and if necessary, present. Having a third party in the room is usually a good idea, "someone who understands the gravity of the situation and who will hold the discussion and details of the termination to be confidential in nature," according to management expert Malcolm Tatum.

Also, be very specific in discussing the circumstances of the firing, citing names, dates, and statistics related to the job and other information such as final pay, expense reports, health insurance and so on. If severance is being offered or unemployment is available, include details on that as well.

With home-based workers, there is less security and thus greater concerns about breaches of confidentiality or dissemination of private information. However, such contingencies should have been covered in the initial telecommuter agreement. If circumstances dictate, you might want to gently remind the employee that he signed a confidentiality or security agreement and it is legally binding.

Terminations are emotional, and the team member may not hear what you've said the first time, so you may have to repeat yourself to make sure everything is understood. Also provide the information in writing and, depending upon the circumstances, perhaps some words of encouragement about finding a better situation with another company that's more commensurate with their skills and needs.

SUMMARY

Thanks to technology and the flexibility inherent in telecommuting, you have a cornucopia of meeting options at your disposal. Employees need to be comfortable and conversant with the technology, or the meetings will be less effective and productive. Team members should also be involved in the various aspects of the meeting, from leading, to documenting results, to providing video clips and other information. Not only will this help grow their skills but it will strengthen their commitment to the project.

Additionally, the type of technology used in the meeting should be matched with the kind of information that's being shared. For instance, explaining a revised minor procedure to a smaller work group lends itself to teleconferencing while launching a sophisticated product with multiple applications may require the sophisticated multi-functions of a web conferencing program such as Microsoft Office Live Meeting.

Managers also need to be judicious in how they use the various types of communication, such as never using e-mail to reprimand someone or send an angry message. Not only does it live forever in the computer (even if erased by the user) but this shows a lack of judgment and poor management skills. Rather, you should seek the most immediate and personalized method available when communicating milestones for the team, from hiring and celebrations to resolving performance issues and conflicts. Dealing with the latter in a face-to-face situation is often difficult, especially when terminating employees. If handled properly however, it is not only legal and ethical but provides the employee with clear-cut information that everyone can hopefully learn from.

CHAPTER 17

Evaluating the Success of Your Telecommuting Program

INTRODUCTION

In the final analysis, the telecommuting program has to be beneficial for the company on many levels, not only for the employees and managers, but also in terms of corporate goals, productivity, cost benefits, and ultimately, customers and profits. This chapter will examine how to evaluate these various factors, as well as what to look for in making a telecommuting program successful.

Sometimes in spite of everyone's best efforts, telecommuting programs fail. This may be due to one or a combination of variables. Since telecommuting will become increasingly integrated into the corporate landscape, managers should closely examine the reasons behind the failure.

CORPORATE GOALS

Telecommuting has enhanced the performance of many companies. The German manufacturer Siemens claimed it cut office space by 35 percent and produced a $3 million annual savings as a result of its telecommuting efforts, along with increasing productivity of some workers by over 20 percent. Similarly corporations such as J.D. Edwards, IBM, American Express, Compaq, and AT&T have derived considerable productivity gains and savings from instituting telecommuting programs, according to the Telework Coalition (TelCoa).

In order to determine whether the telecommuting program is meeting the internal goals of your organization, look at factors such as reduced lateness, absenteeism and sick leave, increased job retention, and ability to attract the highest quality candidates as well as how many people telecommute and for what portion of the work week. You can obtain this raw data from the human resources and payroll departments. Additionally poll both tele-commuters and office workers to get their perceptions regarding these factors. You can then compile the information and compare it against the mission statement and other company benchmarks.

Companies are becoming increasingly sensitive to the environment and community. Therefore you should evaluate the telecommuting effort in terms of such goals as reduced gas consumption, traffic congestion, and time spent on the road, as well as estimated decreases in air pollution. Equal employment opportunity and employee morale aspects can also be considered by asking such questions as: How many additional disabled, elderly, or otherwise unemployable workers were added because of the telecommuting program? How much personal time did they gain? Do they use this time for such healthy pursuits as exercise and family outings? Do they report considerably less stress now that they work from home? Did telecommuting help them lose weight by eliminating the fattening temptations often found in the office? A written or even oral survey of workers can yield answers to these and other questions.

PRODUCTIVITY

A properly organized telecommuting program will have productivity measures in place so you can track how well the telecommuters are doing, either in comparison to the office workers in the same job or by comparing it against past performance prior to instituting the program. Although performance is more easily measured in data and information processing, customer service, and sales jobs because you are looking at numbers as opposed to knowledge products, it is possible to examine productivity in all telecommuting jobs.

The methodology is simple: Ask telecommuters and their supervisors in addition to consumers of your product or service. Questions for workers can include:

- Do you feel you are more productive, and if so, in what way and how much?
- Has the quality of your work improved?
- Are you doing more work in less time? If possible, provide examples.
- Are you more focused while working at home?
- Are you getting adequate technical support while working at home? If not, how does this affect your performance?
- Has working at home affected timeliness in terms of mail delivery or dependable phone and Internet access?
- Has incompatibility in equipment or software slowed you down in any way?
- Do you have the adequate tools at home to perform the job? If not, has this affected your productivity and how?
- Are you able to communicate regularly with your supervisor? Are you able to easily reach him or her to resolve problems and answer questions?
- As a telecommuter do you feel like more or less like part of the team or more or less visible? How does this affect your work?
- Has lack of face-to-face interaction increased or decreased productivity?
- Has telecommuting made you a better and more creative worker? Why or why not?

Questions for managers can include:

- How has telecommuting changed employee performance? Has it improved, deteriorated, or stayed the same? Please provide examples.

- How have employee attitudes changed? Has this made any impact on their work output?
- Do you feel it is easier or harder to communicate with employees? How has this affected productivity?
- Are telecommuters meeting their work goals? Are they accomplishing them faster and more efficiently?
- Do you feel that the telecommuting effort is working well and that it will continue to improve?

Have employees and managers provide specific examples, whenever possible, so they can get a clear idea of what is working and what isn't. Although this evidence is mostly anecdotal, the proof is in the pudding—that is, employees who meet deadlines and produce accurate work, managers who are satisfied with results, and customers who keep coming back for your product or service, in addition to a smooth-running working environment and pleasant interactions.

COST BENEFITS

For accountants, financial analysts, and other number-crunching types, this can be a relatively easy area to measure. Cost savings can include decreased requirements for physical plants or office space as well as outsourcing staff and eliminating the need to pay benefits and retirement if workers are part-time or independent contractors. Improved employee productivity and retention—not having to constantly train new workers—is another cost saving and becoming even more prevalent as the economy shrinks and people become more motivated to hold on to their jobs.

Cost benefits analyses involve comparing data generated for expenses (output) versus that for cost savings. Often expenses are considerably higher at startup than after the project has been going for a while—this should be factored in as well. For example, ARO estimates that setting up a telecommuter costs approximately $2,500, dropping to $500 a year for maintaining the employee.

You'll also need to factor in the cost of organizing the telecommuting effort, such as purchasing equipment, training workers, traveling for interviews and for launching the project, and so forth. In addition to salaries and any benefits, ongoing expenses may include travel, telephone, and Internet costs if they are reimbursed, insurance and liability (if applicable), as well as administrative and technical support, such as using the time of the company secretary or computer repairperson.

Other additional savings may include:

- Productivity increase: X more sales calls made, Y additional written materials published or websites launched
- Decreased sick leave
- Lowered or nonexistent costs in paying utilities

Accounting firms and outside consultants can perform in-depth cost benefits analysis. However, no matter how it's accomplished, remember that often there is a negative or null cost savings in the first or even the second year of a telecommuting effort, but "double digit positive ratios are not uncommon by the fifth year," according to author George Piskurich. When one adds in the cost of establishing a brick-and-mortar facility, there is no question regarding savings. Which is why, during times of expansion, you should seriously evaluate the feasibility of a telecommuting program rather than adding to the physical plant or opening a branch office.

MANAGER SATISFACTION

In order for the program to work efficiently and effectively, managers need to be satisfied with it as well. It may take time to adjust and overcome initial resistance to a new way of working, as discussed in earlier chapters. But once you've been managing telecommuters for a while, take some time to evaluate whether you think the telecommuting program is working and why. Are workers meeting their goals and mileposts? Are communications smooth and responses to problems quick and easily resolved? If other office workers are a part of the team, what are their attitudes towards teleworkers and how does this affect your role as a manager? Also:

- Can you easily and comfortably evaluate employee performance?
- Is there a sense of camaraderie and teamwork in the department?
- Are telecommuters more difficult to manage than office workers? If so, in what way?
- Do you feel teleworkers are harder to control?
- Does managing telecommuters involve extra work? How much and why?
- Are performance problems more difficult to handle? Do you have more or fewer performance problems with teleworkers?
- Are teleworkers more or less productive?

Answering these and any other questions related to communication, productivity, and employee attitudes, both yours and team members', will help provide insight into the success of the overall effort.

CUSTOMER SATISFACTION

This can be a difficult and evasive area to evaluate. For one thing, some companies don't necessarily want their customers to know they're utilizing telecommuters. It should make no difference whether the person answering the customer service inquiry or investigating the insurance claim is working from the corporate office or a thousand miles away in Hawaii. However, there are indirect ways of finding out whether the telecommuting effort is benefiting your customers.

Raw data. Is your customer base growing? Are you getting plenty of positive feedback or more complaints? Do things seem to be running more (or less) smoothly since you've instituted telecommuters?

Surveys. These can be done over the telephone, via the Internet with an interactive website or by sending e-mails, or the old-fashioned way with paper and snail mail. Questions can revolve around the quality and ease of interactions and communications, as well as the responsiveness of the individual and resolution of the problem or question. A rating scale from one to ten can be used or they can check yes or no answers. Surveys should be short and sometimes have an incentive attached, such as a coupon or discount to encourage customers to respond.

Focus groups. Here a group is asked about their attitude toward a product, service, idea, or packaging. Focus groups are effective in evaluating services or testing new ideas. Because they generally involve a smaller number of people and take a longer amount of time, from a couple of hours to several days, to evaluate, you can get in-depth information and insights not normally obtained from the other customer service inquiry methods. However, if numbers are what you're looking for, you may not get the scope of response that you need.

Measuring customer satisfaction can be subjective, so evaluate it in conjunction with other factors, such as profit and loss, productivity, and so forth.

WHEN PROGRAMS FAIL

According to a 2004 study by Gartner, a technology research and advisory company based in Stamford, CT, an estimated 20 percent of employees who volunteer for telecommuting want to go back to the office within six months of working at home.

Programs can fail for a number of reasons. "Sometimes telework ceases to make sense in a particular environment," Bob Fortier, president of InnoVisions Canada, told Techrepublic.com. "Perhaps a new project requires intense on-site participation. Or there is a decline in the quality or quantity of an employee's work. Or it could be because the telework arrangement had a negative impact on others in the work unit."

Other factors contributing to failure may include:

1. **Lack of quality face time where a high level of interaction is needed.** As discussed in the early chapters of this book, certain types of jobs and work situations lend themselves to telecommuting; others do not.
2. **The need for the worker's actual physical presence in getting the job done.** Again, this depends upon the situation; if a high level of coordination and communication is required, working from a distance may be counterproductive.
3. **Loss of creativity.** Some jobs, such as advertising campaigns, require frequent brainstorming sessions where team members meet constantly and bounce ideas off each other.
4. **Disconnection between expectations and reality.** As mentioned in Chapters 12 and 13, once workers begin telecommuting, they may find it not quite the idyll or ideal they expected; hence the 20 percent dropout rate.
5. **Personality mismatch.** The company hired the wrong type of person without considering the telecommuting personality. Blanket hiring of in-house employees for telecommuting jobs can be a mistake. At the very least, the employees should be trained, evaluated, and monitored regarding their ability to handle distance work.

The First Six Months: Toughing It Out

You've worked hard to set up the telecommuting program, and believe it will be cost effective and increase the quality of workers' lives and productivity. It is in the early stages though, and employees are coming to you with complaints about family interruptions and inability to get started and stay focused. Also, they miss their coworkers.

What to do? Adjusting to nontraditional office life can be difficult if you're accustomed to being around others all the time, but certain steps can ease the transition.

If they're physically nearby, allow employees to come into the office for one or two days a week. This will fill their need to be around others in the office and provide valuable face-to-face time. Additionally it may help office workers see that telecommuting is more difficult than it appears and will help forestall resentment and jealousy.

Encourage the employees to join a local professional association where they can meet regularly with their peers. This will keep them abreast of the latest developments and encourage creativity.

Suggest that they add a favorite sport or hobby to their weekly agenda. Again, this gets them get out of the house on a regular basis.

Provide as much support as possible. This can range from tech support in helping them fine-tune their computer system to meet the needs of the job, to administrative assistance in sending out letters and other correspondence. Sometimes just listening to workers' concerns and letting them vent their frustrations helps as well.

The period of adjustment generally lasts between six and twelve months, but if that has passed and things don't seem to be improving, it's time to re-evaluate whether telecommuting is right for the department or jobs.

Here are some steps to make sure programs succeed.

If feasible, rather than making telecommuting a reward, make it mandatory for a specific job classification. Except for management and tech support, all jobs at ARO are telecommuters.

When deciding whether to telecommute, determine how much informal telecommuting already exists. Companies increasingly let employees work at home on certain days and under certain conditions. You may be farther along in instituting a telecommuting policy than you realize.

Look at work processes to see how much technology is being used. If you rely heavily on e-mail, web, and phone conferencing as well as asynchronous methods of communication, rather than constant face-to-face interaction and meetings, the odds for successful telecommuting may indeed be good.

There is also an increasing trend toward remote management. More and more companies and workers find themselves reporting to a boss who is geographically distant, "whether employees are telecommuting or not," observes author Lin Grensing-Pophal. Thus, "managers in general will need the same skill set and style found in managers of telecommuters." In such cases, if it works well with the requirements of the job, it is only a step further to remove employees from the office into a home-based environment.

SUMMARY

Properly implemented telecommuting programs can succeed. However, a number of factors come into play, including how well telecommuting meshes with corporate goals and whether or not it increases productivity and the company's bottom line.

However, some telecommuting efforts fail, either because the workers are ill equipped to cope with the pressures or the jobs are unsuitable, or both. You can take certain steps to forestall these difficulties, such as giving the workers support and time to adjust to the change and making sure that your organization is compatible with telework.

Allowing the program several months to settle and using fine-tuning procedures, as well as being flexible and responsive, can help smooth over the bumps. It may take a while, but if the telecommuting fit between workers and jobs has a solid basis, efforts generally pay off.

The next chapter will discuss trends in telecommuting and how you can grow your telecommuting footprint while reducing the carbon footprint.

CHAPTER 18

Growing Your Telecommuting Footprint

INTRODUCTION

As with any type of forecasting, predicting the future of telecommuting is chancy at best. It is possible to discern trends and make educated estimates as to what might be happening in the telecommuting landscape over the next several years. We'll discuss five major trends affecting the workplace, as well as areas of growth and expansion. Additionally, information on innovations affecting virtual teams and remote work will also be included.

EXPANDING AND DEVELOPING YOUR NETWORK

The Bureau of Labor Statistics report reveals that the likelihood of people working at home varies greatly based on the industry. For example, 30 percent of those employed in management, professional, and related occupations regularly conduct work at home. Almost two-thirds of those who usually work at home are employed in these fields. Twenty percent of sales workers report usually working at home. Conversely, only about 3 percent of those employed in production, transportation, and material moving reported working at home. One-third of people who reported usually working at home are self employed. The percentage of men and women who work at home is nearly equal while those who are married, who have children, or who are college graduates are more likely to work at home than their counterparts.

As individuals and companies struggle to reduce their carbon footprint and gas prices continue to rise, these figures will likely continue to increase. Market forecasters, such as the Yankee Group, Gartner, and Nielson's, estimated the total number of U.S. telecommuters will escalate to about 50 million by 2010.

Where will these workers come from? Author Harriet Hankin, in her book *The New Workforce*, identifies five emerging trends.

1. **An increasingly aging yet active population.** Lifestyle changes and medical advances keep people alive and fit into their nineties, according to the book. Financial pressures and personal desire are also motivators. Nowhere is this more evident than at ARO, where many employees are Baby Boomers or younger retirees. This was not by design; rather, the jobs themselves fit their needs and schedules.

2. **The decline of the nuclear family and the rise of alternative households.** Today the traditional two-parent, 2.5-child family is but a slice of the work force pie, which also consists of single parents, same-sex partners, stay-at-home dads, even grandparents raising grandchildren, among many others. Companies will need to develop benefits programs, flexible schedules, and make other accommodations to meet their employees' varied requirements.

3. **A workplace that also is becoming more racially diverse and blended.** Race, ethnicity, religion, gender, sexual orientation, and nationality come into play here. Thanks to technology, virtual teams can work from anywhere, using anyone who has the proper skills. Along with obvious racial, religious, and other differences, companies need to become attuned to the disparity in cultures as they expand globally.

4. **Multiple generations working side by side.** This starts with the Silent Generation, born before 1946; and extends through Baby Boomers, born 1946–64; Gen X born 1965–late 1970s; and Gen Y (sometimes called Nexters or Millennials), born after 1980. Each generation has its own

code of values, needs, expectations, and styles of work. Savvy companies will understand these differences, using the strengths of each to achieve their goals.

5. **The understanding that it's more than a paycheck—or even a long-term commitment.** Telecommuters in particular are concerned with a work and life balance—otherwise they wouldn't be working remotely. Like their office peers, they look for management that champions trust, mutual respect, and ethical conduct.

The days of supervising employees through fear and punishment have gone the way of the gold watch for thirty years of service to a single company. According to the Bureau of Labor Statistics, the average person born during the later years of the Baby Boom held 10.5 jobs from the ages of eighteen to forty, although nearly three-fifths of the job changes occurred before age twenty-five.

These trends speak volumes about how companies need to rethink the traditional way of hiring, training, and retaining employees. Telecommuters are an increasingly large part of this picture.

VIRTUAL TEAMS OF THE FUTURE

Certain types of virtual workers are more and more in demand. Although some parts of the economy are suffering, those with skills ranging from customer service to information technology (IT) can basically work from anywhere, anytime. This trend makes it harder for smaller firms to compete in terms of salary and benefits packages.

Thus, the stage is set for telecommuting, an ideal arrangement for those with the right personality and training. Gartner, the Stamford, CT technology research and advisory company, predicts that by 2015, IT people will spend more than 80 percent of their time working collaboratively, often across ten or more virtual teams. However, many of their findings can be applied to other in-demand workers as well.

According to Gartner, six emerging rules will govern the work-place of the future:

- The quality of peers will matter
- The competition for qualified talent will be global
- The employment model will change shape
- No two people will approach work in the same way
- Talented people will move around
- Physical gaps between leaders and followers will widen

During the next five to ten years, knowledge workers in partic-ular will increasingly use a combination of global communication and personal devices as well as location-independent technologies, such as blogs and Wikis. Even today, informal social networks like interactive websites allow international groups of profession-als to exchange information and job tips. To recruit qualified team members, companies may find themselves switching from local to globally based job searches.

Gartner also predicts that, while businesses traditionally defined and supplied workers' technology and equipment, techni-cally savvy telecommuters will be purchasing and choosing their own hardware and software to collaborate and meet goals and deadlines. This suits the results-oriented culture of the telecom-muter, in which product and not process is what counts.

As technology becomes more sophisticated and interactive, various glitches and discrepancies between incompatible programs and devices will be smoothed over. An example is the former incompatibility between Windows- and Mac-based applications. Even Apple's website provides tips and information on how users of both can connect to the same networks, share common applica-tions, and exchange data and files.

Two additional trends are at the forefront, although only time will reveal their actual impact on virtual teams.

1. *Virtual worlds.* A computer-based simulated environment intended for a specific group of users, virtual worlds were originally the arena of gamers and fans of fantasy. Participants create avatars, computer-based alter egos, either a three-dimensional representation of themselves or a two-dimensional icon, such as a picture. The computer-simulated world is similar to the real one with its own laws of physics and gravity. It also features motion and sound and objects such as grass, trees, and buildings. While communication can take the form of text, VoIP technology is increasingly being used for real-time interaction.

   A 2008 report by Forrester Research discussed the use of virtual worlds by companies and governmental agencies. Organizations such as BP, IBM, Intel, and the U.S. Army have already begun to investigate what they call the "3-D Internet" as an alternative to doing business (see page 236). Although it's still very expensive and difficult to set up and implement, applications can include a virtual office in which people work physically alongside each other and the sharing of 3-D models of physical and theoretical objects.

   Through nonverbal communication and interaction, the atmosphere of a virtual world can add a dimension of reality to training and meetings. Because they communicate in a more personalized manner, team members can understand ideas and concepts more quickly. This could translate into better-quality work and stronger relationships.

2. *Telecities.* According to author and futurist Joseph N. Pelton, telecities are virtual communities "whose life, direction, and functioning are largely shaped by telecommunications. Proximity . . . will be defined by the speed and bandwidth of networks as much as geographical propinquity."

Additionally, "New York and Singapore may be closer than, say, New York and Arkadelphia, Arkansas."

This has long-range implications for telecommuters, whose access to backup data centers and distributed wireless and satellite facilities would become more important than their actual physical location. Added to this is the bonus of providing telepresence "anytime and anywhere at virtually no cost," he continues. "The speed . . . of modern transmission systems [appears] to be [a] major [driver] in this transformation, not only in the most developed countries but also around the world." Thus employees in Bangladesh could have the same professional advantage as those in Manhattan.

Telecities are also green, eliminating the use of paper and reducing pollution as well as conserving energy through the lack of office space. Workers would be paid electronically—Electronic Funds Transfer (EFT) has already become commonplace in most countries—and since employees are widely disbursed, telecities may reduce the opportunity for terrorist attacks such as on the World Trade Center.

IBM: Futurific

IBM has already begun implementing some of the innovations discussed in this chapter. These range from "on demand job aids such as collaborative online platforms that allow employees to learn from their peers to virtual tools that give them instant access to subject matter experts," states *Training* magazine.

For example, when the Chinese division added 3-D technology to its training program, the change was incorporated worldwide, throughout the 350,000-employee company. The technology enabled new hires "to meet, greet, and work together . . . in simulated online environments. Before their first day, they logged onto a virtual platform . . . replicating their physical offices" and got to know their future peers as avatars.

Another online tool, Expert Tracker, allows workers to interact with IBM and other experts, who list their available hours online as would a college professor. This helps make senior management more accessible as well as encouraging mentoring and peer-to-peer interaction. It also provides better use and control of time.

The simulated online environment is also available through personal Intranets. "When employees log on, the system not only recognizes their name and password, but job role and information needs," according to Nancy Lewis, vice-president of On-Demand Learning. Employees can get answers and best practice information anytime, anywhere, even if they are stranded in a hotel room far from the home office.

Come to think of it, IBM may not need its Armonk, New York, headquarters much longer.

SUMMARY

No one knows what the future holds, but it looks to be bright for telecommuters and by extension, their managers. You can focus on getting the best possible results from employees who are not only motivated to get the job done but are happier and more productive.

Many of the negative things about an office—the pettiness, the physical discomfort of having to work in a uniform environment, the rigid schedules, the commute—are eliminated by telecommuting. As technology evolves, many of the glitches that have occurred in the past will be resolved.

Although telecommuting is not for every job, trends and forecasts indicate that it will become more and more commonplace. So while it may not be in your immediate future, it merits at least some consideration and study since you may find yourself in a remote management position—with or without telecommuters—sooner than you might expect.

Sample Self-Evaluation FAQ for Telework

(To be given to prospective telecommuters)

Am I a good candidate to be a teleworker?
All or part of many jobs are appropriate for teleworking.

Teleworkers usually perform part of their job at their official duty station. You will need to continue to live in a location that enables you to come in to your official duty station on a regularly scheduled basis, and on an as-needed basis for meetings and other special activities.

As examples, telework is feasible for work that requires thinking and writing such as data analysis, reviewing grants or cases, writing decisions or reports. Telephone-intensive tasks—setting up a conference, obtaining information, following up on participants in a study—are also well suited to telework. Finally, computer-oriented tasks including programming, web page design, data entry, and word processing are jobs that favor telework.

Telework is not suitable for employees who need to be in the office to learn the organization, who require on-the-job training, who need close supervision, or who thrive on interaction with co-workers and would suffer from the isolation of working alone.

How should I ask permission to telework if I am a federal employee?

All federal agencies are required to identify the positions that are appropriate for teleworking, and to offer the opportunity to telework to the people in these positions.

Remember that employee participation is voluntary and subject to management approval, and that it is a management option rather than an employee benefit. You are not "entitled" to telework—there must be a clear advantage to the government for your teleworking.

Not all managers and supervisors are equally familiar with teleworking, and some have very real concerns about effectively supervising people who are teleworking. If you think your supervisor is going to be hesitant in approving your teleworking, it is up to you to do your homework thoroughly and make a comprehensive proposal to your supervisor pointing out the advantages to the organization of your teleworking, explaining what part of your job you would do at home, and on what schedule. A description of your home office setup is also important for this approval.

Some of the advantages to your agency are:

- Improves the quality of work and increases productivity. Employees concentrate on the project itself with less distraction from the office environment
- Improves morale and reduces stress by giving employees more options to balance work and family demands
- Saves hours of commuting time, which allows the employee to spend more time on projects, completing them with a higher quality of work in a timelier manner

What will have to happen before I can telework?

You will need to reach an agreement with your supervisor on a number of aspects of the telework assignment, including what part of your work will be done at home, your work schedule, how and when you will communicate with your supervisor and colleagues, and how your work will be evaluated.

You will probably be required to sign a telework agreement with your agency.

You will need to identify an appropriate work location in your home that is safe, comfortable, free from distractions, with adequate working space and access to all the resources you need to carry out your job. You don't need to devote an entire room for your office at home. Some teleworkers have successfully developed a part of an existing room, a garage, an attic, or even a closet for their workstation. Working on the couch in front of the TV is not a good idea.

It may be necessary for your agency to place government-owned computers and telecommunications equipment in your home or at other alternative worksites before you can begin your teleworking.

You may need to be trained in the use of this hardware and software, and arrangements need to be made for technical assistance and hardware maintenance.

Your agency may decide to provide you with a telephone credit card. Agencies are authorized to use government funds to install telephone lines, and necessary equipment, and to pay monthly charges in any private residence or private apartment of an employee who has been authorized to work-at-home.

Your agency may ask you to conduct a safety inspection of your telework workspace before you may start to use it for teleworking.

How can I make sure that my teleworking works for both me and my company?

Establish a routine: Once you start teleworking, you will have twenty-four-hour access to work. You may be tempted to work longer hours. However, working too much can cause stress and stress-related illness. Knowing when to stop is essential for effective performance. One way to get around overwork is to implement specific business hours. Set firm starting and stopping times, and communicate these to your manager and coworkers. At the office, there are routines that structure your time. If you work at home, it may help to establish your own routine so that you don't overwork.

Establish goals: Develop a list of goals and assignments for the days you telework. At the end of the day, go over the list and see how much you've been able to accomplish. It's helpful to start the list a couple of days before you're teleworking. This helps to plan for all the resources you'll need to support your activities at home.

Set deadlines: While teleworking, follow the same rules for deadlines as if you were in the office. If you're mailing reports to the office, send them so they arrive the day they're due or earlier. If you're sending your work electronically via a computer, it should also arrive on time.

Avoid distractions: Avoid teleworking on days when there may be friction at home, such as family quarrels or problems. If you have an elderly family member, an infant, or a toddler needing care, it will be difficult to telework and complete any work. Telework is not a substitute for childcare or eldercare.

Maintain regular communication with your manager: As a teleworker, you'll need to keep your supervisor informed about the status of the programs you are working on, your progress, and any difficulty encountered. Think of your manager as a client that needs information on a timely basis.

Be accessible: Stay in touch with the office during teleworking days. Set up a system (mobile telephone, voice mail, e-mail, answering machine, or pager) so that you can be reached easily.

To be a successful teleworker, you should be an organized, disciplined, and conscientious self-starter who requires minimal supervision.

Your teleworking should not adversely affect either your own performance or that of your coworkers. Thus, if your job involves frequent interaction with your coworkers or customers, you will be expected to be available at the same times as when you were in the work office for this interaction via email or the telephone.

Although telework will give some employees more time for their family responsibilities, you may not use duty time for providing dependent care or any purpose other than official duties.

You must have a safe and adequate place to work off-site that is free from interruptions and that provides the necessary level of security and protection for government property. If this is not available in your home, you may still be able to telework in a telework center.

Sample Work Agreement/Contracts

FOR A COMPANY/CORPORATION:

Certification by Customer Service Representative of Company X

Comes now _____ *[name of Customer Service Representative],* who is a Customer Service Representative of Company X and who will be handling calls for the _____, and certifies the following:

1. I have never been convicted of a felony. I have never been charged with any crime involving theft, identity theft, or embezzlement.
2. I will protect the confidentiality of all _____ information on the _____ System, including, but not limited to, Personal Health Information ("PHI"), Social Security numbers, names, addresses, phone numbers, salary information and hours of work, by refraining from disclosing the information, in any way to any unauthorized person.
3. I will protect the confidentiality of all Employer information on the _____ System, including, but not limited to, the number of hours for which contributions were made, the amount of contributions made, addresses,

phone numbers, and the location and types of projects being worked, by refraining from disclosing the information in any way to any unauthorized person.

4. I will maintain my computer terminal in a dedicated home office, with an office door separating it from the other rooms in my home. I will keep the office door shut at all times when I am taking calls concerning the _____ or accessing the _____ System and when I am not on the premises.

5. If any other adult is within hearing distance when I am taking a call, I will take whatever steps are necessary to prevent them from overhearing confidential information, including, but not limited to, lowering the volume of my voice, asking the other adult to leave the room, or refraining from stating a name, Social Security number, health status, or any other confidential information.

6. I will not print or e-mail any information from _____ _____ System or allow anyone else to do so.

7. I will not download or copy any information from _____ _____System to my computer or to any other computer or hand-held device.

8. I will not damage or destroy any information on _____ _____ System or allow anyone else to do so.

9. I will not alter, damage, or destroy any programming codes on _____ System; take an action to change, damage or disrupt the functionality of _____ System or allow anyone else to do so.

10. I will use passwords to access the _____ System; and will not disclose the password to any unauthorized person or post the password on my workstation or anywhere else easily observed.

11. I will log off of the _____ System at the end of each work period and any time I leave the premises at which the computer is located.

12. I will not access the _____ System via a hand-held device or via a laptop that has been taken out of my dedicated home office.

13. I will not access the _____ System if unauthorized individuals may see what is on my computer's screen.

14. I will maintain updated protection against malicious software.

15. I will promptly report to COMPANY X any breach of or failure to follow any of the above requirements. I will promptly file a written report with COMPANY X if any information is disclosed in any way to any unauthorized person.

Dated this _____ day of _____ 20____.

_____
Signature

_____
Print Name

Courtesy of ARO. Used with permission.

FOR A GOVERNMENTAL AGENCY:

U.S. Department of Education Flexiplace Work Agreement

The following constitutes an agreement between:

_____ and _____
Principal Office   Employee Name

of the terms and conditions of the Flexiplace Program. The supervisor and employee agree:

The Type of Flexiplace Schedule is: Fixed _____ As Needed _____

1. To adhere to the applicable guidelines, policies, and procedures of the Flexiplace program.
2. To develop and/or amend performance agreements as needed for work performed away from the official duty station. The employee will meet with the supervisor to receive assignments and to review completed work as necessary or appropriate. The employee will complete all assigned work according to work procedures mutually agreed upon by the employee and the supervisor in the employee's performance plan.
3. The employee's official duty station is not changed by participation in Flexiplace. All pay, leave, and travel entitlements will be based on the employee's official duty station.
4. Where applicable, the employee will complete a new alternative work schedule that incorporates the days and times at the alternative work site consistent with the Collective Bargaining Agreement.
5. Requests for leave should be made in accordance with applicable law, OPM regulations, Department policy, and, where applicable, the Collective Bargaining Agreement.

6. The employee will continue to work in pay status while working at his/her alternate worksite. If the employee works overtime that has been approved in advance, he/she will be compensated in accordance with applicable law, OPM regulation, Department policy, and, where applicable, the Collective Bargaining Agreement. The employee understands that the Department is not required to compensate unapproved overtime work.

7. The employee must ensure a safe and healthy work environment and will sign a self-certification checklist that proclaims the alternative work site free of work-related safety and health hazards. Management may deny or rescind a Flexiplace agreement based on safety problems in the home. Provided the employee is given 48 hours advance notice and management has reasonable cause to believe that a hazardous work environment exists, management may have the home office inspected for compliance with safety requirements.

8. The employee is covered under Federal Employees' Compensation Act if injured in the course of performing official duties at the alternate duty station.

9. If the employee borrows government equipment and/or software, the employee will protect the government equipment and/or software in accordance with the applicable procedures. Government-owned equipment will be installed, serviced, and maintained by the government. Government-owned software and data files will be checked for viruses. Government-supplied equipment shall be returned immediately upon request and the employee has no expectation of privacy therein. If the employee provides his/her own equipment, the employee may be responsible for installing, servicing, and maintaining it. However, the government will provide virus-checking software.

10. The government will not be liable for damages to an employee's personal or real property during the course of performance of official duties or while using government equipment in the employee's residence, except to the extent the government may be held liable

by claims arising under the Federal Tort Claims Act or the Military Personnel and Civilian Employees Claims Act.

11. The government will not be responsible for operating costs, home maintenance, or any other incidental cost (e.g., utilities) associated with the use of the employee's residence. By participating in this program the employee does not relinquish any entitlement to reimbursement for authorized expenses incurred while conducting business for the government, as provided for by statute and implementing regulations.

12. The employee will apply approved safeguards to protect government or agency records from unauthorized disclosure or damage and will comply with Privacy Act requirements set forth in the Privacy Act of 1974, Public Law 93-579, codified at Section 552a, title 5 USC, and specific Agency confidentiality requirements.

13. Standards of conduct (34 CFR Part 73) continue to apply to employees working at alternate work sites.

14. For purposes of the Flexiplace program and provided the employee is given at least 48 hours advance notice, management may inspect the employee's home worksite at periodic intervals during the employee's normal working hours. An employee may request that a Union representative accompany management on an alternate worksite visit.

15. The employee agrees to limit performance of officially assigned duties to his/her official duty station, Agency-approved alternate duty stations, or other locations approved by the supervisor. Failure to comply with this provision may result in loss of pay, termination from the Flexiplace program, and/or other appropriate disciplinary action.

16. The employee, after two weeks notice or less if agreed to by the supervisor, may terminate participation in the Flexiplace program. After two weeks notice, management has the right to remove the employee from the program for legitimate management reasons including, but not limited to: the employee's performance; changes in organizational needs that require the employee's presence; or adherence to Flexiplace procedures contained herein.

17. At intervals specified in the Flexiplace program guidelines, the supervisor and the employee will complete surveys to evaluate the Flexiplace program.

Approving Official	Date

Supervisor	Date

Employee	Date

Agency Flexiplace Coordinator	Date Reviewed

Employee's Alternative Workplace Address and Phone Number:

_____

_____

_____

Flexiplace Coordinator will maintain original and provide copies within five (5) workdays to the following:

    Participating Supervisor
    Participating Employee
    Human Resources Group
    Principal Office, Executive Officer
    Principal Office, Labor Management Partnership Council

Home Office Inspection and Safety Guidelines

The following information is provided to assist you in conducting your inspection. It has been provided as a guide to familiarize you with many of the hazards that can be found in a home/office work environment. If you suspect that something is hazardous, but are not sure, you can contact your Agency/Regional Safety and Health Manager for assistance. It is recommended that you maintain this guide as a reference source.

Working or Walking Surfaces: Surfaces should be level and free of tripping, bumping, or slipping hazards. Things to look for include: torn carpet, electrical or telephone cords in walkways, partition support brackets, waste baskets, file cabinets with drawers that open into aisles, bookcase doors that open into aisles, misaligned furniture, temporary or permanent storage that narrows or obstructs aisles, doors that open into aisles or narrow halls, etc.

Electrical Safety: There are numerous safety considerations involved in the use of electrically powered equipment and appliances. These center around three hazards: shock, burns, and fire.

Grounding: Generally most homes/buildings are provided with three-wire grounded electrical outlets. These must be checked for correct wiring and adequacy of grounds by the owner and/or appropriate electrical inspectors. You should look for cracked or broken outlets, missing covers with exposed wiring, or signs of arcing or burns around the outlet. Another consideration is excess heat. Feel wall switches and surfaces around outlets. If surfaces feel hot, have them checked by an appropriate authority.

The subject of grounding for office-type equipment is difficult to cover in this amount of space. As a general rule, if an appliance comes from the manufacturer with a three-prong plug, it should be internally grounded. The ground pin should not be broken off nor should the device be used ungrounded via an adapter or extension cord. Large appliances such as refrigerators, computers, copiers, etc., as well as heating devices such as coffee pots, hot plates, etc., should also be grounded. If you have any doubt about a particular device, contact your Agency/Regional Safety and Health Manager.

Electrical Cords: Appliance and equipment cords should be checked on a regular basis for proper connection to the device, frayed or damaged insulation, defective plugs, and exposed wires. The use of extension cords in the workplace should be limited and closely controlled. Before using extension cords, attempts should be made to rearrange furniture or add additional electrical outlets.

Extension cords are to be used only on a temporary basis. When they are used, they should be of the same or larger wire size as the cord being extended and have a compatible connector plug. Adapters must not be used to connect the device to an extension cord.

CAUTION: Extension cords must never be draped over furniture, partitions, equipment, etc.; extended across aisles or walkways; nor extended through doors, walls, ceilings, etc.; and never located under carpeting.

Electrical Outlets: A major cause of fire is overloaded electrical circuits. This usually occurs through the use of multiple outlet adaptors or extension cords with a multiple outlet connector. Limit the number of devices connected to any outlet to the number of receptacles provided by the outlet. If additional outlets are needed, they should be properly installed by a qualified electrician.

Electrical Equipment: Most inspections on electrical equipment require some special training and testing equipment. You can, however, determine if it is properly connected with a cord in good condition, that the device is not generating excessive heat, and that it is operating as intended. After looking it over, ask someone about the equipment. Does it function properly? Does it ever give you a mild electrical shock, etc.?

Fire Protection & Suppression: Fire protection and suppression take many forms. Some of the most common are: fire extinguishers; alarm systems; fire hoses and standpipe systems; smoke detectors; sprinkler systems; and heat detectors. Where they exist, they must be in proper working order at all times to better ensure safety.

Fire Alarm Systems: Generally speaking, homes or buildings above one story in height have or are expected to have some type of approved fire alarm/notification system. There are many different types of systems, from very simple to very complex. A basic system, one that can be found in quite a few of the buildings in which people work, is comprised of an annunciator panel, which identifies locations of wall-mounted pull stations and indicates if the system is working properly or if the alarm has been activated.

There are many different ways a fire alarm system can be activated. Some of the most common are through the use of a pull station or via a smoke or heat detector. All employees should know how to activate the fire alarm system that protects the homes and buildings where they work.

Fire alarm system questions that should be asked periodically include:

- Is the system working properly?
- Are the activation devices easily identifiable?
- Can the alarm be heard and/or seen by all of the building's occupants?
- Is the alarm tested and inspected regularly?
- Does the alarm notify the local fire and/or police department or a local alarm-monitoring company?

- Are all of the building's occupants familiar with how the system works and sounds?
- Is there a sufficient number of activation devices?
- Do the activation devices work properly?

Fire Extinguishers: There should be enough of the proper type of fire extinguisher. Extinguishers should be permanently mounted in an accessible location. If the view of an extinguisher is obstructed by partitions, furniture, corners, etc., then a directional arrow fire extinguisher location sign or some kind of marking is needed. The access to a fire extinguisher should never be blocked, even temporarily. The distance to reach an extinguisher should not exceed 75 feet.

All fire extinguishers should be checked regularly and inspected at least annually. They must have a tag attached showing the inspection date. Fire extinguishers must be hydrostatically tested every five to twelve years. Look for a metal tag or decal showing the last test date.

If the extinguisher has a gauge, check to see that it is full. Examine the fire extinguisher's hose and discharge nozzle for damage. Also check to see that the handle locking pin, or wire, is intact. If not, the extinguisher could have been used and now has to be refilled.

If the extinguisher has any damage, especially surface damage such as dents, or has been discharged or tampered with, it must be re-inspected by a qualified person.

Sprinkler Systems: Some facilities have automatic sprinkler protection. If your alternate work area has this, check to see that the sprinkler heads have not been painted. Paint can clog the sprinkler head and prevent it from operating properly. Storage under and around sprinkler heads should be limited to no closer than 18 inches in any direction to allow ample clearance for the water spray. Do not permit anything to be attached to or suspended from a sprinkler head. Ideally, the sprinkler system should be tied into the building's fire alarm system so that when a sprinkler head is activated, the proper authorities are notified immediately.

Fire Prevention: For the most part, the materials used in constructing and outfitting most buildings have a varying degree of fire resistiveness. That is, they have predetermined flame and smoke spread characteristics. It does not mean they are fireproof. Furniture, drapes, books, paper, and chemicals are typical examples. The amount of flammable or combustible material in your work area should always be held to a minimum. Look for excessive amounts of paper products, unused furniture, etc., and attempt to dispose of them.

Storage: The storing of any item on top of tall furniture or cabinets should be avoided. To permit this practice sets the stage for many types of injuries. Employees attempting to place things on top of furniture or cabinets can strain themselves. They can fall if chairs are used in place of ladders or even if ladders are used incorrectly. The items themselves can fall, striking employees. It is best to limit storage to designated storage rooms or areas. Properly arranged, such rooms will have secured shelves, adequate aisles, proper lighting, and will be maintained in a state of good housekeeping.

A good practice is to limit storage height to maintain a minimum of 18 inches clearance from the ceiling in general, and from light fixtures and other electrical equipment in particular. If sprinkler protection is provided in the work or storage room, maintain as much clearance between stored items and the sprinkler head as possible; again 18 inches is a good minimum clearance. Check to see that heavy items are stored on lower shelves. Have a ladder or approved step stool available so you can safely reach high places within the work or storage area.

Office Practices: Certain office practices can be hazardous. File cabinets can cause accidents in many ways. If located near entrance doors or aisles, drawers left open can become a bump or trip hazard. If the upper drawers are fully used while the lower drawers are nearly empty, the cabinet can tip over when the upper drawers are pulled out. A good rule to implement: Never open more than one file drawer at a time. Always close drawers when leaving the file cabinet—even for a brief period.

Sharp implements such as scissors, razor blades, or letter openers should always be put away after use and never left on top of file cabinets or other locations where they can fall. Razor blades, or similar extremely sharp instruments should, always be stored with a cover or holder so that the blade is not exposed. They should be stored in a properly marked central location. Chairs and other office furnishings should be checked for structural integrity and defective items disposed of promptly. If any equipment is determined to be defective, it should be clearly marked "DANGER" and "DO NOT USE" until it is disposed of properly.

Fans: If used, fans must be fully guarded so that there is no opening near the blade greater than half an inch in any direction. The only exception is if the fan is installed seven feet or more above the floor or working surface. Metal-framed electric fans should be grounded. Care must be taken to ensure that a fan's electrical cord does not become a tripping hazard.

Heaters: Portable heaters in the work area are authorized only for medical reasons, with a doctor's certification, and if applicable, with the permission of the Department. When such heaters are authorized, be sure that the heating element is guarded against accidental contact, positioned a safe distance from furniture or other combustibles, and that a tip-over switch cuts off electrical power to the heating element if the heater is knocked over. This feature could prevent the heater from starting a fire. Kerosene heaters in the work area are not permitted.

Coffee Pots or Similar Items: Use of coffee pots and similar items in the immediate work area must have a "use permit" that is available for inspection. They should be placed out of normal walk areas and on a noncombustible surface. Never place such a device in a storeroom, closet, or other location where it cannot be observed. If the device is in a location where it cannot be observed, it could smolder, start a fire, and spread beyond control before being detected. Should an electrical short circuit occur, quick action is necessary to prevent a fire. Be sure that all of these types of electrical equipment are turned off at the end of the day. Immersion-type water heaters for coffee or tea cups are prohibited in department-approved workspaces.

Radiators: Some older homes and buildings use radiators for heat instead of the more modern forced air systems. If your work area has radiators, be sure not to place combustible or flammable articles on or near them. Also check to ensure that electrical power cords are not allowed to drape across them.

Video Display Terminals: Video Display Terminals (VDTs) are word processors or computer terminals that display information on a television screen. Safe use of VDTs can prevent employee injury. Because of the expanding use of VDTs, concerns have been expressed about their potential health effects. Complaints include excessive fatigue, eye strain and irritation, blurred vision, headaches, stress and neck, back, arm, and muscle pain. Other concerns include physical discomfort, cumulative trauma disorders, and potential exposure to radiation.

Visual symptoms can result from improper lighting, glare, distance from the screen, positioning of the screen, or copy material that is difficult to read. VDT operators can reduce eyestrain by temporarily looking away from the VDT, doing eye exercises, switching to other work, or adjusting the brightness of the VDT screen.

VDT operators are subject to the risk of developing various musculoskeletal and nerve disorders, such as cumulative or repetitive motion disorders. Carpal Tunnel Syndrome (CTS), a cumulative trauma disorder, is caused by repetitive wrist-hand movement and exertion. When irritated, the tendons and their sheaths housed inside the carpal tunnel swell and press against the nearby median nerve. The pressure causes tingling, numbness, or severe pain in the wrist and hand. CTS can be reduced by stopping or limiting

VDT activity, by maintaining proper posture, or as a last resort, surgery.

Another issue of concern for the VDT operator is whether the emission of radiation, such as x-ray or electromagnetic fields in low-frequency ranges, poses a health risk. Currently, there is no conclusive evidence that the low levels of radiation emitted from VDTs pose a health risk to VDT operators.

In the office environment, the workstation consists primarily of a work surface of some type, a chair, VDT equipment, and other related items. At home, as well as in the office, an employee must have adequate workspace to perform each of the tasks required by the job. Individual body size must be considered and will influence the design of the chair, the height of the work surface, and access to various elements of the workstation, including the video display section. A height-adjustable work surface is an advantage. In general, a good VDT work surface will provide as many adjustable features as possible.

Ergonomics Guidelines and Information

HISTORY OF ERGONOMICS

As a formal field of study, ergonomics began during World War II. During this time, scientists and engineers began to consciously study how to improve the design of military equipment, in particular, aircraft, from the human point of view.

In Great Britain, these classically trained scientists coined the term "ergonomics" for this application. The term is taken from Greek roots: *Ergon* for "work" and *nomos* for "rules." Literally, the term means "the rules of work."

To this day, more ergonomics studies have been performed on the aircraft cockpit than on any other single workstation. Indeed, the aerospace industry is the source of much of the data and concepts that are now being applied in the workplace.

Physical Versus Cognitive Ergonomics

There are two major divisions in the field of ergonomics. The first is physical, that is, on physical things like working position, reaches, chairs, and furniture.

The other area is cognitive, which has to do with how we perceive information and react to various types of signals. For example, a tremendous amount of work has gone into Human-Computer Interface (HCI), which focuses on designing the operation of computers to be more user friendly. The prime example is using a mouse to click on an icon, rather than the old way of memorizing commands that you had to type (very precisely) onto a blank screen.

LIGHTING

Technically, the correct term is "illumination," which is the amount of light falling on a surface and is usually the variable that is measured in an office environment. Illumination is measured with a light meter, a pocket-sized device that is inexpensive and easy to use. The readout is in lux (metric system) or footcandles. The guidelines for lighting are:

Reading and desk work: 50–80 footcandles or 400–550 lux
Computer work: 20–40 footcandles or 50–400 lux

You can see from the standard that the lighting requirements for computers are considerably more dim from those for reading or writing with paper. If you regularly spend six or more hours at a time at your home office, then proper lighting can increase productivity and accuracy, while minimizing fatigue and eye strain. Poor office lighting can cause eye irritation, eye strain, headaches, and a decrease in your eye's ability to focus. It can also cause you to lean forward when reading, resulting in neck and back strain.

The eye can adapt to a very wide range of light levels, but it can only adapt to one light level at one time. When one looks at a bright computer monitor on a dark background the eye doesn't know whether to adapt to the bright monitor or the dark background. When this happens hour after hour, day after day, fatigue sets in. The same thing can happen when looking at a brightly lit sheet of white paper in a dark room.

Lighting the home office

In most homes, the type and level of lighting provided is not suitable for office work. Office tasks, whether computer-based, paper-based, or a combination, require different lighting than most other areas of the home. The most common lighting problems include glare that reflects off your computer monitor into your eyes and inadequate task lighting. To eliminate these problems, you need to control and balance two different types of lighting in your office:

- Ambient lighting
- Task lighting

Ambient lighting is general room illumination. It's a combination of natural light and artificial light. Natural light typically comes in through windows. Artificial lighting originates from interior lights, such as ceiling fixtures, track lighting, fluorescent lights, or floor lamps.

Task lighting provides direct illumination for activities such as reading or writing. It illuminates your keyboard or other areas on your desk without reflecting any glaring light onto the computer screen.

To work comfortably, you need to control and balance both ambient and task lighting in your office. You need to tailor the lighting levels for the types of tasks you do.

To improve the lighting in your home office, you can:

- Use adjustable desk lamps to provide task lighting for reading and writing.
- Use floor lamps or light fixtures with globes to provide ambient lighting. Avoid using light fixtures with exposed bulbs because they can increase glare.
- Dim or turn off the ceiling lighting if you often use a computer. Consider installing a dimmer switch that will allow you to tailor your ambient office lighting levels.
- Replace incandescent light bulbs with fluorescent bulbs that screw into regular light bulb sockets. They last up to thirteen times longer than regular bulbs, use less electricity, and provide even lighting with less glare.

- Use curtains, shades, or blinds on windows to control the amount of natural light in your office.

ADJUSTING YOUR OFFICE CHAIR

It's extremely important to have an adjustable chair, particularly if you sit for long periods of time. Many chairs allow you to adjust your chair height, backrest, lower back support, and armrests.

How you adjust your chair depends upon the type of work you do. The following discusses how to adjust your chair to work comfortably while using a computer and standard keyboard.

Chair height

If you have a height-adjustable keyboard tray:

1. Adjust your chair height so that your feet are flat on the floor and there isn't too much pressure on your seat bones or behind your knees.
2. Adjust the height of your keyboard tray to a position where your wrists are in the same plane as your forearms and your elbows are hanging naturally at your sides. Keep in mind that your elbows do not necessarily need to be at right angles. You can slant your keyboard upward or downward.

If you do NOT have a height-adjustable keyboard tray:

1. Adjust your chair height so that you are working at about elbow height. Be sure that your wrists are in the same plane as your forearms.
2. If your feet do not reach the floor, use a footrest. The footrest should be high enough to support your feet solidly with no pressure behind your knees. One way to check this is that you should be able to slide two or three fingers between the seat cushion edge and the back of your knees.

3. If your feet touch the ground, but your knees are raised from the front of your chair, there may be too much pressure on your seat bones. If you have an adjustable desk, you can raise the work surface.

Otherwise, raise the keyboard by purchasing an adjustable keyboard tray or purchase a taller desk.

Backrest

Angle: Try tilting the back of your chair all the way back, then all the way forward. You can use this adjustment to change your angle throughout the day. It helps you to keep moving so you are not sitting in one static position for a long period of time. For example, you can use this adjustment to lean back in your chair while reading or forward while writing.

Forward and Backward Position

In some chairs, you can change the forward and backward position of the backrest. This feature provides lumbar support if you work sitting in a forward position most of the time. The adjustment is often made with a knob that is under the chair. You may need to get on your hands and knees to find it. Often it is a very simple mechanism: You just loosen the knob, push the backrest in whichever direction you want, and tighten the knob again.

To adjust your backrest for use with a computer keyboard:

1. Be sure that the back of your knees do not come in direct contact with the front edge of the chair seat. There should be two to three inches between the edge of the seat and the back of your knee.
2. If your knee is hitting the edge of the chair, adjust the back of your chair forward. If your chair is not adjustable, consider buying an adjustable chair.

Height

Some chairs allow you to adjust the height of the backrest. The purpose of this adjustment is to change the height of the lumbar support so that it fits the small of your back. If you are tall, you would raise the lumbar support, and if you're not very tall, you would lower it. Your goal is to fill the arch in your lower back, so that you keep the S-curve.

Often, the knob for this adjustment is on the back of the backrest itself and you may need to stand up to change it. Typically you loosen the knob by turning it counterclockwise, change the backrest height, and then tighten the knob again. If you have this type of knob, you may need to stand up and change it a few times to get it right.

If your chair doesn't have built-in support, you can use a rolled towel or lumbar pad to support your lower back.

Armrests

Adjust the armrests so that your elbows and lower arms rest lightly on them. This helps eliminate shoulder strain. Usually, your armrests should be at the same height as your keyboard.

If your chair has fixed armrests that are too low, wrap some padding around them. If the armrests are fixed and too high, you may be able to remove them or consider purchasing another chair.

Seatpan

An adjustable seatpan is helpful when you alternate between working in a forward position and leaning back in your chair. In many cases, the seatpan adjustment is interconnected with the adjustment of the angle of the backrest. When you tilt the backrest forward, it also tilts the seatpan forward, so that you keep the proper orientation of your upper body in relation to your thighs.

You can use this adjustment to change your position throughout the day. It helps you to keep moving so you are not sitting in one static position for a long period of time.

ADJUSTING YOUR WORKSPACE WITHOUT AN ADJUSTABLE CHAIR

If you spend even a few hours a week working in your home office, you should consider purchasing an adjustable chair. An adjustable chair allows you to work more comfortably. Sitting with your body in alignment and changing positions stimulates blood circulation, improves health, and helps prevent stress and strain on your body.

With an adjustable chair, you can:

Maintain good posture while you work.
Easily move and change positions.

However, if you don't have an adjustable chair, here are some tips to help you work more comfortably:

- Maintain proper wrist alignment by adjusting your keyboard up or down. Be sure your wrists are in the same plane as your forearms.
- If your chair does not have a padded seat, you may want to purchase a chair cushion.
- If your chair has fixed armrests that are too low, wrap some padding around them. If the armrests are fixed and too high, you may be able to remove them.
- If your chair doesn't have built-in back support, use a rolled towel or lumbar pad to support your lower back.
- If your feet do not reach the floor, use a footrest. The footrest should be high enough to support your feet solidly with no pressure behind the knee. You should be able to slide two or three fingers between the edge of the chair and the back of your knees.
- If your feet touch the ground, but your knees are raised from the front of your chair, there may be too much pressure on your seat bones. You'll need to purchase an adjustable chair, or use a taller chair.

ERGONOMIC TIPS FOR LAPTOPS

- When in your home office, attach a separate keyboard to the laptop and use this keyboard instead of the laptop's built-in keyboard. This will allow you to raise the laptop screen to a more appropriate height.
- If you don't have access to a separate keyboard, use the laptop's keyboard following the ergonomic principles you have just learned. Be sure your elbows are level with or slightly higher than the keyboard. Be sure your wrists are in the same plane as your forearms, and your upper arms hang relaxed at your sides.
- When you look down at the screen, be careful not to bend your neck and head forward. Instead, tilt your chin down, keeping your head and neck balanced over your spine.

STRETCHING EXERCISES

Print and post these near your desk, to remind yourself to stretch regularly.

Do exercises gently and cautiously throughout the day. Fifteen seconds for each stretch is usually sufficient. Do them slowly. Repeat them several times.

- Stretch arms up, back, and down. Gently pull your fingers back and expand them out.
- Turn your head to each side. Rotate your shoulders from front to back in circular motions
- Stand up, place your hands on your buttocks, and stretch backwards.

Glossary and Definitions

Acceptable Use Policy (AUP): An organization's policy for employees and computer networks that defines and possibly restricts the nature of their use or the basis on which access privileges are granted.

Application Service Provider (ASP): A company that provides computer applications and software from a central location to other organizations for leased remote access, much as an Internet Service Provider (ISP) allows access to the Internet.

Bandwidth: Refers to the speed of transmission of information over a communications pathway, often measured in frequency (Hertz) or bits per second (bps). The lower the bandwidth, the slower the access to remote data or downloading of rich media.

Bookmark: A direct link to an often-visited site that you've saved in your Browser for easy access.

Broadband: A high bandwidth transmission pathway or service capable of supporting a wide range of frequencies (Hertz) or high-speed data as measured in bits per second (bps).

Browser (web Browser): A software application that allows the user to interact with the world wide web. Examples include Microsoft Explorer and Netscape Navigator.

Cable Modem: Refers to modems that use the cable television provider's coaxial cable link to the home or business to provide "always-on" high-speed, broadband connection to the Internet.

Client Server: A common form of distributed system in which software is split between server tasks and client tasks. A client sends requests to a server, according to some protocol, asking for information or action, and the server responds.

Coaxial Connection: A type of cable used to carry high-frequency signals. It is commonly employed by cable companies to reach your house and distribute signals throughout.

Collaborative Technologies: May include capabilities of advanced telephone services, computer networking, e-mail, and group applications to enable distributed and remote workers to share all the immediacy and benefits of the enterprise's virtualized collaborative communications environment.

Compensatory Time: Hours worked but not paid that will be used as time off later. Although this may become a part of the telecommuters' compensation procedures, any policies relating to it should be decided upon before beginning telecommuting.

Compressed Work Week: A variation on a typical work schedule in which employees work the standard number of hours in fewer than the standard number of days. For example, employees can work four ten-hour days, rather than five eight- hour days. Telecommuting may incorporate some aspects of a compressed work week.

Computer Aided Design (CAD): A computer and its related software and peripherals used to design and engineer components and products with complex graphical representations and design rules.

Computer-Based Training (CBT): The use of computers as a primary distribution method for either text or visual training.

Computer Conferencing: The use of computers for conferencing, either in "real-time" (synchronously) or through use of an electronic bulletin board within a designated time (asynchronously).

Core Time: The hours employees are expected to be at the main work location. They may, however, spend the rest of the work week elsewhere. When someone is beginning or considering telecommuting, they can spend a decreasing amount of core time in the main office to see how they adjust to working at home.

Customer Relationship Management (CRM): Enterprise-wide software applications that allow businesses to manage and track all aspects of their customer relationships.

Desktop Applications: Common computer software applications such as word processing, spreadsheets, presentations, database access, calendar, and contact manager used to support the productivity and connectivity of workers.

Desktop Scanner: A peripheral optical scanning device used to capture an image of paper documents as a graphic file to input to a computer for use with graphic packages, Optical Character Recognition (OCR), and document management applications to help enable and manage your workflow.

Desktop Suite: An integrated set of desktop software applications commonly used by an employee and including such standard functions as word processing, spreadsheet, presentation, database management, calendar, and contact manager.

Digital Subscriber Line (DSL): A technology that uses ordinary copper telephone lines to deliver high-speed information over modest distances between customer premises and a telecom provider's facilities while still carrying regular voice traffic.

Domain Name: A unique name that identifies a world wide website and becomes part of the address of a series of individual related web pages.

Download: To go online to an enterprise server or sites on the world wide web and pull down or retrieve a file from the remote location into your own computer. The opposite of Upload.

e-Commerce or Ecommerce: Electronic commerce, utilizing the Internet to conduct business and execute transactions such as online shopping and Business-to-Business (B2B) procurement.

e-Learning: Electronic learning; utilizing the Internet to learn something or take classes from a distance.

Encryption: The transformation of data into a form unreadable by anyone without a secret decryption key for the purposes of privacy and security.

Enterprise Resource Planning (ERP): Any software system designed to support and automate the business processes of medium and large businesses. This may include manufacturing, distribution, personnel, project management, payroll, and financials.

Ergonomics: The study of the design and arrangement of equipment to optimize the end user experience in comfort, health, and efficiency. As related to computer equipment, ergonomics is concerned with such factors as the physical design of the keyboard, navigation devices, display screens, and related hardware, and the manner in which people interact with these hardware devices.

Ethernet: A standard Local Area Network (LAN) connection in which data is broken into packets and transmitted to a destination without error in the presence of other data packets and traffic.

Extranet: A semi-private enterprise computer network accessible to a defined group of outside participants, usually customers or strategic partners.

Facsimile Equipment or Fax: Equipment that allows images of hard copy documents or from computer files to be sent through the switched telephone system and printed out at a remote location.

Fiber Optic Cable: A bundle of optical fibers that each uses the transmission of light to carry high volumes of data through flexible glass or plastic fibers, or wires.

File Transfer: Transmission of data files between computers over direct cable connection, a Local Area Network (LAN), or between remote computers utilizing the Internet or other connections.

Firewall: A combination of hardware and software that sits between network elements to prevent unauthorized access, enforces security policies, and limits the exposure of a computer or a network to outside attack.

Flex-time: A system that allows employees to choose their own times for starting and finishing work within a broad range of available hours or even days. For telecommuters, this applies to the hours they will work at home as well as any time spent in the office or on the road.

Graphical User Interface (GUI): A visual interface that allows users to control programs and manipulate commands in those programs by using a pointing device, such as a mouse, to navigate a graphical screen image.

Groupware: Software applications that allow multiple people to simultaneously participate in joint projects, managing document review and revision, work flow, and conferencing by sharing files and resources.

Hoteling or Hot Desking: An unassigned office that is shared by others and is equipped with a workstation and telephone. This office can be reserved by a dedicated teleworker for one or two days while performing his job.

Hot Spot or Hotspot: A geographic location supported by a Wi-Fi wireless access point.

Hub: A central device at the core of a Local Area Network (LAN) connecting computers and peripherals to each other and external resources.

Hyperlink: Alternately known as a "link" or "hot key." Usually appears different in size, color, or will initiate a transfer to another web page.

Hyper Text Markup Language (HTML): The programming language used to build most web pages and understood by all browser applications.

Hyper Text Transfer Protocol (HTTP): The underlying protocol for transmitting hypertext documents and rich media around the Internet.

Information Technology (IT): A synonym for data processing or management information systems (MIS).

Instant Messaging (IM): The ability for computer users to communicate text messages with each other instantly and conveniently. May depend on proprietary standards that can be bridged by enterprise-grade Instant Messaging systems.

Internet Service Provider (ISP): A company that charges monthly fees for providing Internet access, user account support, and perhaps specialized content. ISPs often lease their telecommunications connection from other service providers.

Job Sharing: A system whereby two or more employees share one normal work week job and the commensurate pay.

Intranet: A private computer network limited to one department, company, or organization.

Local Access Architecture (LAA): The capability of telecom providers to connect teleworkers and various local facilities in a direct fashion staying on the provider's network, bypassing the public Internet for performance and security considerations.

Local Area Network (LAN): A short-distance data communications network used to link computers and peripheral devices under some form of standard control and protocol such as Ethernet.

Mobile Wireless Access: The ability to roam with Personal Computers (PCs) and Personal Digital Assistants (PDAs) around the enterprise or in a Wide Area Network (WAN) via data transmission over radio frequencies.

Network: A system for connecting various, usually computer-related, devices such as desktop computers, servers, hubs, routers, and peripherals.

Network Administrator: An employee whose main responsibility is the configuration, maintenance, security, and evolution of enterprise network systems, as well as possibly providing assistance directly to end users.

Operating System (OS): An operating system is the program that, after being initially loaded into the computer by a boot program, manages all the other programs in a computer, such as Microsoft Windows, Mac OS, Linux/Unix, etc.

Optical Character Recognition (OCR): A software application designed to identify written words and convert them into text via an optical scanner or from existing graphic images of documents.

Paging: To send a number or brief text message to display on a beeper or personal receiver.

Parallel Port: A computer connector for sending low speed to a printer or attaching various input or mass storage devices.

Peer-to-Peer (P2P): Peer-to-peer is a communications model in which each party has the same capabilities and either party can initiate a communication session.

Personal Communication Services (PCS): A form of cellular telephony at different radio frequencies licensed to increase competition for mobile voice and data services.

Personal Computer (PC): A computer for one person's use, as opposed to mainframes and mini-computers, usually in a desktop or laptop form.

Personal Digital Assistant (PDA): A small portable computer usually held in the hand and used to keep track of notes, phone numbers, addresses, appointments, etc. Often used with a stylus and handwriting recognition and synchronized by docking in a cradle attached to a PC. May also have a miniature keyboard, wireless connectivity, slots for expansion cards, an embedded camera, and various other functions and ports.

Point-to-Point Protocol (PPP): A standard Internet protocol for interconnecting computers and remote equipment and allowing the transport of IP packets over a simple link.

Public Utility Commission (PUC): Each state has a regulatory body with oversight of various aspects of the regional utility industry including many aspects of telecommunications deployment, management, and pricing.

Random Access Memory (RAM): The primary memory and temporary data storage area in a computer in which data can be accessed in any order or at random.

Remote Work (Telework) Centers: Smaller, corporate-owned facilities located away from the main office, usually in a suburb. Depending upon the company's requirements, workers may be expected to be there during the entire week or part-time, working at home the rest of the hours. Telework centers are especially practical in foreign countries where living space is limited or cramped. (See Satellite Officing.)

Return on Investment (ROI): The internal accounting calculation about the long-term payback or value of making any specific investment in capital equipment, facilities, or human resources.

Rich Media: An Internet advertising term for a web page ad that uses advanced technology such as streaming video, downloaded applets (programs) that interact instantly with the user, and ads that change when the user's mouse passes over it.

Router: A device that directs or routes data traffic and messages between computers. May incorporate firewalls, address and content filtering, and other administrative and security functionality.

Sales Force Automation (SFA): Sales automation software is a type of program that automates business tasks such as inventory control, sales processing, and tracking of customer interactions, as well as analyzing sales forecasts and performance.

Satellite Officing: Secondary offices owned or leased by a corporation. They can range in size and location from a single room to an entire building, but generally are designated for certain employees on certain days or times. As with remote work centers, telecommuters can divide their time between the satellite office and home. (See also Remote Work Centers.)

Satellite Transmission: A form of transmission that sends signals to an orbiting satellite, which amplifies them and returns the signals back to a receiver, such as a mobile phone, television receiver, or computer back on Earth.

Server: A shared computer on a Local Area Network (LAN) serving any of a variety of special functions such as managing and distributing software applications and data, running specific applications as a shared service, powering an enterprise website, or connecting peripherals and various resources to end users.

Shared space: The use of an office at different times by more than one employee, such as telecommuters, who may be scheduled to work there at specific hours. (See also Team Spacing.)

Small Office Home Office (SOHO): SOHO is a term for a small business office based in commercial space or a residence as well as a home office environment from which a teleworker may operate.

Synchronize: To align data and files between servers, PCs, PDAs, and other devices.

Tape Drive: A peripheral data storage device for computers that reads and writes on magnetic tape. Frequently used as backup for primary applications and data and may be stored offsite for business continuity purposes.

Team Spacing: In lieu of a traditional office where everyone has a specific desk or work area, this group space is shared by all team members, virtual and otherwise. Since no one has an assigned cube, this eliminates scheduling conflicts and facilitates team activities, such as group meetings. (See also Shared Space.)

Telecommuting: Periodic work out of the principal office one or more days per week, either at home, a client's site, or in a telework center.

Teleconferencing: A term for a conference of more than two people linked by telecommunications through a conference bridge, including audio, video, and computer-based conferencing. (See Videoconferencing.)

Telework: Any form of substitution of information technologies (such as telecommunications or computers) for normal work related travel; moving the work to the workers instead of moving the workers to work.

Total Cost of Ownership (TCO): The internal accounting calculation about the total cost of not only purchasing a piece of equipment, but supporting it and its user over its entire useful service life.

Unified Messaging: A synonym for integrated messaging, which allows voice, faxes, data, images, and video to be managed from a universal message inbox.

Uninterruptible Power Supply (UPS): A power supply with battery backup that continues to provide power to a computer in the event of interruptions and failure of the incoming electrical power.

Upload: To go online to an enterprise server or sites on the world wide web and send a file there from your own computer. The opposite of Download.

Videoconferencing: Real-time bi-directional exchange of audio and video content between remote locations over high-speed broadband connections utilizing dedicated equipment or PCs. (See Teleconferencing.)

Virtual Office: Basically, anywhere the teleworker is—home office, a coffee shop, car, etc. Rather than a physical location, a virtual office can be anywhere that has Internet access and the capability of conducting business. Initially salespeople worked from virtual offices, but the concept has expanded to include many other types of telecommuting jobs as well.

Virtual Private Network (VPN): A highly secure network created utilizing public networks with a combination of telecommunications equipment, computer hardware, software, and the Internet.

Virus: A program, usually hidden in a file or email, which can infect a computer by altering or deleting files. Servers and PCs should run applications to detect and protect against viruses, updating their definition files frequently.

Voice over Internet Protocol (VoIP): A protocol for the transmission of voice telephony over data networks bypassing the Public Switched Telephone Network (PSTN).

Voice Recognition: A program designed to identify spoken words and digitize them into text for control of computer equipment or input to application programs.

Web Server: A dedicated computer that stores and serves up the files that form web pages to web users over intranets and the Internet utilizing Hypertext Transfer Protocol (HTTP).

Wide Area Network (WAN): A data network typically extending a Local Area Network (LAN) outside a facility over telephone common carrier lines to link to other LANs in remote locations.

Wi-Fi: a high-frequency wireless local area network.

Wireless Access Point (WAP): A wireless local area network (WLAN) node for connecting various PCs, information appliances, and peripherals over short-distance wireless networks. May be integrated into a router.

Wireless Local Area Network (WLAN): A Local Area Network (LAN) using high-frequency radio waves rather than wires to communicate between devices and nodes. May be configured quickly and cheaply, but is often not as fast as wired LANs and may pose additional security concerns.

ZIP Drive: a small, removable media, high-capacity storage device for computers operated similarly to a floppy drive.

FOR MORE INFORMATION

The following is a selected list of resources for information about telecommuting. Teleworkers should use caution—some websites and companies promise them jobs but only take their money. Managers should be cautious as well, especially when looking to hire effective workers. Telecommuting and work from home sites come and go with amazing frequency. This list encompasses some that have been around for a while.

Gil Gordon Associates
www.gilgordon.com
Operating since May 1995, the site, although slightly outdated, consolidates a wide variety of information from around the world, and offers many different perspectives on the subjects of telecommuting, teleworking, the virtual office, and related topics. An acknowledged expert in telecommuting and telework, Gil Gordon has won numerous awards and the site contains everything from answers to commonly asked questions to resources on all aspects of telecommuting to downloads of existing telecommuting programs that may provide ideas for implementing programs.

International Research Center (IRC)
www.researchedge.com
While not a telecommuting website per se, it is the location of an excellent resource: *The Enterprise Telework Guide*, formerly known as the AT&T Telework Guide. Written by IRC owner Mark Goldstein and sponsored by Cox Business Services

(*www.coxbusiness.com*), it contains complete and comprehensive information on setting up a telework system as well as resources, advice, and definitions. Along with providing background and technical knowledge to aid companies in evaluating and implementing telework programs, it can also assist the telecommuter in equipping, connecting, and using the tools and applications necessary to support their remote work activity. The guide can be found in its entirety on the web.

JALA
www.jala.com

Co-founded by Jack Nilles, "the father of telecommuting" frequently quoted in this book, this international—and virtual—group of consultants helps business and government organizations in three main areas: telework, telecommuting, and virtual organizations. They support telework program strategy development, program planning, teleworker and technology selection, training, program implementation, and evaluation—including cost-benefit analysis.

Additionally, they provide:

* Advice to organizations and teleworkers
* Applied futures research, including telework and energy use forecasting
* Technology assessment
* Investigation of the potential impacts of new technologies

The site also has resources for learning more about telework and its potential impact as well as some basic information about designing a program.

The Telework Coalition
www.telcoa.org, www.telecommute.org
Mailing address:
The Telework Coalition
204 E Street, NE
Washington, DC 20002
202-266-0046

Dedicated to promoting the benefits of teleworking, the coalition brings together a diverse array of organizations, companies, and individuals with the common interest of promoting awareness and adoption of existing and emerging telework and telecommuting applications, including telemedicine and distance learning, as well as addressing access to broadband services that may be needed to support these applications.

The organization has the following goals:

- To promote and expand the utilization of telework applications through the education of federal, state, and local elected officials, and employers and employees in both the public and private sectors, as to their benefits
- To work with policy makers in developing incentives, including tax credits for employers and employees who engage in telework programs, accelerated equipment depreciation, and establishing pilot telework, telemedicine, and distance learning programs
- To inform the public of these available incentives to accelerate their adoption and use
- To assemble a group of experts in the telework field who can address and resolve the specific concerns of agencies and businesses that inhibit the implementation of beneficial telework programs

- To address the ever growing concerns about traffic congestion, the environment, and work/life balance
- To build awareness of telework as a critical component in the
  establishment of a decentralized and distributed work force
  that is necessary when addressing business continuity and
  disaster recovery planning

Therefore, to help convey the concept that "work is something
you do, not someplace you go." The site is also a useful clearing-
house regarding trends, information, and ongoing legislation.

www.telecommuting.com

TeleCommuting.Com Inc. manages a collaborative environment between corporations and their potential teleworkers. Along
with posting jobs, they have a comprehensive library section which
contains over 400 articles on telecommuting. Additionally their
site has helpful links to sites that can provide additional information and reputable resources, from several on this list to international teleworking organizations, such as InnoVisions Canada.

BIBLIOGRAPHY

"10 Tips for Managing the Transition to Alternative Officing." *Workforce,* November 2007, p. 5.

Allert, Jeanne. "You're Hired, Now Go Home" *Training & Development,* March 2001, p. 56.

"Any Time, Any Place, Anywhere: Broadband And The Changing Face Of Work." White Paper published by The Positively Broadband Campaign. (Washington, DC: The Winston Group, 2002).

Atkinson, William. "Telecommuting: The Remote Control Risk," *Risk & Insurance,* April 17, 2000, p. 27.

"The Bare Essentials For Effective Telecommuting,"online article, *Hub Pages,* nd (*http://hubpages.com/hub/ The_Bare_Essentials_For_Effective_Telecommuting*).

Caher, John. "Taxing of Telecommuters To Go Before New York State's High Court," *New York Law Journal*, January 2005, p. 87.

"The Challenges for Payroll When Employees Telecommute," *IOMA's Payroll Manager's Report*, March 2006, p. 5

Charrier, Sylvie. "You Can Work in Your PJs," online article,inyourpjs. com, nd (*http://telecommute-resumes.com/successful-telecommuter .htm*).

Cooney, Michael. "Telecommuting: Security a Top Issue As Teleworking Grows," online article, *Network World*, March 19, 2007 (*www.net workworld.com/community/node/12633*).

"Customer & Technical Support-Telecommute," online article, *Virtual Vocations*, nd (*www.virtualvocations.com/jobdetails/job/7957/customer-technical-support-telecommute.html*).

Davis, Debbie. "What to Do When Your Telecommuting Program Isn't Working," online article, *Tech Republic*, August 22, 2000 (*http://articles.techrepublic.com.com/5100-10878-1052410.html*).

Deam, Jenny. "Not So Workable: Parents Who Combine Job, Home Life Find the Flexibility Has Flaws," *Denver Post*, June 9, 2003. p. F01.

DeMaria, Michael. "Telecommuting: Keeping Data Safe and Secure," online article, *Network Computing*, November 26, 2001 (*www.network computing.com/1224/1224ws1.html*).

"Digital Age Demands Talent Search," online article, *CIO UK*, May 16, 2007 (*www.cio.co.uk/industry/construction/news/index.cfm?articleid=1299*).

Duarte, Deborah and Snyder, Nancy Tennant. *Mastering Virtual Teams, 3rd ed.* (San Francisco: Jossey Bass, 2006).

"Establishing a Corporate Telecommuting Program," online article, *Auxillium West*, nd (*www.auxillium.com/telecomu.shtml*).

"Examples," online article ATI, Alabama Telework Initiative, nd (*http://telework.eng.uab.edu/examplesMore.htm*).

"Eye-to-Eye Video: Solving the Eye Contact Problem," online article, *ITOD*, July 23, 2004 (*http://itotd.com/articles/254/eye-to-eye-video*).

"Facts on Health Insurance Coverage," online article, National Coalition on Healthcare, nd (*www.nchc.org/facts/coverage.shtml*).

"Federal Government Teleworker Growth Outpaces Private Sector," online article, *Network World*, March, 19, 2007 (*http://findarticles.com/ p/articles/mi_m0EIN/is_2007_March_ 19/ai_n27184406*).

Fisher, Kimball and Fisher, Mareen Duncan. *The Distance Manager.* (New York: McGraw-Hill, 2001).

Fulbright, Jenny. "What Qualifies for a Home Office Tax Deduction?" online article, *Power Home Biz*, 2006 (*http://www.powerhomebiz.com/ vol22/taxdeduction.htm*).

"The Future of Social Security," online article, Social Security Administration, SSA Publication No. 05–10055, May 2007 (*www.ssa.gov/ pubs/10055.html*).

"The Future of Virtual Teams: Collaboration in 3D web," online article, *Leading Virutally*, nd (*www.leadingvirtually.com/?p=26*).

Blog, posted by Lisa Galarneau on May 9, 2007 (*http://terranova.blogs .com/terra_nova/2007/05/synthesizing_vi.html*).

Gould, David. "Basics About the Virtual Team," online article, June 5, 2006 (*www.managementhelp.org/grp_skll/virtual/ virtual.htm*) .

Gould, David. "Leading Virtual Teams," online article, June 5, 2006 (*http://www.seanet.com/~daveg/ltv.htm*) .

Grensing-Pophal, Lin. "Training Supervisors to Manage Teleworkers— Employees Engaged In Telecommuting," *HR Magazine*, January 1999, p. 19.

Grensing-Pophal, Lin. *Telecommuting: Managing Off-Site Staff for Small Business* (Bellingham, WA: Self-Counsel, 2001).

Griffin, Frank, "Personality Traits of White-Collar Telecommuters: Perceptions of Graduating Business Students,"*Journal of Education for Business,* May, 2001, p. 25.

Gurvis, Sandra. *Careers for Nonconformists* (New York: Marlowe, 2000).

Gurvis, Sandra. *Management Basics* (Avon, MA: Adams, 2007).

Hankin, Harriet. *The New Workforce* (New York: Amacom, 2005).

Harris, Jade. "Comparing Apples to Apples With the 'Bible of Telecommuting,'" online article, September 1, 2006 (*www.telecooler.com/content/view/137/58*).

Hayes, Brigitte, "Project Management Marries Collaboration: A New Technology for Distributed Project Teams," Paper presented at the PMI Global Congress Proceedings— Prague, 2004.

Henricks, Mark. "Musical Chairs—Companies That Utilize Hotel Offices." *Entrepreneur*, April 1999 (*http://findarticles.com/p/articles/mi_m0DTI/is_4_27/ai_60036403/pg_2*).

Human Resources, August 21, 2002 (*http://ucsfhr.ucsf.edu/files/telecomm_supervisors_checklist.pdf*).

"Hiring a Virtual Worker, the Good, the Bad and the Ugly," online article, the JS Group, November 30, 2007 (*http:// thejsgroup.typepad.com/my_weblog/2007/11/hiring-a-virtua.html*).

"Home Office/Work Space Safety Tips," online article, Home Safety Council, nd (*www.homesafetycouncil.org/safety_guide/sg_homeoffice_w001.aspx*).

"Independent Contractors vs. Employees," online article, IRS (*www.irs.gov/businesses/small/article/0,,id=99921,00.html*).

"Internet Usage Statistics," December 2007, online article, (*www.internetworldstats.com/stats.htm*).

Iskold, Alex. "Best Of Software For Virtual Teams," online article, February 28, 2007 (*www.readwriteweb.com/archives/software_for_virtual_teams.php*).

Jacobs, Sonji. "New Tax Breaks to Promote Telework: State Firms to Get Credits If Workers Stay Off the Road," *The Atlanta Journal–Constitution*, April 21, 2006. p. G1.

Kalensky, Debra A. "Telecommuter Work/Life Balance Survey Executive Summary Brief" online article, nd, (*www.tjobs.com/tcsrvyrslts_a.shtml*).

Kanarek, Lisa. "Ergonomics for Teleworkers," training materials, nd, Harrington Software Associates, Inc.

"Lead: Mentoring," online article, Small Business Administration, nd (*www.sba.gov/smallbusinessplanner/ manage/lead/SERV_MENTORING.html*).

Lindenberger, Judith. "How to Write A Job Description," online article *Business Know How*, nd. (*www.businessknowhow.com/manage/jobdesc.htm*).

Copeland, Lennie. "Managing a Multicultural Workforce," online article, *California Job Journal*, December 31, 2006 (*http://www.jobjournal.com/article_full_text.asp?artid=1888*).

"Managing Telecommuting Employees, Part II," online article, March 28, 2002 (*www.nfib.com/object/1584031.html*).

Mariani, Matthew. "Telecommuters," *Occupational Outlook Quarterly*, Fall 2000, p. 10.

Meyer, Mathias. "Hourly vs. Fixed Pricing," online article, May 4, 2007 (*http://freelanceswitch.com/money/hourly-vs-fixed-pricing*).

Moody, Diane and Ingrid Steinberg. "Training for Teleworkers," *Training Journal*, April 2002, p. 20.

Nilles, Jack M. *Managing Telework*. (New York: Wiley, 1998).

"Number of Jobs Held, Labor Market Activity, and Earnings Growth among the Youngest Baby Boomers: Results from a Longitudinal Survey," online article, Bureau of Labor Statistics of the U.S. Department of Labor, August 25, 2006 (*http://www.bls.gov/news.release/pdf/nlsoy.pdf*).

Pate Dwyer, Kelly. "Ten Tools for Remote Teams," online article, bNet, nd (*www.bnet.com/2403-13059_23-166425.html*).

Pelton, Joseph. "The Rise of Telecities: Decentralizing the Global Society," Peterson, Stevie and Storr, Velda. "Why Virtual Teams?" online article, 2000 (*www.managementhelp.org/grp_skll/virtual/defntion.pdf*).

Piskurich, George M. *An Organizational Guide to Telecommuting.* (Alexandria, VA: American Society for Training and Development [ASTD], 1998).

"The Pros and Cons of Hiring Independent Contractors," online article, Forbes.com, October 11, 2006 (*http://www.forbes.com/2006/10/10/contractor-IRS-union-ent-law-cx_nl_1011nolo_print.html*).

Publication 15a Employer's Supplemental Tax Guide Supplement to Circular E, Employer's Tax Guide (Publication 15), IRS.

Repsher Emery, Gail. "Study: Flextime Workers Are More Productive But Telecommuters Prone to Overwork," online article, *Washington Technology*, November 20, 2000 (*www.washingtontechnology.com/cgi-bin/udt/im.display.printable?client.id=washingtontechnology&story.id=14943*).

"Retirement Plans, Pensions, and Social Security," online article, FindLaw.com, nd (*http://employment.findlaw.com/employment/employment-employee-wages-benefits/ employment-employee-wages-benefits-retirement-top*).

Roberts, Lisa. "Tele-Resentmen—Industry Trend or Event: Overcoming Colleagues' Envy When You're the Teleworker," *Home Office Computing*, April 2001, p. 10.

Rogers, Cathy. "What Is Shared Office Space?" online article, nd (*http://www.wisegeek.com/what-is-shared-office-space.htm*).

Schindler, Esther. "Getting Clueful: Seven Things the CIO Should Know About Telecommuting," online article, cio.com, May 9, 2007 (*http://www.cio.com/article/108501*).

"Secrets for Finding Good Telecommuting Jobs," online article, Updated August 2, 2004. Originally reported for TechTV, 2001 (*www .pamdixon.com/telecommutejobs.htm*).

Smith, A. E. "Tips for Rewarding Telecommuters: How To Ensure That Off-Site Workers Get Their Due," online article, *Manage Smarter*, March 5, 2007 (*www.managesmarter.com/msg/content_display/sales/ e3i9bdfd14f0f781f5d03095719eb3af98c*).

Smith, Susan Mary. "Telecommunication" online article, Search Mobile Computing website, May 28, 2007 (*http://searchmobilecomputing .techtarget.com/sDefinition/0,,sid40_gci213115,00.html*).

Stones, Lesley. "Employees to Call More Shots in Future," *Business Day*, June 21, 2007, p. 17.

"Supervisor's Checklist for Telecommuters." University of California San Francisco Human Resources, August 21, 2002 (*http://ucsfhr.ucsf .edu/files/telecomm_supervisors_checklist.pdf*).

Tan-Solano, Margaret and Brian Kleiner. "Virtual Workers: Are They Worth the Risk?" *Nonprofit World,* November/December 2003, p. 20.

Tatum, Malcolm. "How To Fire Employees," online article, How to Do Things, June 8 2006 (*www.howtodothings.com/business/a3074-how- to-fire-employees.html*).

The Futurist, January/February 2004, (*www.wfs.org/futcontjf04.htm*). p. 28.

"Top 10 Mistakes Home-Based Business Owners Make," online article, nd (*www.allbusiness.com/specialty-businesses/home-based- business/3981-2.html*).

Training Course for Telemanagers, online training course, Office of Personnel Management, nd (*http://www.leadership.opm.gov/programs/ Management-and-Supervisory-Skills/MCW/Index.aspx*).

"Telecommuting Case Study: IBM," online article, 2007, (*www.valley metro.org/Rideshare/Telework/Resources/Case_Studies/IBM.htm*).

"Telecommuting Has Mostly Positive Consequences For Employees And Employers," online article, *ScienceDaily*, November 20, 2007 (*www.sciencedaily.com/releases/2007/11/071119182930.htm*).

"Telecommuting: Trend or Not?" online article, HR Answers, November 11, 2002 (*www.hranswers.com/general/trends.cfm?trendid=25*).

"Ten Tips for Managing Creative Types," online article *All Business*, nd (*www.allbusiness.com/human-resources/ workforce-management/2975119-1.html*).

Trunk, Penelope. "Virtual Office Is What You Make It," *Boston Globe*, October 1, 2006.

Twentyman, Jessica. "Keeping Tabs," *Personnel Today*, October 23, 2007, p. 22.

"The Virtual Worker," online article, *Strategy Week*, nd (*http://strategy week.com/thevirtualworker.php*)

von Hoffman, Constantine, "Managing Telecommuters," *Harvard Management Update*, reprint No. U9803D.

Weinstein, Margery, "Virtually Integrated," *Training*, April 2007, p. 4.

"What Is Hoteling?" online article, nd, *Search CIO* (*http://searchcio .techtarget.com/sDefinition/0,,sid19_gci1067496,00.html*).

Zbar, Jeffrey. "Training to Telework," *Home Office Computing*, March 2001, p. 72.

INDEX